W9-BNV-943

Winning Marketing Strategies

BARRY FEIG

PRENTICE HALL

Library of Congress Cataloging in Publication Data

Feig, Barry.
Winning marketing strategies / Barry Feig.
p. cm.
Includes index.
ISBN 0-13-644907-7 case
1. Marketing--Management. I. Title.
HF5415.13.F447 1999
658.8'02—dc21 99-114543
CIP

© 1999 by Prentice Hall

All rights reserved. No part of this book may be reproduced in any form or by any means, without permission in writing from the publisher.

Printed in the United States of America

10 9 8 7 6 5 4 3

ISBN 0-13-644907-7

ATTENTION: CORPORATIONS AND SCHOOLS
Prentice Hall books are available at quantity discounts with bulk purchase for educational, business, or sales promotional use. For information, please write to: Prentice Hall Special Sales, 240 Frisch Court, Paramus, New Jersey 07652. Please supply: title of book, ISBN, quantity, how the book will be used, date needed.

PRENTICE HALL
Paramus, NJ 07652

On the World Wide Web at http://www.phdirect.com

Preface

"So much to do, so little time." That's the mantra of today's marketer. Because of growing competition in every segment of industry, today's marketer has to be more knowledgeable and creative than ever before. You must produce now!

This book is meant to inspire you to create new marketing strategies and to give you the tools you need to compete— and win. One thing is constant: If the product doesn't sell, marketing is going to take the heat. But marketing is also a fun way to make a living, even if it is sort of a perverse enjoyment.

Winning Marketing Strategies is a how-to book on achieving your marketing goals, whatever they may be. It's a compendium of ideas.

Here are some of the problems the book will solve.

- How to have an idea accepted by management.
- How to take that idea and build a comprehensive marketing program around it.
- How to conduct research that really works without busting a budget.
- How to make trade shows work.
- The hows and whys of marketing on the Internet—and whether to use the Internet at all.

The book contains over 1000 ideas strategies and examples that you can mix and match for your particular situation. These are not recycled or worn-out ideas, but new strategies that break rules as well as classic approaches that have withstood the test of time.

This book presents the essential tools—as well as the basics—of marketing and sales on every page. It's a comprehensive blending of marketing and sales strategies that you can use instantly.

As marketer, you're on the front lines. Everything starts and flows from you, or at least it should. This book has the full arsenal of marketing weapons—how to's, tips, tactics, strategies—all proven. It's as useful for the marketer who is starting his first day on the job as it is for the experienced marketer who is racking her brain for the next BIG marketing idea.

Don't feel like you have to read the book from cover to cover. Thumb through it randomly and adapt the ideas for you particular marketing situation. I've tried to keep the writing light and informal. I've intentionally eschewed the marketing jargon of most business books.

By the way, you can help me out by dropping me an e-mail. Let me know how you used a strategy or built one of your own from the ideas in this book.

Happy Marketing.

Barry Feig
newmex@aol.com

Dedication

I dedicate this book to my college-bound kids (for making this book necessary), and all my loved ones who stood by me for all these years.

Contents

CHAPTER ONE
Proven Strategies to Build Marketing Success
1

CHAPTER TWO
Strategies for Developing Action Plans
16

CHAPTER SIX
Strategies for Choosing Advertising Agencies and Other Suppliers 111

CHAPTER SEVEN
Strategies for Point of Sale, Impulse Items, and Trade Shows 130

CHAPTER EIGHT
Strategies for Pricing and Adding Value
153

CHAPTER NINE
Selling and Marketing Strategies that Create Record Sales
172

CHAPTER TEN
Strategies for Speeding up the New Product Development 187

CHAPTER ELEVEN
Strategies For Making Distributors and Merchants Ecstatic 204

CHAPTER TWELVE
Proven Strategies for Turnaround Situations and Repositionings
220

CHAPTER THIRTEEN
Strategies to Make Your Package and Product Name Sell...Sell...Sell
233

CHAPTER FOURTEEN
Strategies for Marketing Through the New Media
00

CHAPTER NINETEEN
Strategies for Contests and Sweepstakes
343

CHAPTER TWENTY
Exploring Alternative Marketing Strategies
358

Index
369

Introduction

A while ago, I was playing racquetball with a businessman who was a wholesale seafood purveyor. Actually, it really doesn't make much of a difference what kind of business he was in. In all businesses—even nonprofit concerns—the prime directive is to sell something to someone. This particular businessman had learned marketing from the old school: Buy low, sell high; when the customer flinches or stops coming by, lower your prices; when something works you add to your marketing repertoire; when it doesn't work, you try to fix it or jettison it. The hard part is finding anything that works, or even just finding the time to create and execute a marketing strategy, let alone a breakthrough strategy.

The after-game discussion centered around his son, who had just graduated college and was thinking of entering the business. But the son didn't want to do things the old ways, and his father was a little displeased.

"Why does he think he's so smart? What can you teach in school that you can't learn from being in business—seeing what works and building on your mistakes? There is so much to know about business and sales that you can't get in school."

"Marketing," I explained, "is always changing. There are new methods, new tactics and new markets to target. While business school is mostly fluff and theory, the case histories they use in classes can be adapted."

I explained to the businessman that a company called Foxy Lettuce turned the produce world upside down by packaging their lettuce in little plastic bags. Did the wholesale fish merchant give new packaging any thought as a way of boosting sales?

"Too expensive" he said, "and I could never get my employees to take the time to do it."

Then I told him about the Orville Kent Company. They started by selling potato salad to supermarkets. They gave their product a brand name (anathema in a commodity category) and they commanded higher prices for their goods.

"Nah," said the businessman. "All retailers want is the lowest price and they all pay late. I can't tie up my money with crazy marketing schemes."

"But what about the Smartfood Company? They sold cheddar-flavored popcorn, and when they were out of advertising dollars, they spent their last resources dressing women like giant popcorn bags on ski slopes and beaches. Demand became so strong that retailers were forced to carry product. Eventually, they sold their company for a great sum of money to Frito-Lay."

"Yeah, but I don't sell popcorn," said the businessman. "I sell fish and they can go bad."

Produce in plastic bags. . .brand images. . .nubile women dressed in popcorn bags. That's part of what new marketing strategies are all about. I tried to explain to the businessman (who happened to be my brother) that when you do things the way you've always done them, you're going to get the same results you've always gotten. *Marketing is a business of learning about options and weighing strategic alternatives.*

"But marketing is so expensive, who has time to come up with ideas?" he countered.

That statement is what caused me to write this book. The important part of the story is that he was so wrapped up in the details of running his business that he forgot he was a marketer.

This book will furnish you with the options and strategies you need to create successful marketing forays. It will furnish you with the tools, in the form of strategies, you need to succeed. It will show you what worked for many companies and also what didn't work.

But the book will only work if you keep an open mind and rid yourself of preconceived notions. Unimaginative marketers might argue that a specific strategy may have worked for a particular product or category, like office equipment, but where is the strategy for selling turnips? Surprise—it's in the same place. The key to using this book is to *adopt* and *adapt*. Adopt what has worked and adapt it for your particular product or marketing environment.

This book is proactive. It suggests you take the initiative in your marketing excursions instead of forcing yourself to be creative only when it is brought upon by negative business forces. It's easier and safer to have strategies in your pocket to use before a calamity hits (and it will).

As you read through winning strategies in this book then, keep these three tips in mind:

- *Remember to be a marketer.* Don't get so caught up in day-to-day details that you forget the importance of marketing.
- *Keep an open mind.* Be alert for new marketing ideas and look for ways to adapt proven marketing strateies from other companies.
- *Implement new marketing stratiegies as you go along.* Don't get stuck doing things the same old way and don't wait for things to go downhill before trying out new marketing strategies.

CHAPTER ONE

Proven Strategies to Build Marketing Success

Think Like a Marketing Superstar

Marketing is a people function. It's a position of opportunity, responsibility and creativity. Marketers must often work around situations that are not of their doing. By successfully doing so, they can become corporate heroes. When marketers are consigned to doing things the way they've always been done, they're going to get the same old tired results they've always gotten.

Marketing strategies are needed even before you think of profits, or even your product. Strategic marketing starts with your thought processes and mind-sets. To be a successful marketer, it helps to think like one.

Something about the ad or brochure for this book caught your attention. What was it? It could have been the title. Or maybe it was something in the advertising. Perhaps it was the familiarity of my name. In any event, the book caught your attention. Something is urging you to read the next sentence. You've been hooked. It's my job to keep you interested and excited.

As a marketer you have to keep developing new hooks to capture your customer's attention.

Successful marketers need different sense organs than other people in an organization. Marketers listen, keep people excited and generate ideas. Successful marketers have the ability to sniff out an opportunity that could be half a world away. They do this by being part of everyone's world—even when they're not particularly wanted. They know the pulse of their market and the heartbeat of the company they work for.

This means interacting with everyone even though corporate turf is guarded zealously. Everyone in a corporate environment is dealing with a different aspect of the product than you are. While the plant foreman may say that he is in the process of making widgets, your job is to sell those widgets; so you must know how they are made and how to make them more customer-friendly.

While the Research and Development (R & D) person may define his job as coming up with new engineering triumphs, it is your job to make sure R & D comes up with something that will be bought and to gently guide R & D to a consumer safe-haven. The best engineering in the world will fail if there is no market—or no enthusiastic marketer—for a particular product.

While the sales manager might say his job is to sell, it is your job to grease the salesperson's selling wheels.

Generate Excitement Through Strategic Thinking

As well-known philosopher Yogi Berra supposedly said, "half of baseball is 90 percent mental." Like baseball and most sports, marketing is a "head" game. It's a game of inner strength. The so-called motivational speakers like to talk about this inner strength as a certain toughness. But you don't have to be tough. You have to be prepared. And you have to be flexible, because new markets open and close weekly. That sounds basic and simplistic, but many marketers work from set-in-stone preconceived notions. Or they define their product only in corporate terms when it should be defined in a customer-oriented manner. You also need to know the brand's emotional or motivational hooks that really drive the product.

It's a way of thinking—not about yourself—but about the potential of the product you are marketing. If successful marketers have one thing in common, it is the ability to become missionaries for their product. They extoll the virtues of a product or strategy to anyone who might be interested. You're in the enthusiasm business. It's your job to create and generate excitement. Now you may say, "I'm marketing toilet paper, who is going to be interested in that?" Ask a person who needs toilet paper in a hurry if he's interested. Successful marketers know that there is no stronger interest than self-interest. *Successful marketers think of their products in terms of their customer's self-interest.*

Twelve Key Strategies for Successful Marketing Thinking

1. *Solve problems.* Think in terms of benefits rather than features. Successful marketing propositions don't start with a product, but with the answer to a customer's problem. Know what customers want to buy and WHY they're buying it. If you don't know the driving forces, learn them. That way there are no misdirections or expensive false starts.

2. *Learn to manage chaos and manage in chaos.* Things don't happen in order, even though management types often crave linear time and work flows. The successful marketer manages chaos—in the corporate world, and in buying patterns. He finds sales patterns where none seem to exist on the surface and builds on them.

3. *Build relationships as well as sales.* Most people can sell a good product once. But it's the relationship that spurs future sales. Especially in a service environment, the company is buying you, not just your product.

4. *Stay in tune with your customers.* Know that consumers buy on emotion first and physical benefits next. How one sells to the consumer is just as important as how it is sold. There will be much more on this in the coming chapters.

5. *Borrow ideas from the competition.* Do this freely and without remorse. Know how the competition will react to your marketing strategy and the plusses and minuses about competitive products. Become your competitor's best friend and customer until you know almost as much about competitive products as they do.

6. *Listen.* Listening is an underrated art form. Customers will give you as much information as you need if you probe correctly. Successful marketers ask—and then listen! The second part is where most people go wrong. It's physically impossible to talk and listen at the same time and the weak marketer spends more time babbling than listening. Customers will tell you everything you need to know about how to make them buy your product when you ask the right way. Successful marketers ask questions and know when to shut up.

7. *Continuously think of ways to make your product better.* Constantly evolve your products and your strategic thinking. Avoid tunnel vision by always looking for peripheral strategies and markets. The ideal product and target market has never been invented. Improve your product and look for new target markets even *before* the product or strategy hits the market.

8. *Never see yourself as a victim.* It's an easy mind-set to get into: You feel your product is not ideal, the competition too strong. These are all temporary conditions. Moses had hundreds of thousands of followers hanging on to his every word. But many people don't know that Moses had a speech defect (Exodus). There always will be negatives but you will overcome almost any negative with solid marketing that puts a spin on the product and turns a negative into a selling point.

9. *Think proactively 100 percent of the time.* Locate problems before they occur, along with potential solutions. There are always going to be problems that you didn't think of when you started a strategy. Find remedies for potential dysfunctional situations before they occur.

10. *Fill your head with minutia about anything and everything.* It doesn't have to be related to the task at hand. Mind chatter feeds on those little scraps of information you keep in your head. The answers to questions rest in your subconscious waiting to be set free at the proper moment.

11. *Live and breathe marketing.* Keep a twenty-four hour vigil for new opportunities. Opportunities don't come and kick you in the butt; they always have to be probed and ferreted out. And opportunities don't work the 9-5 shift. In our business society we have put marketers on a daily nine-hour schedule. But our body and brain rhythms don't fit that schedule. New ideas usually opt to surface at weird times when you're actually thinking of something else—i.e., driving a car, taking a shower, and even making love (unfortunately).

12. *Take a break now and then.* Having time away from work isn't just a good idea. It's mandatory. Continuous work brings circular thinking. When batteries are recharged during a vacation, you get a fresh look at your ideas and your marketing proposition.

Marketing and Selling

There is a great deal of dead wood in most corporate bureaucracies. Some companies could cut their work staff in half and get twice as much work done. A tremendous number of people sit behind desks shuffling e-mail and hoping that nobody notices them—and it often happens that way. They have no great impact on the company. Nobody really knows about them. Nobody really cares.

Not so with marketers or sales managers. The results are out there for everyone to see. If sales plummet, guess who takes the blame? (If sales rise, *everyone* takes credit, but this is a fact of corporate life.) So, in effect smaller companies, mid-sized companies and even corporate giants are at the mercy of the marketing and sales function and ride their coattails to success.

Marketers and salespeople are true entrepreneurs. The business is yours to grow through your own nonstop marketing efforts.

Think of Yourself as a Salesperson

Marketing is just another word for selling, despite what it says on your business card, and vice versa. Everyone is a salesperson in one form or another, maybe not of goods and services but of themselves. Selling starts the second you're born when you learn that crying will get you attention. It continues as you sell yourself to your teachers and your future mates. You've learned what motivates your "customers." You've practiced which hot buttons to push and how to push them and that is a primary tenet of marketing.

Look at your business card. It says marketer. Forget it. While you're at it, forget all you were told in the job interview about being a "marketer." Your function is to sell goods and services. Eliminate that space on your resume where it says job objective—marketing. There's really no such position. You're really a salesperson, whether you embrace the title or not. Marketing and sales are joined at the neck.

I know in MBA school they teach a lot about marketing but almost nothing about selling, but that's only because Marketing 101 sounds a lot more impressive than "Introduction to Salesmanship" or "Selling 101."

But if you've been in marketing for any length of time, you know the importance of selling. When they handed you your MBA certificate what they really gave you was a license to sell. Even if your business card says marketing, you're really a salesperson. Yes, the business is yours to grow, but you have to sell to a bunch of people before your idea ever reaches even one potential buyer.

Selling Your Ideas Within the Company

Selling is the engine that makes your new product move. All new products start and end with the consumer buying something. But people won't buy until it is sold to them. Even your best ideas will go nowhere unless your management buys into them. If you're an entrepreneur, substitute the words "banker" or "venture capitalist" for "management."

Let's suppose you have an idea that you think will open up the gateway to a profit nirvana. You have no tangibles although you may try to impress people with prototypes and charts on an overhead projector. What you're trying to communicate is air. You've got to sell this "air" to many people.

First you have to sell the idea to:

- Your task force
- Boss
- R & D
- Upper management
- Company president

While you won't be pitching personally to all these people, you have to instill your enthusiasm into every person on the purchase totem pole.

And that's only the beginning.

Then you'll have to sell it to your sales force...who must sell it to the distributors...who must sell it to their store clients...who must sell it to their salespeople...who must sell it to the consumer...who probably doesn't give a damn.

Whew! Sounds tough? It is. But remember, when you stop selling, you stop the presses. Nothing happens without your brilliant idea and you pitching it.

The Salesperson-as-Marketer Strategy

People who successfully sell to other human beings are a strange breed. The great ones feel that they are true entrepreneurs carrying the company's success on their shoulders. How can they be the entrepreneurs if you are? Because you're both the same person, except you're selling through media and the salesperson is doing his or her job through personal contact. The salesperson can't function until he has a message and tools created by you. The good salesperson will consult with the marketer as a doctor consults with other specialists.

But even salespeople can't be there to physically place your product in the consumers' hands all the time. You have to sell by proxy. Your product has to be there in your place. The product has to sell itself not once...not twice...but at least four times. This may vary depending on whether you're selling a product or a service, but the principle of the four times sale remains the same in most situations.

Four Times the Product Must Sell Itself

On the shelf, or in the service business, while making your pitch.

A product or service needs a one-sentence hook. You should think of your product and your selling premise as a three-dimensional ad with a strong headline. The headline is of key importance, because no matter how great your product or service is, it's going to be summed up in one sentence. Your pitch can take three hours to make. Your commercial may have taken months to produce. But your product or service is going to occupy only one sentence in a person's mind. You can produce a half-hour infomercial demonstrating every feature of a new vacuum cleaner, but the consumer is going to remember something like "it was pretty efficient."

The one-sentence mnemonic conquers information overload as it cuts through the repetitive blather of other selling pitches. In most selling propositions, consumers buy what affects them at the moment of purchase. If it connects with their lives at the key moment of decision, they're interested. If it doesn't connect, they're not prospects for the product.

At the cashier or when the client signs the contract.

The initial impression you or your product makes is obviously really important, but first impressions don't always close the sale whether the product is that 49-cent roll of toilet paper or a ten million dollar advertising account. The customer is going to look at every aspect of your product to see why he or she should NOT buy it. Your concept must exert so much power that your product almost forces the buyer to sign on the dotted line. At this point, the emotional benefit is even more important than the physical benefit.

In use, or in business-to-business scenarios, when the deliverables are received.

You should always deliver MORE than the customer expects. In business-to-business situations, always show progress and how your product will increase the buying firm's chances of meeting its goals.

After use, or after the project is completed.

Like a great entertainer, your product should leave the consumer wanting more.

Six Quick Product Marketing Strategies

Here are some fundamental ways to keep your product strong and viable.

1. *Develop new uses.* Give your product or service a new function that the other guy hasn't thought of yet. It makes the buyer feel smart, like he's getting something for nothing. Be a hero for solving two problems for the cost of one. It's a great way to preempt a category. The WD 40 company has built its whole product line (which consists solely of WD 40) around new uses for the product. If a new computer scanner can function as a copy machine and a fax machine—and save money—the buyer will be delighted.

2. *Make a minor cosmetic change.* There are a zillion computers on the market, but Acer did something special: They made theirs black. It's high-tech, and also fits nicely into home decorating schemes. Frank Purdue created a frenzy in the chicken business when he capitalized on the fact that his chickens had a brand name and yellow skin. This convinced consumers that Purdue chickens were healthier, prime chickens. It reassured them that they were buying the best for their families and it gave them a point of comparison when they put their yellow-branded Purdue chicken next to pale chickens. (By the way, Perdue's chickens are yellow because he feeds them crushed marigold petals.)

3. *Develop a new name.* Choose a name that buyers can remember. Stay away from neutral names that no one really loves or hates. Snuggles is a great name for a fabric softener, especially when it's positioned for kids clothes. Gobblestix, a name for a turkey jerky product targeted to moms and kids may sound simplistic at first to us marketing mavens...but not to moms and kids.

4. *Make it more convenient.* But don't make it too easy. Your package should allow consumers to rationalize the added expense. When Colgate

introduced its first pump back in the fifties it was considered frivolous and didn't sell. But in the eighties the company learned that consumers would rationalize the added expense of the pump as being easier and less messy for kids to use. The Internet offered the greatest information retrieval system known to man, but it was the user friendliness and easy-to-use graphics of the World Wide Web and America Online that really sparked interest.

5. *Put in a new performance cue.* Then tie it into a product benefit that stirs emotions. A wall and floor cleaner without a strong, or even obnoxious residual scent is considered ineffective by consumers because it fails to reinforce the fact that the user has done her job.

6. *Make the product fun.* Don't be afraid of a little whimsy. My computer keyboard is black, yellow and purple. Why did I buy it? Because it caught my eye. Even a product as simple as basic household sponges can be fun when we cut them into shapes like little animals.

All of these strategies will be discussed in detail in later chapters. And all of these are products of marketing creativity.

Creativity in Marketing and Sales

Creativity is a must for the strategic marketer. It's another aspect of the strong marketer's personality. Creativity is as important as dollars spent when it comes to marketing. Creativity will actually enable you to cut down on marketing expenses when it allows you to break through buyer ennui.

Creativity is a buzzword these days. Companies are paying big bucks for so called "facilitators" who claim to make you more creative. Marketing is really applied creativity. The good news is that everyone has creativity in one form or another and you don't need to spend tons of money learning how to be more creative.

Everyone has the spirit and knows how to be creative but most don't know how to use it. That's because you're taught from youth NOT to use your creative powers. In school you're taught to color between the lines. As you grow older in your high-school years, you're told that only the book or the teacher is right. At work, you're told that creativity is best left to the so-called right-brained creatives in advertising agencies. You're told not to break certain sacrosanct marketing rules even though in marketing there are no hard and fast rules.

Of course, some creativity is inate. Just as some people are born to be more athletic than others, some people are more creative. But most of us can be taught to throw a ball even if we can't attain 90 mph fast balls. We all can be taught to be much more creative than we are.

One-Minute Strategy for Improving Creativity

You can teach yourself to be creative if you know how the creative process works. It starts with something that goes on in your brain constantly. We talked about it a few pages back. It's called *mind chatter*. It's those inane thoughts that jump in your head all the time...while driving to the store for a half gallon of milk or while waiting for a light to change. People who make their living through creativity have merely learned how to channel their mind chatter. They have disciplined their minds to discern the good from the useless. It's simple, really.

Fill your brain to overflowing with all sorts of stimuli and catch the overflow with a pen. ALWAYS carry a pen. The great idea that can strike you at any second can get lost just as quickly as new mind chatter invades your synapses. You may not have the answer at the beginning of your personal brainstorming session but it will surface. Somewhere in all that mind chatter garble, you will discern the answer if you let it happen and a 29-cent Bic will encase the idea in cement.

A Fail-Proof Creative Method

The one-minute strategy above is a good way to open up your mind to creative thinking. But as a long-term, proven strategy for boosting creativity, I recommend the following five-step formula:

- Immerse
- Stimulate
- Leave it alone
- Restimulate
- React

Step One: Immerse Collect all the information about a problem you can think of. Immerse your brain with information from anything even remotely concerned with the problem. Input is the food of big ideas. These can come from anywhere. We must have something to react to. To the dedicated marketing pro, supermarkets, stores and malls are more than places to buy things. They're ongoing labs to products and product ideas.

Step Two: Stimulate Every product in the store should feed or stir a creative spark in you. Write that burst of electricity in your brain down. Any product that crosses your path should be a springboard to a new idea. But you don't have to come up with a new idea instantly. That's the trouble with most "brainstorming" groups. They want to create an idea in a concentrated—usually two a day—time frame. Look instead for idea seeds and build on them later. Fill your head with minutiae, wherever you are. It doesn't even have to be a category you're working on. Force one category into another and see how it fits your objective.

Step 3: Leave It Alone Let your brain do the work on its own while you go on automatic pilot through your daily routines.

I always procrastinate at the start of a project or article. But in that time, I'm subconsciously thinking of solutions. When I finally sit at the computer the ideas magically come out. I write my first sentence. Then I usually watch a video. I jump up every five minutes or so when a new idea pops in my head. I'll edit out the bad ideas (which most of them are) but I'm putting ideas on paper so I can react to them later.

Here's an analogy: Think about a puzzle you're trying to do. You can sit there for hours trying to figure out a word or solution but you can't get it. You decide to go to the store and while you're in the car turning out of the driveway, the answer pops out. It seems obvious. Why didn't you think of it before? Did you get any smarter while driving the car? Of course not. Your mind just learned to unscramble all that data in your head, and to finally make some sense of it.

Step Four: Restimulate Keep going back to different venues to restimulate your mind. Each time you go back you'll get more ideas and more idea seeds. Use the ideas you wrote down before and react to them again. Everything you allow to enter your psyche and every bit of idea that you put down on your note pad becomes a trigger for a new idea that you hadn't thought of before.

Step Five: React Fertilize your written idea seeds by reacting to them even further. Bounce ideas off your kids or your spouse. Then listen. Their responses will give you new ideas. Build on their responses. They'll grow into the big idea you've been looking for.

A Quick Brainpower Exercise

A couple of pages back, you read about six quick product marketing strategies. Now let's use them. First, put yourself into a relaxation mode. Recall the six strategies (you can peek if you want) and relate them to a task at hand. Guide your thinking into the six strategies, and write down everything you think of. Now go watch TV or play a video. Quit for the day.

Tomorrow, look at your notes, react to what you wrote and watch your new ideas fly. Watch them soar. Now comes the hard part—sharing the results of your creativity with others.

Streamline Your Marketing Team

The president of a leading computer chip manufacturer recently said, "There are two kinds of companies—the quick and the dead."

Of course, you can say that's true for the computer industry which reinvents itself every day of the week. But remember it's true of all industries. All businesses should work at the speed of a formula-one car racer.

As a marketer you can streamline and turbocharge your organization with a commitment to speed and success.

The main reason for sloth and wasted movement is because there is a logjam of people who just aren't motivated. Some companies now take as much as two years or more to bring a product from conception to market. Sometimes it takes a year and a half just to develop a concept. That's ridiculous.

A couple of years ago an ailing financial services firm was looking to develop new financial products and reposition some old, sagging ones. Its bureaucracy had gotten so intimidating and so swollen with the MBA mentality that no one could—or would—make a decision for fear of the consequences. They started a project and spent a half million dollars and two years to reach a critical nondecision point where they called in an outside firm. It took six hours to go through deck after deck of overheads, with each department contributing their own subtle nuances. They called it being thorough. It was really a mindless waste of time.

The firm said it could complete the project in three months. The financial services company leaned on them to do it in six weeks. It was the smartest decision they could have made. Working on a project with little time to spare is better than spreading it out. The length of a project always expands to fit the time available but the more time a project is given, the harder it is to stay focused and interested.

This work-intensive project was a huge success. Five new products were successfully developed.

Why Strategic Plannings Go Slowly

Fear. Fear of failure keeps people generating more and more paper work and makes the product totally obscure and boring. The project continually stretches out as more and more reports are written.

Strategy to avoid this: Inspire your people to focus on end results. Challenge them to work harder and speak of the credit they will get when the strategy works.

Sheer number of people involved. Our marketing ideas have to be sold to others throughout the organization. But few of the people you sell to are ever going to be there in time to make a decision. There's just too much middle management. Managers are forced to be errand boys for the core idea even if the idea has no more meaning after everyone has made their "subtle" changes.

Strategy to avoid this: Make sure your management is on board for every element of the strategy from the beginning.

Too many people doing too many things. The buzzword in companies today is to act as teams, but most of the time the key task force acts together separately. Can you tell me why R & D is frequently locked away in a building separate from marketing—often in another state?

Strategy to avoid this: Get everyone involved from the beginning so that they will have a vested interest. Instill your team with vigor from the first start-up meeting. Don't work in a compartmentalized way. Make sure every member of your team sees the whole picture and not just his or her own role.

Too much time. When too long a time frame is established, there's a tendency for too little meaningful work to be produced.

Strategy to avoid this: Come up with an unrealistic timetable, then cut it in half. Most creative people and business people are used to working under deadlines. They thrive under pressure. Consider that a new newspaper—virtually a new product—is printed every day. Working aerodynamically does not mean working carelessly. It means preempting the competition. For a small company, speed provides the one sure advantage of overpowering the big companies.

Ten Strategies for Launching Your Project

1. If you're developing a team approach, enlist people with different personalities and mind-sets. They'll feed off each other. Get every discipline you can involved in the project.
2. Look into far-out ideas. Stretch the envelope at the beginning. You can pull back later. Nothing is more motivating to a person than to know her idea will be acted upon.
3. Don't sweat the details. If you can make money, they'll all fall into place.
4. Embrace management's goals when they're specific and attainable—but there must always be a specific goal to shoot for.
5. Start every project off with an informal brainstorming meeting where mission goals are specified. You can adapt the five-point brainstorming method on page 38. Let the results germinate.
6. Dodge corporate constraints at the beginning. If the idea or strategy is sound, corporate higher-ups will come around.
7. Ignore any research report for a project that started more than six months prior. It's hopelessly outdated. Question accepted wisdom. If it's wrong, it's neither wise nor acceptable.
8. Always have tight deadlines for every aspect of a project.
9. Don't get caught up in the "Not Invented Here" syndrome. Nobody really cares as long as you can develop profits.
10. Ignore preconceived notions. Start every project with a blank slate.

The Ten Commandments of Marketing

Thou shalt look at the customer's interest before thy own.

Thou shalt enjoy the thrill of success.

Thou shalt listen before thou speaks.

Thou shalt honor the product and nurture it until it grows.

Thou shalt immerse thyself in the customer's wants and needs.

Thou shalt wallow in the beauty of ideas.

Thou shalt use the tools of emotion in every sale.

Thou shalt not immerse thyself in self-pity.

Thou shalt blaze trails to the customer.

Thou shalt respect thyself and thy abilities.

CHAPTER TWO

Strategies for Developing Action Plans

Marketing isn't brain surgery. But you wouldn't know it by listening to managers who jabber breathlessly and write tomes for and about their marketing strategies. They treat each aspect of their product as if it were an untouchable part of the holy grail. Marketing gets more complicated as managers and entrepreneurs get bored with the simplicity of it all.

Clarify Your Basic Message

Put your ideas down on paper and refine, refine and refine until you have a crisp, workable strategy: which products you make, who your competitors are and how you can outmaneuver them. Everyone in your company should be privy to this information.

There's an easy and convenient prototype that you can follow for your marketing plan. And surprise—it's been staring you in the face for years. It's a newspaper. If you read the newspaper this morning, you had in your hands the basic foundation of a marketing strategy.

Not counting the actual editorial content of a story, there are two key grabbers that are in every well-written newspaper article.

The headline. The headline grabs your attention and gives you the gist of the story. It sucks you in fast. If the cover headline doesn't grab your eye, you might not even buy the paper.

The lead. In this short sentence, the newspaper communicates all you need to know. A good lead has five points. It tells WHO it happened to, WHAT happened, WHERE it happened, WHEN it happened, WHY it happened and HOW it happened.

Look at the following headline and lead sentence:

Three New Mexicans Get Top Award

Three Albuquerque Marines were given a medal of honor at the White House today for their bravery in the Gulf War

The headline and the lead gave you the information you need to know. If the newspapers can communicate a shorthand message every single day for about thirty stories an issue, then you can develop a succinct product story and consumer strategy the same way. Use the lead story strategy format as your cornerstone.

Let's take the introduction of a new refrigerator storage bag. Here's the headline, lead and your positioning strategy:

Introducing Glad Lock Bags
with the Color Change Seal.

So simple, busy husbands and on-the-go kids close it right every time.

Let's take it apart.

WHO (is the product for): Anyone with kids or significant others who never close kitchen bags or wrap up foods.

WHAT (is the product): A new storage bag that let's you know the bag is closed correctly.

WHERE (can the product be used): In the refrigerator.

WHEN (should the product be used): Whenever you have food that can go bad.

WHY (should the consumer choose the product over the competition's product): It saves them effort, time and prevents spoiled food.

HOW (does the product make the consumer's life easier): They know when the bag is closed airtight. No more dried leftovers.

The 5 W's & H statement is your marketing strategy on the head of a pin. Developing this strategic statement early on makes it that much easier to develop your marketing plan because you and your task force can stay focused.

Although many products are more complex than storage bags, you still have only one brief sentence to make the earth move for someone.

Five Steps to Developing a No-Nonsense Marketing Plan

Let's jump from newspapers to a piano. Think of a marketing strategy as a collection of piano keys. You can plunk a few keys at random and eventually you may come up with a tune. But if you plunk the keys in a predetermined order, you'll come up with the tune you want, maybe even a masterpiece much faster with a whole lot fewer errors.

The notes that should be played are:

- Identify strategy
- Segment strategy
- Focus strategy
- Attack strategy
- Evolve strategy

Identify Your Opportunities

Marketing can be considered a process of identifying markets and targets and satisfying them uniquely. There are many things that must be satisfied, not the least of which is your own company's goals. If you can't get your idea out of the conference room, you won't be able satisfy your ultimate buyers.

Identify Your Company's Goals

No matter how strong your product and strategy is, your first strategic goal is to get upper management on your side.

Marketing and management groups are growing farther apart. This makes it harder to determine what the company really wants from you. Often the company itself really doesn't know what it wants except to please stockholders. You and management are coming from different places, headed toward different goals. For instance:

You want to earn market share and know that it may take time. Management wants immediate profits.

You are beholden to management and yourself. Management is beholden to stockholders.

You know there will always be risks involved. Management wants a sure thing.

You're close to the consumer but no matter how much you beg, management finds it beneath themselves to attend focus groups, or even watch the focus-group tapes.

A key to working successfully with management is to be on the same team psychologically.

Seven Strategies for Working Successfully with Management

1. *Sell the dream of more profits by setting specific and almost realistic sales goals.* Share the process with management from start to finish.
2. *Define your company's corporate mind-set and build on it.* In your planning and meetings talk about your new marketing ideas in terms that specifically relate to the existing corporate culture. Know what the company can do and what it can't do. Build on the positives. Knowing when management feels comfortable and when it is uncomfortable is critical. Play into the financial, marketing and category safe havens. For instance, some companies like to be number one in everything they do. Others will settle for a comfortable number two or three status.
3. *Plan all your work on a strategic basis.* Show how every element of your program fits in with the company's overall market strategy. If it doesn't fit exactly, force feed it through your presentations. You may have to fudge a bit and use semantics.
4. *Insist that management "come clean" and present you with the whole picture, not just your role.* Get agreements on all plans at the beginning to prevent any miscommunication. If you don't have clear mission goals, then wounds will fester.
5. *Always show progress in attaining your goal.* Show learning and the next steps.
6. *Explain changing customer needs.* It's hard to go against the "let's do it the way we've always done it" mind-set. But management is usually too far from its markets. You're closer to your customers than it is. Use published data in all your meetings and correspondence to clearly demonstrate new markets and necessary marketing changes brought on by evolving consumers. Position yourself as the market expert.

7. *Be innovative, not imitative, unless there's an opportunity to exploit.* If you believe that your role in your company is to innovate new products and new businesses, get agreement before the fact. If your company is a follower—and many successful companies are—have that understanding up front. Whether your task is to be the first or a profitable also-ran, get agreement.

Seven Proven Tactics for In-House Communications

Agree to a future product strategy.

Define your company's corporate comfort zone.

Communicate evolving consumer needs.

Understand the rewards of being innovative, not

imitative, and vice versa.

Think entrepreneurealy, not like a manager.

Operate strategically, not just tactically.

Think personal risk, not personal safety.

Identify Your Competition's Strengths and Weaknesses

Part of any strategy is recognizing the strengths and vulnerabilities of your competitors. Entrepreneurial companies often create intriguing products for niche markets, then watch helplessly as the big guys steal them. As soon as a product area becomes big, large companies will try to take over. This doesn't have to happen. By factoring in the heavy players as your marketing plan, you can preempt them with new enhancements to your product before they can read it.

It's imperative that you know, what your competitors might throw at you. It's easy to spot a competitor who's staring you down through ads and sales. But often the competition is not that obvious. The manager of a hamburger chain might define his competition as other fast-food chains. But he should be thinking of an even bigger picture. The hamburger chain's competition might include supermarkets who are selling microwavable "handheld" food products, or convenience stores, some now set up like mini-delis.

You should know the history of your competition as well as strengths and weaknesses. Corporate pride can have as much to do with a competitor's reaction as well as the tiny market share you might be carving out. Just as important as the physical stature of the competition, are the business personalities of rivals. Every company has a certain philosophy of doing business, a guiding belief system. You need a deep understanding of a competitor's mentality in order to anticipate how that competitor will react.

Bob Frey is CEO of Cin Made, a Cincinnati maker of plastic and cardboard tubing that is used to hold motor oil as well as other materials. When he bought the company in 1984, oil companies were turning to plastic containers instead of cardboard. Frey found that with only a relatively small investment, he could make these plastic canisters. Even more important, he also knew that his competitors did not have the machinery or knowledge to do the same thing. When he retooled, he eliminated much of his competition.

Eight Strategies for Assessing Competition

Use established research services like AC Nielsen

Hobnob at trade shows and visit your competition's booths

Interview former and existing employees when they apply for jobs

Collect Dun & Bradstreet reports regularly

Talk with mutual suppliers

Peruse trade magazines and secondary research

Keep your ears open for hearsay

Conduct primary market research with customers, suppliers and dealers

Now put this information to use. For instance, if you learn that a competitor is cashed strapped you can go after their old customers. It may sound ruthless, but it's a good way to pick up new business.

Illustration 2.1

A Competitive Matrix: How to rate your competitors and their weaknesses.

Competing firm name:	1 ______	2 ______	3 ______	4 ______	5 ______
Rate 1 - 5 with 5 being highest:	1 ______	2 ______	3 ______	4 ______	5 ______
Market position in segments you want:	1 ______	2 ______	3 ______	4 ______	5 ______
Estimated level of consumer satisfaction:	1 ______	2 ______	3 ______	4 ______	5 ______
Regional strength of competition. Regions you are considering:					
Region 1	1 ______	2 ______	3 ______	4 ______	5 ______
Region 2	1 ______	2 ______	3 ______	4 ______	5 ______
Region 3	1 ______	2 ______	3 ______	4 ______	5 ______
Region 4	1 ______	2 ______	3 ______	4 ______	5 ______
Region 5	1 ______	2 ______	3 ______	4 ______	5 ______
Use actual numbers or rate 1 - 5 with 5 being highest:					
Financial performance:					
Profits/sales ration	1 ______	2 ______	3 ______	4 ______	5 ______
Estimate return on investment (ROI)	1 ______	2 ______	3 ______	4 ______	5 ______
Number of employees	1 ______	2 ______	3 ______	4 ______	5 ______
Physical plant size	1 ______	2 ______	3 ______	4 ______	5 ______
Financial resources and leverage	1 ______	2 ______	3 ______	4 ______	5 ______
Price position relative to a category (high, low, midrange):	1 ______	2 ______	3 ______	4 ______	5 ______

Rate 1 - 5 with 5 being the highest:					
Product quality (actual and consurmer perceived)	1 ______	2 ______	3 ______	4 ______	5 ______
Innovation	1 ______	2 ______	3 ______	4 ______	5 ______
Scope of product line	1 ______	2 ______	3 ______	4 ______	5 ______
List:					
Product areas that are missing	1 ______	2 ______	3 ______	4 ______	5 ______
Management personality (i.e., are they slow to react? Aggressive? Conservative? Combative?):	1 ______	2 ______	3 ______	4 ______	5 ______
Rate 1 - 5 with 5 being highest:					
Marketing strategy and effectiveness	1 ______	2 ______	3 ______	4 ______	5 ______
List channels in order of perceived strength					
Distribution channels used	1 ______	2 ______	3 ______	4 ______	5 ______
Summary of key strengths and weaknesses	1 ______	2 ______	3 ______	4 ______	5 ______

Identify Your Target Consumers and Their Physical Expectations

When you identify your potential customers' lifestyles, you can build an ongoing relationship with them. You do this by identifying the expectations and the satisfactions they are looking for.

This sounds obvious but when a person buys a product, she expects to receive certain performance cues. The products have to taste good, look good, or perform at a certain level. Customers also expect certain cues that the product is working. If there are no performance cues, consumers have no reason to buy the product again, even if it works.

For example, a carbon monoxide detector may be a necessary protective device but if there is no signal, such as a blinking red light, to show the person the product is actually working, the consumer will have doubts.

Did you ever wonder why duct tape is always silver? It used to be brown. But the Duro Dyne company wanted to sell duct tape that people thought was better performing. They gave it a silvery backing. It was a better tape and the silver tape told buyers that it was special. Not only that, it blended in nicely with galvanized ductwork and gave the appearance of a neater job. Now *all* duct tape is silver.

Your objective is to make your product do something faster, better or cheaper than anything on the market—and prove it whenever the customer uses the product.

Identify Your Target Consumers and Their Emotional Expectations

Consumers buy end results. But it can be difficult to determine what the end result of using your product actually is. There is a fine line in determining if your product benefit is physical or emotional. Use key psychological hooks along with physical benefits. Duro Dyne used a great deal of buyer psychology to create a market for its product.

Identify Your Leadership Position

Every company does something better than anyone else. At least they should make that claim. Make your product stand out by being number one in some aspect of your category that consumers care about.

Illustration 2.2
A diagnostic model to indentify your leadership and grow with it.

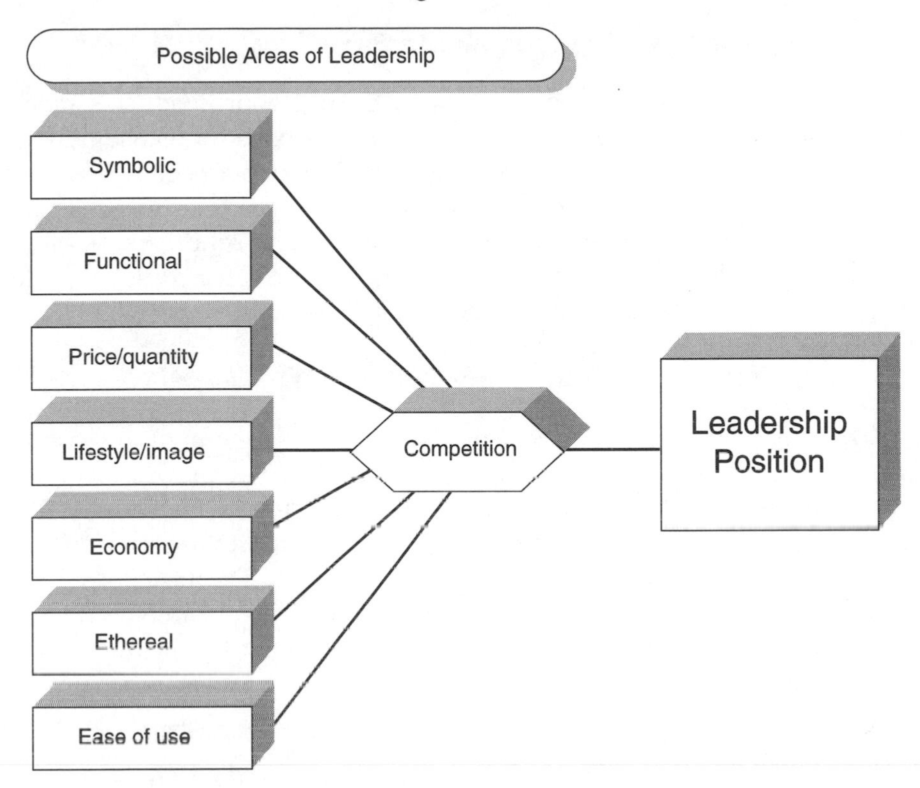

Identify Cultural and Transcultural Opportunities

Bagelmania is rampant.

Mexican style "wraps" are taking off across all prepared food categories.

Caucasians won't buy sneakers unless they are endorsed by "cool" African-Americans.

The cultural mosaic of America is one of constantly changing preferences and buying habits. Strategic marketers should learn cultural anomalies and take advantage of them.

Identify—Or Create—Economic Opportunities

Don't be afraid to reinvent the wheel. Even if your product is mature, don't jettison the product. Rethink it. Identify new ways to please new customers. A mistake that many marketers make is to go for the "whole enchilada." They see a huge mass of people and try to market to them. That's a mistake because the "whole market" is usually an amorphous mass of people with no underlying sameness. Identifying and satisfying niche markets is a great deal safer because the niche is more efficiently targeted.

Plant, Nurture and Prune Your Decision Tree

There is going to be a time when you and management are going to decide whether a market is big enough to profit from, or whether you're better off forgetting the whole thing. While marketing is always a bit judgmental, you can drastically increase the odds of succeeding by building a decision tree based on the market you've identified. The branches can be pruned or allowed to sprout based on how many factors you've identified. Once you've identified your primary market and honed your message, it's time to segment.

Strategies for Segmenting

Segmenting is one of those buzzwords that pop up now and again in marketing. The basics of segmentation are simple. Markets are divided into targeted opportunities. The depth of these opportunities help managers make decisions about the quantity and the quality of their marketing efforts. Successful niche marketing is the product of segmentation. A key part of segmenting is defining a broad, targetable base of consumers whose latent needs are not satisfied by existing products.

There are still bucketloads of opportunities out there if you look with an open, creative mind. In the United States there is a market for absolutely anything. Even bat guano is sold to farmers for its nitrogen-giving properties. But you have to find the farmers who need guano. The ultimate segmentation goal is to reach and sell to a concentrated number of people that are already disposed to the product.

There are only two basic segmenting theories. Both work:

1. Find people who need what you make and sell it to them the way they want it sold to them.
2. Change your product to appeal to certain groups—for instance, a good/better/best product development strategy might target people in several economic segments.

Segmenting can be fraught with danger if you don't do it methodically. By nature, a segmentation strategy that will appeal to one group may turn off another. You must sometimes say different things to different people—at the same time. When Levi-Strauss branched out into designer clothes, sales actually dropped. Their core users were not hearing and seeing what they expected to hear and see from Levi-Strauss.

Ten Segmentation Strategy Disconnects

The wrong person is targeted

The psychology is wrong

The timing is wrong

The selling proposition is confusing

The market is too amorphous

The market is not amorphous enough

Not enough planning of the "sale"

The program is too focused

The program is not focused enough

The product is too focused

The product is not focused enough

The first rule of marketing is to know your customers. The primary mission of segmentation is to satisfy those customers. Your product should be special for some reason. The trick is to find your leadership position and appeal to a consolidated audience who share similar interests. Markets can be segmented in much more sophisticated ways than marketers usually think of, but to be effective you need to understand your audience very well.

Broad-Based Segmentation Strategies

Many broad-based segmentation strategies are built upon customer profiles. If you ask a person to describe himself he will usually describe himself like this:

"I'm a 34-year-old insurance salesperson with a wife and three kids. I like gardening and racquetball."

This statement offers at least eight ways to approach this prospect though various segmentation strategies.

1. He's a man.
2. He's a white collar worker.
3. He's married.
4. He has three young children.
5. He's athletically inclined.
6. He fits into the 30-40-year-old age group.
7. Since he plays racquetball, he's probably health-conscious.
8. Since he likes gardening, he's probably receptive to offers to buy flowers and seeds.

Here are some of the most common segmentation and subsegmentation opportunities:

Sex There are two kinds of product groupings—male and female. Some products, like toothpaste and premixed, low-alcohol drinks are usually bought by females. Some products, like shaving supplies and strong liquors, are usually bought by males. Now you may say "naturally, men's shaving cream is bought by men." But many shaving cream buyers are women and they buy it for themselves. You may be able to create a strong, preemptive positioning by targeting a new men's shaving cream to women.

Age Age is our largest affinity group. People gravitate to people of similar ages. Products can be marketed to children, to teenagers, to young singles, or to middle-aged consumers.

A rule of thumb in segmenting to kids is to always show kids older than your target market. Little kids aspire to be bigger kids.

When appealing to people nearing fifty, on the other hand, show people younger than that age and show them in action and in social settings.

The Mature Market This category is not lumped into age segmentation because it is large, growing and full of subsegments. This group is growing faster than the overall population. This market can broken down into four subcategories, each of which has different needs.

Age 50-64 (older)
65-74 (elderly)
75-84 (aged)
85 plus (very old)

Contrary to a common misconception, mature households have more money to spend than any other demographic. Disposable income (i.e. after tax) per capita is higher among mature households than among groups having a head of household under 50.

Occupations If you ask people to describe something about themselves, they'll usually mention their job connection first. It is what defines them. In advertising, it helps to market to an occupational aspiration. For instance, if a person works on an assembly line place him in situations where he can become a foreman.

Social Class Despite the belief that we live in a classless society, people know what social class they are in. People will reject a marketing strategy that is either too "uppity" or too "downscale."

Geographics People in different parts of the country behave very differently. Here are five extreme generalities, and segmentation possibilities, to give you a start in your marketing foray.

1. *California and the West*: They are very trendy and like to try products with a unique twist.

2. *Midwest*: As the bromide goes, these are "show-me" down-to-earth type people. They are more prone to a reason-why type of approach.
3. *South*: These people, like those in the Midwest, tend to be more traditional. They are often slow in picking up new ideas and products. They respond best to advertising and new product offerings from names and brands they have had relationships with.
4. *Northeast*: These people are more difficult to categorize. They are early adopters, but there are pockets in Maine and the other Northern states that take slowly to new ideas.
5. *Northwest*: This is the fastest growing segment. Northwesterners are trendy and like to give lip service to environmental issues. Typically these people, recently relocated from the West and the East, want to leave their old ways—and products—behind them.

In general terms, when segmenting geographically, choose the area that is easiest to market to logistically. Market and tailor your communications programs to the above basic characteristics.

Family Life Cycles Another significant segmentation variable is based on how many people live at home and help in the family's buying decisions. Families can be further broken down into:

- Singles
- Older single-parent families
- Newly married couples
- Full (traditional) families
- Newly single
- Empty nest couples

Consumer Role As people grow older, they enter new consumer roles. For instance, when a woman becomes a grandmother she is more likely to buy more expensive, even extravagant toys for grandchildren than she was apt to buy as a mother. Teenagers entering the adult phase in their consumer lives will often buy the product that their mothers used successfully.

Ethnicity Hispanics, Blacks, Asians, Native Americans—virtually all ethnic groups have their own buying habits. Granted, all groups are becoming homogenized to a certain extent. But, the greater the concentration of ethnic grouping in a locality, the more they will cling to the "old ways."

Products and flavors "from the old country" are, of course, readily accepted and highly prized by the elders in these groups but also, not surprisingly, by their kids.

How Marketing Based on Emotional Hot Buttons Works

Satisfaction Sought	*Strategy*
Desire for control	Show how consumers can control their lives through a product.
Desire to be loved	Show how the product will make the user more popular with other people, especially a loved one.
Desire for prestige	Show how the product will increase the buyer's status with other people.
Desire to love and nurture	Play to the nurturing instinct by showing how your product can give someone else care.
Desire to be a better person	If your product can help one break a bad habit or become a better person, shout the message loud and clear.
Desire for belonging	Create an affinity group that a person can aspire to through the use of your product.
Desire to save time	You can't buy time, but show the consumer how to make better use of available time.
Desire to reinvent oneself	Show the consumer how to leave the old baggage (i.e. bad debts, obesity, bad habits, etc.) behind and start anew.
Desire for self-gratification	The desire for pleasure or a self-reward has always been a strong motivator.
Fear of losing something	Promise the consumer protection from the outside world. Show how your product will protect the things and relationships the buyer treasures.

Focus on Heartfelt Segmentation

Use psychology, not statistics, when building your customer base. Heartfelt segmentation can be considered a new kind of segmentation. In heartfelt segmentation you push the users' emotional hot buttons rather than sell the physical benefits. In groups where people are naturally segmented by their emotional inner drives, your product should deliver emotional as well as physical gratification.

Segment by User Status

Segment by people who have bought your product before. This doesn't have to be the exact product. It can be a similar product or one that is directly competitive to your product.

One direct-mail marketer looks at how much money a consumer has invested in a particular interest. If a person has $500 dollars invested in cookbooks, for example, then the person will be a very willing prospect for cookware and gourmet foods.

Four User-Status Segments

1. The buyer has heard of your company but has never bought from you.
2. The buyer has tried your product; it is one of a group of products she uses.
3. The buyer uses your product often.
4. The buyer uses the product because nothing is available. (She has never heard of your company or your product.)

Segmentating by Occasion

A quick way of segmenting is according to various occasions. Merchants like to gear up for concentrated seasonal rush. For many marketers, it can be more efficient to concentrate a campaign around a particular buying time than to keep up the selling momentum all year round. Seasonal segmentation opportunities are:

Valentine's Day
President's Day
Easter
Mother's Day

Father's Day
Memorial Day
Vacations
Fourth of July
Back to School
Christmas
New Year

A Six-Step Strategy for Segmentation

1. Identify bases for segmenting the market.
2. Put a human face on your target market.
3. Identify the efficiency of reaching your market.
4. Select the market.
5. Identify the positioning.
6. Attack.

Strategies for Planning Your Focus

An old poster reads, "When you're up to your butt in alligators, it's hard to remember that your job was to drain the swamp."

Focusing means going after your objective and market in a singular way. No matter what marketing monsters come your way (and they will), you'll have to deal with them by staying focused. Straying from your objectives and marketing strategy will dilute your resources in terms of money and energy.

Consider yourself a specialist using your vast (or less than vast) resources to solve one consumer problem that no one else is solving. The focus key will help you get past the giant marketers who are obsessed with megalomania. You're probably not going to fight off Microsoft or Nike "mano a mano" but you can focus on solutions to problems that they are not addressing.

There is a difference between focusing and segmenting.

Segmenting is planning. *Focusing* means harnessing your research for the attack. Focusing is determining where and how to implement your resources. Once you've identified your segment and window of opportunity, it's time to isolate those areas that have market potential. The thrust of focusing is to determine how to best position your product and to decide on the strategic directions you should take with your brands.

Five Proven Focusing Strategies

1. Create, explore and exploit new consumer and trade opportunities that you have identified. This should be done on an ongoing basis.
2. Hone in on consumer needs not met by existing products as identified in the Identify and Segmentation strategies.
3. Create products and enhancements based on perceived consumer needs:

   Develop and feed niche market segments that you've uncovered.

   Develop clearly superior products where existing products and markets already exist.
4. Leverage your technical advantages of products and product lines that are demonstrably better than any other product on the market.
5. Develop new marketing channels and distribution alternatives.

Three Sample Market Focus Strategies

Focus on Activities Sneaker manufacturers have revolutionized the formerly moribund running shoe business by creating and positioning products for running, walking, and basketball, thus virtually changing the footwear industry.

Focus on Seasons Aries has built a business on its Isotoner glove which has a very profitable six-week selling life per year.

Focus on Distribution Hanes has built a business out of a utilitarian, parity product by developing and continuously updating its original L'Eggs merchandising strategy.

Eleven Questions to Help You Focus

1. What is the strongest leverageable appeal?
2. How should the benefits of the product be communicated?
3. Who should they be communicated to?
4. How can the selling concept be expanded to develop even more profit opportunities?
5. What level of consumer represents the strongest target consumer base?
6. What is your truly leverageable product difference?
7. How should it be leveraged?
8. How should it be positioned against current and possible future alternatives?
9. What products would it replace?
10. How and when would the product most likely be used that differs from competitors?
11. What strategic imagery elements need to be developed in addition to your product's intrinsic benefits?

Strategies for Attacking the Market

Any reasonably well-stocked bookstore features a wide variety of works on how to attack a market. All the marketing disciplines have adherents who brag that the way they do it is best. But the best way to attack is to use all the disciplines to create an integrated effort. The remainder of this book is about attack strategies, so I'll just offer a brief outline for now.

The key words are to *adapt* and *adopt*. Adapt your products and strategies to your market. Adopt the most promising positioning to deliver on these needs. This means changing your product to fulfill consumer demands. *While you've been thumbing through the above for strategies and information, you were actually planning your attack.*

- You've identified the vastness of your market so you can create materials to sell.
- You've put a human face on your target market so you can create ads and positionings that speak to these people specifically.
- You've identified your leadership positioning so you can broadcast it to distributors.
- You've identified your competitors so you can rub their noses in your product, or you can keep out of their way.
- You've segmented your products so you can focus on the right distribution outlets.
- You know the economic opportunity so you can go ahead with your plan.

The best way to attack is to do it on all segmented fronts. Segmentation strategies targeted to a single market are not always the best. They tie the firm to a single market segment. If that segment declines in size or if a market's taste changes, your sales can erode.

Illustration 2.3
Three attack "schematics" to help you plan your attack.

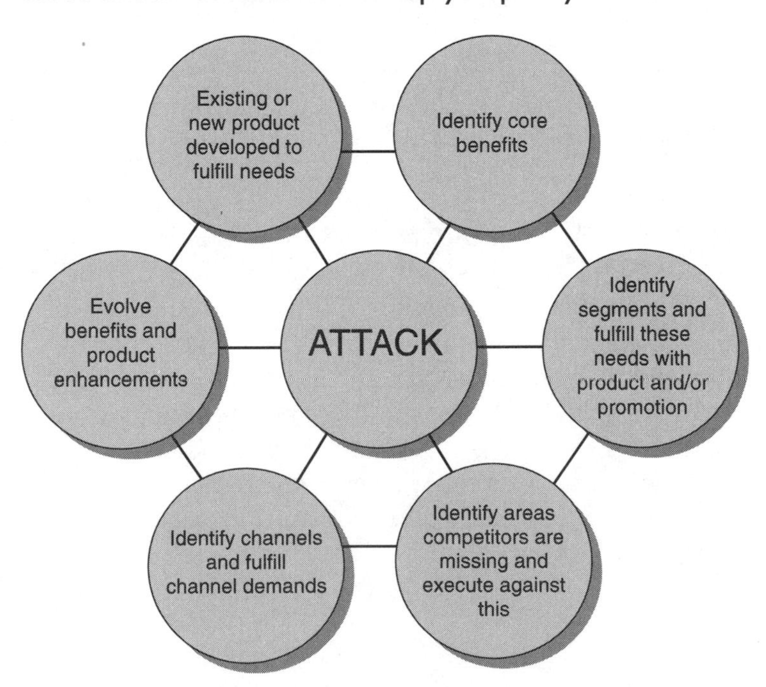

Illustration 2.4

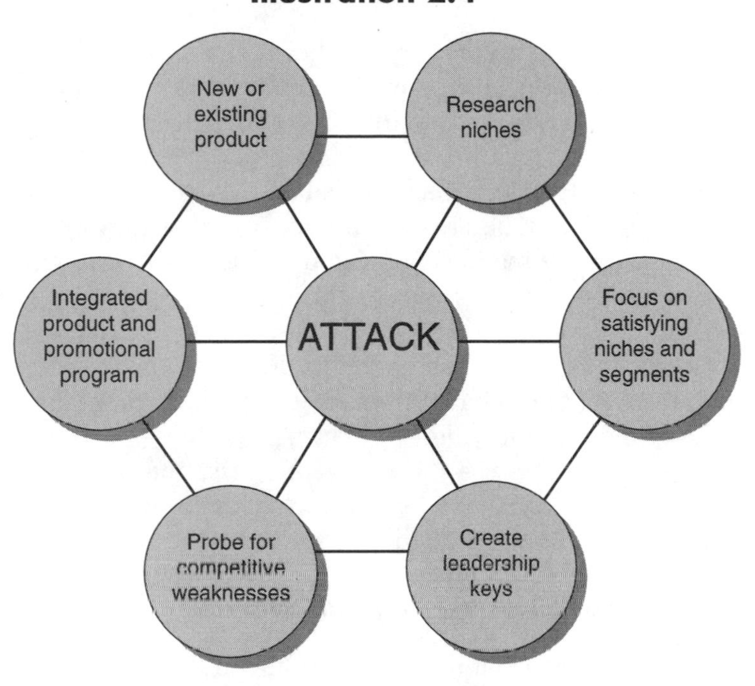

Illustration 2.5

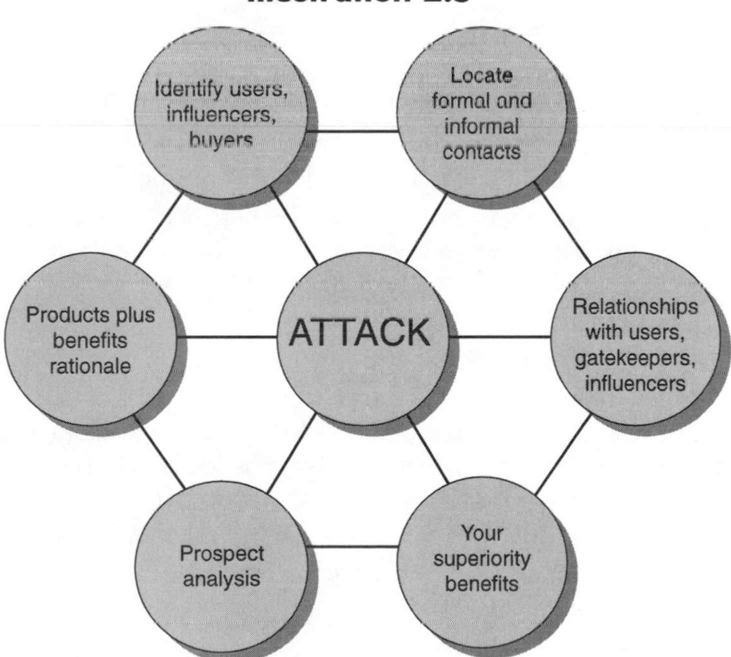

Strategies for Evolution

Strategic planning was the war cry of the eighties but it fell out of favor because companies didn't factor in the evolvement of markets and products. You're marketing in a constantly changing market and you need to make provisions for changes.

Most product and sales forecasts assume that sales and profits will flow from market share. They don't take into account that new competitors will always be changing the market. But if you've identified your competitors in advance, you're not going to be too surprised.

Changing environments require new strategies and tactics because a tactic becomes old as soon as a competitor learns to use it. Constantly evaluating and assessing your changing market and your competition will keep you alive, growing and glowing.

As mentioned in the example of Levi-Strauss, entering unfamiliar territory can be disastrous. That's why it's important to evolve in a way that's going to be accepted by your ultimate customers.

Five Strategies for Assessing and Evaluating Your Market

1. Do formal and informal research in your product and your customers. (See Chapter 3.)
2. Contact a sampling of your customers by telephone at least every quarter.
3. Create feedback mechanisms and strategy sessions at least every month.
4. Continuously do store checks and distributor checks.
5. Do internal "paranoia checks" every month to determine whether or not your objectives are still current, feasible and measurable.

One-to-One Marketing Strategy

The airlines do it. Joe's Service Station does it. Capital Concierge does it. Does what? They avoid the customers-as-statistics syndrome because they work with their customers one by one.

They develop strong relationships with their existing customers, which is a great deal less expensive than developing new customers. The airlines treat their frequent fliers to the best seats and special promotions. Joe's Service Station inputs license plate numbers to instantly identify customers by name and get information on their preferences, like whether they want their oil checked and their windshields cleaned. Capital Concierge, a company that takes care of the special needs of travelers and executives, keeps a database of their customers' needs and preferences. That way, they know in advance what their customers want—sometimes even before the customers themselves, know what they want.

One-to-one marketing carries the five strategic steps—Indentify, Segment, Focus, Attack, and Evolve—to new heights. It requires learning about your individual customers so that you know who are most valuable to you. It then means customizing your product or service to enhance your company's value to these particular customers. In the past, this practice was called "stroking." Let's face it, everyone likes to be stroked.

One-to-one marketing is becoming imperative with the stiff competition in goods and services. As you learn more about your customers you can use this knowledge to create new products and services for your most valuable customers.

Seven Effective One-to-One Marketing Strategies

1. *Get all the information you can about your customers.* Use polls, sweepstakes sales transactions, website hits to build a strong, usable database.
2. *Calculate each customer's true value.* Figure what a customer may spend and what it will cost you to keep this customer.
3. *Know what and when the customer is likely to purchase.* For example, figure out when a customer's next business trip or vacation is coming up and time your marketing material to meet that person's needs. Once again, this info can be obtained through polls, giveaways (with data collection) and personal or telephone contact.
4. *Listen to and solicit complaints.* These can be opportunities in disguise. When a person knows his complaint is taken seriously, he is more likely to bond with a company. How can he complain if you fixed up his problem according to his specifications?
5. *Get information about other potential customers.* People prefer to buy from a company that was recommended. In all of your contact work,

ask for the names of friends and associates. Send a thank you note to the customer for getting the name.

6. *Cultivate your top customers.* In catalog operations, building relationships is much more difficult. It's obvious that you can't build strong relationships with 20 million customers, many of whom will never talk to you or meet you. But you can analyze your customers through sales figures to find out which ones are valuable enough to warrant the extra effort of building a relationship with them.
7. *If you're a retailer, keep notes on each customer's preferences.* For instance, if you own a dry cleaning establishment, keep files on whether a customer likes their clothes with no starch, folded or on hangers.

CHAPTER THREE

Strategies for Conducting Successful Market Research

The poorest view of a market is from your office.

Research is the art of making the unseen, seen. Well-planned research will tell you everything you need to know about your market, dramatically increasing the odds of your success. Strategically planned research encourages your customers to tell you their inner secrets—what makes them buy what they buy. But misguided research will do the opposite. It will channel your energies into the wrong markets with the wrong message.

Avoid Common Research Mistakes

Because research is so critical, but all too often mishandled, this chapter will focus as much on what NOT to do as it will on what to do. We'll leave the realm of the esoteric for another book. Our concern here is to ensure that all your research efforts will provide useful information that you can act on.

Even this is not an easy approach. When I first began writing this chapter, I called on Bob Stevens, former head of research at Procter & Gamble. I told him I was looking for research tactics. He got a little emotional and told me that there are so many questions that need answers that you can't just list tactics. He's right, of course. There are many, many research tools and there's a tremendous amount of overlap.

I have roughly broken down some of the better tactics as to research and fulfillment needs. And I am indebted to Bob for sharing his knowledge with me.

Of course, I haven't defined every research tool here, but many are self-descriptive and others can be found in common research books.

Much Research Wastes Time and Resources

David Ogilvy pointed out the dangers of research in one pithy (and probably by now shop-worn) sentence. "Managers use research like a drunk leaning on a lamp post—for support rather than illumination."

All too often, research accomplishes little more than churning out reports by the pound; reports that ultimately do little more than sit in vacant cubicles where they gather mold and mildew.

Yes, many researchers can tell you in theoretical terms what kind of buyers are out there, what they eat for dinner, and even what colors the buyer's shoes are. But all too often research misses the point, which is whether or not consumers will actually *buy* your product, and under what circumstances. (See page 43 for the most common mistakes made in research according to Bob Smith.)

True Stories from Research Hell

My daughter was ambling through the local mall in Westchester, N.Y., when she was nabbed for a study.

"How old are you?" the guy asked, clutching his trusty clipboard.

"twenty one," she replied.

"No," she was told, "you're going to be thirty for this study."

She watched a commercial. He checked off all the boxes without asking any of the questions.

"I don't have time for your answers," he said. "I need to get more people. I do this all the time."

Incredible? Here's one from the client's side.

After working for three months on a new package and positioning for a company, the client said she was going to field a study using a blank, white package.

"But we worked three months to get the packaging and the positioning just right," I complained.

Bob Stevens' Eight Research Pitfalls

1. Incorporating incorrect stimuli that biases respondents one way or another.
2. Asking respondents to answer too many questions. This reduces the validity of the responses.
3. Conducting research out of context. For instance, cold drinks are taste-tested straight when consumers usually dilute them with ice; coffee is taste-tested black when the consumer uses additives; research is conducted in a simulated environment when real environments are possible; questions are asked of the wrong family member, and so on.
4. Including too many questions in a single study.
5. Asking respondents questions when they do not have the necessary facts to answer the questions, for example, asking the appropriateness of a price when relevant prices are not available.
6. Asking respondents to read things without compensating for illiteracy or slow readers.
7. Conducting interviews even when it appears there is a discrepancy in the interview. It may be the question is not as obvious as was thought. There are multiple (correct) ways of answering the same question.
8. Not giving the consumer adequate time to assess the results of a product they are testing.

"That's okay," I was told, "that's the way Research wants to do it."

"But nobody will want the product! The name, the package and the positioning are the key components. They're going to drive the business."

"That's okay," she said, "that's the way Research wants to do it."

Heres's another: A famous textile cooperative actually separated its product into 89 different tangible physical characteristics and had researchers ask people to rate each of them separately.

They never quite understood that consumers wanted the product because it was seen as natural, luxurious and upscale.

Two Practices that Doom Research to Failure

There are two key factors that result in research that is doomed to failure. The first has to do with how the research is handled and the second with a poor understanding of how communication works.

First, research is serious business. Yet, all too often the future of corporate America's million-dollar investments in new products is in the hands of part-time workers earning $6 an hour. I call them housewives (or teenagers) bearing clipboards.

It's not that these people are bad. I'm sure they want to do their job right. But their goal is to fill in the blanks, not to get the right answer. Fill-in-the-box questionnaires can be dangerously misleading.

You and the clipboard-carrying researcher have different goals. You want to obtain consumer opinions for your strategy. Your clipboard-carrying researcher wants to fill in X number of reports and go home for the night. Even if you acknowledge the plus or minus 5 percent error, your study is missing the one thing that is most important—caring. The second inherent flaw in most research projects is poor understanding of the interplay between questioner and respondent.

Even a simple "yes" answer on a will-you-buy question can be fraught with meaning.

It could mean:

"I'm too polite to say no."

"I'd buy it IF you gave me a coupon."

"Yeah, if I felt rich and was consumed with hunger at the moment."

"Yeah sure...gotta get home for dinner."

Good research flows from the marketer who is on top of every aspect of the research program. It's not enough to delegate the research function to researchers. You have to be there to hear what is said and why it's said.

Choosing the Right Research Methods

Be wary of what research methods you use. Not all research methods are effective. In fact, some are downright misleading.

Avoid Syndicated New Product Research Services

What really surprises me in quantitative research is that companies adjust their concepts to fit in with research protocols. For instance, many companies use B.A.S.E.S. by Burke. B.A.S.E.S is supposed to be able to predict how well a product will perform in the real world. I have found Burke's method and others like it B.A.S.I.C.A.L.L.Y. inadequate, giving thumbs down to many products that would do well. The "controlled circumstances" methodology of B.A.S.E.S and similar companies rule out the quirks and inanities of real-world consumer behavior that can drive a go-against-the-norms new product. That's one reason many products look the same.

Try a Better Approach—Context Research Strategy

The high-strategy way to do market research on new products is to match your test products as closely as possible to what you will deliver to consumers in the real world.

For instance, if a company develops a product through focus groups and uses imagery and packaging to create a message, that's what should be presented to consumers in research. Consumers don't buy a product in controlled circumstances. They buy a product because something about it turns them on at a given moment. It could be the name, the product taste, the company that manufactures it or a clever copy line. That's why research in context is so powerful.

Conduct Goal-Oriented Research

Like all of marketing, research works when you have a goal. A study fielded to "learn about my market" or "reduce my risk" is not reason enough to field a study. You should have clear-cut goals. The idea is to spot problems before they occur and to help you uncover new business opportunities. Even if you think you know your product, strong research will surprise you by uncovering new wants and desires.

Nine Strategic Goals for a Research Program

1. *Buyer Analysis*: What is the basic customer profile, in terms of economics and demographics?
2. *Problem Identification*: What are your customers' wants and needs? How do they want you to satisfy these wants and needs?
3. *Needs Identification*: What would they be buying when they buy your product in both emotional and physical terms? How do you need to court your customers?

4. *Product Troubleshooting*: What are the strengths and weaknesses of your product? How can you overcome your perceived weaknesses?
5. *Market Analysis*: Who are your competitors? How can you get advantage over them?
6. *Asset Leveraging*: What can you offer your customers based on your equities? How elastic are your equities?
7. *Communications Development*: What is the vital one-sentence message that you need to get across?
8. *Idea Generation*: How can you further enhance your market position?
9. *Product/Positioning Evaluation*: What products and packaging can you develop to resolve unmet needs and to return profits?

No, you don't need ten different studies to get the answers to these critical questions. Many of these can be answered in a well-thought-out concentrated project. But nothing will start until you take the initiative. Only when you have thoroughly defined your goals, can you attempt to fulfill them.

Take Advantage of FREE Research

Yes, research can be expensive. But it doesn't have to be. There is a group of people who will give valuable information to you for free. To get FREE research before you do anything else, contact the media.

This is a group of people who have a stake in your success. They are happy to enrich your knowledge because they want you to enrich their wallets through future advertising. These people are the editors of trade magazines. Editors are on top of the market and are a highly underused source of information. They should be your first stop. Ninety percent of the editors I have spoken with have been extremely helpful and courteous.

They are also very busy. Be brief and have your questions prepared. They can give you information about target markets, competition, new developments and anything else you want to know about a given market. The most it will cost you is a subscription to their magazines and, if it's a trade magazine, the subscription may even be free.

As you learn about your market, you'll be developing a learning tree that you can rely on. Undoubtedly, your editor will suggest that you check with a trade group.

I have had mixed results with trade associations. In a best-case scenario, they will give you a few specifics about their markets, but many will

Six Strategic Questions to Ask an Editor

1. Who are the basic players in your specific industry or market? Who are the leaders?
2. What is the sales volume of a category and its niches?
3. Who seem to be the strongest and weakest players?
4. What are the hot new trends or products?
5. Is the market expanding or contracting?
6. Who else should you speak with?

clam up if you're not a member. The main goal of trade associations is to propagate the species.

Check Out Sources of Secondary Research

What we've been talking about so far has been what's called *primary research*. It's the kind of research that you do when you go straight to the source. But there's another kind of research, called *secondary research*. These are basically rehashes of other people's work. But some of it is surprisingly detailed. A library is a good source; most libraries now have strong search engines that you can access by computers. Also, SVP Find in New York, has research reports about a number of industries. These reports will give you a good overview of your market and the competition. Additional sources for good secondary research are trade associations (very general, but in some cases helpful), governmental agencies (terrific for hard numbers and census data), newspaper archives, universities, the World Wide Web and the Internet.

Eventually though, if you think the market is strong enough to invest in, you're going to have to do your own research.

Ten Research Techniques to Eliminate Marketing Guesswork

1. *Interactive consumer groups*. Commonly called *focus groups*, these are among the most used research tools. Essentially, a focus group is a selected group of people with similar purchase habits or demographics that

meet to discuss your product. They are the most helpful research tool, and the most misused. More about focus groups later in this chapter.

2. *Point-of-sale research.* Point-of-sale research is done before introducing a a new package to the market.

This approach consists of having your actual products or samples on display in a supermarket. Real-world evaluation yields better results than a study done in a simulated environment—and what could be more real than a store? Point-of-sale research can help determine the consumer's perception of quality, value, appearance, and purchase probability. Point-of-sale research is more economical than other forms of research and yields a quantity of very helpful respondents.

3. *One-on-One stimulus response strategy.* In this kind of study you and your task force interview consumers and show concepts, products or other ideas to stir the consumer's psyche. In order to make this method effective all members of the task force should actively interview respondents. Research facilities in a local mall can set up the interviews for you. Interviews should run no longer than five or ten minutes.

4. *Telephone studies.* These studies provide a very general overview of the market. They can be somewhat helpful for the marketer on a budget or one who wants a very broad overview of a market. Names can be dug out of your customer database, specialized mailing lists or even a phone book.

5. *Multivariable research.* While it may be "purer research" to test only one variable of a product at a time, testing all variables at once yields faster and better results. In multivariable research care is taken to learn about the synergistic effects of all the variables that will usually drive the product in the real world. These can be done in focus groups or in one-on-one interviews.

6. *Consumer complaint tracking.* This strategy is coming into vogue now that companies are finally learning that dissatisfied customers are their best source of feedback. Complaint patterns are checked through calls to 800 numbers. These callers can then be targeted for mail and telephone studies for possible product improvements.

7. *Faux ad/concept testing.* Here's a research method that can be done via interactive groups, one-on-one interviews, the mail, or touch screens. Consumers react to concepts that are rendered into hypothetical or "faux"

ads. Consumers react to all the parts of the ad as well as the entirety of the concept.

8. *Package design research*. Package design research is the most neglected area of product research. Five major areas of the product should be assessed. These include functionality, protection, appearance, communication, image projection. In this protocol, actual products are placed on the shelf. In-store interviews are conducted among buyers and rejectors.

9. *Store checks*. Oh so basic, but many marketers seem too proud to venture in the "dirty world" of the consumer. Store checks can tell you who the key players are, how well they are doing and what products are selling. They are lab settings for product improvements and other enhancements.

10. *Forced choice assessment*. This is another research method that can be done in focus groups, in one-on-one interviews and even in telephone studies. Respondents are asked to choose from a range of similar products. The marketer makes conclusions based on the pattern of responses.

Three Ways to Research Product Performance

1. *Negative Brand Share*. Want to find out why a product is failing? Here's how. A study of Negative Brand Share can tell you why consumers are not purchasing the brand that looked so good from the confines of your desk. This technique focuses on why consumers buy another brand over the tested brand. It shows how to increase share in a general category and how to attack specific competing brands.

2. *Disposable test markets*. These are mini test markets. Displays are set up in stores in a particular region with the fully packaged product. Careful attention is paid to sales and purchase behavior near the displays. Hidden cameras can be set up to record reactions or researchers can probe customers for the acceptance or rejection of the brand. Disposable Test Markets use real stores, real shoppers, real money and delivers real purchase data.

3. Assessment in context studies. Once again, the fully dressed or mocked up product is shown to consumers. Goals of these studies are to assess value, package, display, brand differentiation and market readiness. Focus groups and one-on-one interviewing are used to collect this vital info.

Eight Methods for Finding and Filling Consumer Needs

Opportunity Development

Objective: Uncover ideas that will enhance your market position with new products, line extensions or product evolvements.

Tasks:
- Improving an existing brand
- Uncovering evolutionary changes in a category
- Uncovering paradigm shifts

Research strategies: Focus groups, complaint tracking, market segmentation studies, technical publications analysis, negative brand share, ideation sessions.

Market Analysis

Objective: Determine the current market as it relates to unmet consumer needs.

Tasks:
- Assess the value of the benefit, and the range and strength of appeal
- Confirm the need for the product
- Estimate the frequency of needs and determine the market size
- Define the competition and the perceived effectiveness of your product vs. the competition
- Assess the corporate fit

Research strategies: Focus groups, internal sales analysis, published proprietary sales data.

Concept Development Enhancement

Objective: Develop the communication of a solution to an unmet need in the consumer's own language.

Tasks:
- Develop the "reason to believe"

- Develop the reason for being
- Assess the appeal, uniqueness and market potential

Research Strategies: Focus groups, ideation sessions, one-on-ones.

Product Development and Evaluation

Objective: To develop a product that delivers on the promise.

Tasks:

- Assess the effectiveness of delivery on a technical basis
- Assess the consumer's perception of delivery

Research Strategies: Lab tests, clinicals (lab and public), spot blind use tests, focus groups.

Package Research

Objective: To develop effective packaging that has acceptable performance, a motivating appearance, communicates the concept, and stimulates trial.

Tasks:

- Assess functionality, appeal, and communication. Evaluate product protection, durability, ease of use and visual appeal
- Ensure that the package supports and communicates the image as it relates to the concept, especially in graphics and copy
- Make sure the package should also facilitate "ease of location" on the store shelf

Research Strategies: Focus groups, home use tests, one-on-one stimuli/response interviewing, spot tests on handling, opening, dispersing, closing, and disposal, point-of-sale research, disposable test market.

Brand Development Evaluation

Objective: To develop the basic parts of the brand and ensure maximum appeal.

Tasks:

Optimize:

- Product
- Package (this includes everything within a market-ready package including the name, art, colors, instructions, and so on)
- Positioning
- Promise
- Price

Research Strategies: Focus groups, one-on-ones, disposable test market, spot tests for aesthetic choices.

Advertising Development Evaluation

Objective: To determine an effective communications program.

Tasks:

- Assess the level of intrusiveness and persuasion
- Assess the effectiveness of various levels of spending

Research Strategies: Many commercials are shown at a time to see if a particular commercial or product stands out.

Day after recall, clutter reels, focus groups

(consumers are asked what commercials were seen to gauge their memory)

Market Readiness Evaluation

Objective: This step is much like a dress rehearsal. It is the first time the brand has been brought together with all the controllable market variables, including competition.

Tasks: Assessing the universal appeal, impact on the market, and value perception in the market context before major financial investments are made

Research Strategies: Disposable test market, point-of-sale research.

The "Make Nice With R & D" Research Strategy

There is usually a dichotomy between Marketing and R & D. Marketing says make what we can sell. R & D says "We came up with this new yellow glop. Put a name on in, package it and sell it." This "pox on your house" attitude helps no one. The key to putting the D into R & D is to treat R & D as a member of the marketing team. It also means that you must be a member of the R & D team. To effectively deal with R & D you must deal with it on an intersecting plane.

So what does this have to do with research? It means that R & D should be an active participant in your research, attending all focus groups and overseeing hands-on research. R & D should actively interview consumers and be included in all ideation sessions.

By including them, they will have a vested emotional interest in the product and not feel like they are forced to react blindly to your mandates. At the beginning of your program, they will usually say something like "that's not my job." But a funny thing happens when they first interview consumers. They want to do it more and more. They enjoy working with consumers and having consumers respond to their ideas. The sacred wall between R & D is broken down—and that's precisely what you want.

Define Your Opportunities and Purchase Triggers Simultaneously

What's wrong with the following scenario? R & D and marketing have worked together and developed a new kind of fabric softener. Consumers are to attach it to the dryer and it will soften clothes for three months. It sure beats using a new dryer sheet with every load. You and R & D are genuinely excited until it hits the market and is clobbered by the dryer sheets.

That's exactly what happened with Free & Soft. It was a pouch you put in the dryer and you forget about it. And that's what consumers did. They put it into the dryer and forgot about it—forever.

If R & D and marketing had looked for purchase triggers at the same time they came out with the product they would have learned that consumers WANT to add something to the dryer. They wanted to feel like they are doing something.

Focus Groups: Let Customers Write Your Sales Pitch

Imagine getting ten or so sales prospects in a room and having them tell you not only *what* they want to buy—but *how* to sell it to them. That's what well-executed focus groups are all about.

Focus groups are easily the most popular form of research used today and with good reason. They're fast and relatively inexpensive at about $3000 per group.

A focus group is an interactive gathering of people of similar backgrounds assembled to have a "focused discussion" on a certain topic, product or product category. They discuss how they use the product and what might have caused them to buy it. It's analogous to eavesdroping at a coffee klatsch or poker game and knowing you're the one that's being talked about.

When properly choreographed and run, focus groups reflect what a microcosm of society thinks and feels. When properly spaced over a variety of geographically dispersed locations, they accurately reflect how a cross-section of buyers will react to concepts in the real world. Used correctly, focus groups allow companies to "test market" ideas on an extremely efficient basis and learn a great deal about a category. It can be marketing's unique R & D Department, building on ideas through trial and error.

People will tell you that focus groups are NOT projectible, diagnostic, objective or precise. They're wrong on all counts. The problem is that focus groups are misused.

A great deal of misuse stems from a desire to control what consumers say and do. Staying flexible and making adjustments is key. Negative feedback in a focus group is as important as positive feedback. Ideas that are discarded by consumers shows companies possible pitfalls, prevent marketing pratfalls and point out things to avoid. They give companies the raw material of consumer viewpoints on which to structure a successful product or ad.

It's the intensity of consumer reaction that focus groups allow that is a key part the process. One insight gleaned from one stirring concept or question makes it all worthwhile. It's these insights into consumer reaction that allow marketing breakthroughs to be achieved.

Many focus groups go awry because marketers want respondents to become marketing experts or to intellectualize what they buy. That's wrong. YOU'RE the alleged marketing expert. All you want is to have consumers react just like they do in the real world.

How to Use Focus Groups Step by Step

Earlier we talked about research in context. What can be more contextual than developing advertising for your product and getting consumer reaction to it? The reason we create ads is simple. If you cannot create a selling premise for your product, you really don't have a product to sell. The best way to use focus groups is to set up a stimulus reaction method using "faux ads."

1. *The heart of the process.*

Instead of asking consumers what they want in a product, show it to them and let them react. Don't develop a single concept, price, or positioning and test it in isolation. Create actual ads for hypothetical products (or services). Develop as many alternatives and variations as you can.

Consumers don't know what they want until you put it in front of them. Usually consumers aren't even aware of a problem until you show them your solution.

2. *Make consumers react emotionally.*

Present these faux ads to your target consumers. Don't try to find winning ads. Look for a consumer hot button. See what excites the respondents.

Interact with consumers to seek out emotional responses rather than meaningless "head nodding." Obtain insights into purchase triggers rather than dangerously misleading "I'd buy it if I had a coupon" responses. Use your ads to probe into consumer needs, desires, and perceived problems, then identify solutions. Make consumers react to real-world products, solutions, and purchasing stimuli, instead of theorizing about them.

Five Strategic Questions to Ask in Focus Groups

- What about this product is different?
- When would the product be used?
- What would it replace?
- What's so good about it?
- Would you buy the product?

3. *Keep going back to consumers.*

Use different geographical areas to make sure your ad will play to wherever your target market is. Keep evolving your creative inventory until your respondents say "Yes, I want that product."

Strategic Cures for Common Focus-Group Ailments

Now for the bad news. A focus group is also the quickest way to kill a good strategy. Here are ten symptoms of focus group malaise and ten solutions.

1. *Death by preconceived notion.*

Every offhand remark heard in a focus group is gleaming evidence of what you wanted to hear going into the group. Symptoms include quotes in the back room like, "I knew they would say that" or "We knew that already, why are we here?" If something is said or done unexpectedly (or goes against preexisting research) dismiss the results by saying, "That's group dynamics at work." "She really doesn't mean that," or "She's the odd-ball in the group."

The cure: Keep an open mind, stay flexible.

2. *Understimulated respondents.*

Signs of a bored group are easy to spot: glazed eyes, yawns and requests for coffee, NO DOZ or their respondent's fee.

Sure, you're paying respondents thirty-five bucks, but that doesn't mean you should bore them to death. Bored consumers don't want to admit they like anything, because then they're going to have to sit there and discuss it!

It's easy to bring ennui to focus groups. Show white-card concepts that have no relation to the real world, or use no concepts at all. Just talk.

The cure: Excite the consumers with real world probes, products and advertising.

And then watch their eyes light up when they see something that turns them on.

3. *Give up on your concept or new product too quickly.*

If the consumer dislikes an idea, drop it right away, before anyone finds out whose idea it was. Don't even think of it again.

The cure: A minor change in positioning or product form.

This may be the difference between the success or failure of a product. Consumers buy product benefits and emotional benefits together. When you separate the two, your product will get shot down every time. Rejection of a pet product or ad hurts, but watching your rival come up with the same idea you let a focus group shoot down hurts more.

4. *Insist that your idea is good, whether consumers agree or not* (the converse of rule 3).

Batter the consumers into submission. Try hard enough and they'll say anything you want them to say. Keep harping on the product idea until they're forced to say something good about it. Then recommend a "go" to your company. "The consumers loved it. They wouldn't leave until we promised to mail them free samples."

The cure: Be reasonable.

A product is good when consumers insist they would buy it—without coupons.

5. *Kill a product based on one set of groups or one geographic location.*

Remember, America is a homogeneous collection of people with equal values, economic situations and likes and dislikes. If it doesn't play in New Jersey, it's not going to play anywhere else.

The cure: Not everyone is going to like your concept.

In fact, there are whole regions who may take your concept, ad or product as a personal affront. If at first you don't succeed, try, try again—but somewhere else.

6. *Over-analyze the results of a group.*

(This one is committed mainly by MBAs, with some help from psych minors and bored researchers.) Analyze the results to death. Listen to the tapes over and over. Over and over. Over and over. Take apart the concepts. What did the consumers really mean and why did they mean it? Attach deep psychological meanings to everything. Of course, the consumers raved over the product, but what do they know? They swore they would buy the product as soon as it was marketed. But does that mean they like it? How well will it graph?

The cure: When you show consumers something they like, you'll know.

A simple, emotional response (yeah or nay) is a lot more valuable than a 125-page pseudopsychographical analysis.

7. *Ask consumers to read something.*

Sure, reading is a very private matter. And a focus group, where people are meeting other people for the first time, is a stressful, unnatural situation. It's virtually impossible to get consumers to comprehend anything about your idea solely by making them read it. But make them do it anyway.

The cure: Read the concepts to consumers, then let them react.

8. *Death in absentia.*

Encourage as few people as possible to attend the groups. They probably won't believe what the consumers said, but at least they'll be out of your hair.

The cure: Attend the groups.

Try to get everyone else there, too, instead of waiting for the book (the 125-page moderator's report that you requested but will never read). The most important parts of the focus group are the people behind the mirror.

9. *The know-it-all.*

The know-it-all respondent and the know-it-all respondent who speak "for the buying public" and the know-it-all marketer who knows the buying public so well he translates everything the consumers are saying while they're saying it. Any one of these will shortcut any progress.

The cure: Shoot 'em.

10. *The midnight postmortem.*

You've been sitting in a darkened room for six hours, trying to grasp more facts than the new IBM Million K computer can hold. Make a decision right now that will affect the whole life of the project.

The cure: Don't resist all urges to recap.

Go back to your hotel and sleep. Wait until the next day or so and you'll be amazed how everything comes together.

Focus Groups as Marketing Tools

Get a good moderator, stimulate your groups well and listen to the people you're trying to sell. Focus groups are more than research tool, they're a marketing tool.

Interviewing Consumers

Just ask what interests you. If you can't think of an aspect of your product that piques your curiosity, then get out of marketing.

Never Break this Research Rule

Being there is the one cardinal rule in focus-group research that should never be broken. The only way you can learn about consumer desires is to hear them verbalized and to watch their body language. Keep a hard and fast rule: if you can't attend the groups, you can't comment on what was said.

How to Make Management Buy in

The best way to get management to buy into your programs (if they won't attend the groups) is to put your concepts or ideas on a wall or chart and discuss each one. Than, you can tell management that you are not guessing about the market, you are giving consumers what they want.

Stay on Top of the Project

When you field a study, make sure you know how it is carried out—the key people who are actually doing the study. Make sure the supplier stays on top of the project from day one. Make unannounced visits to research sites and try to get interviewed.

Use Long-Form Questions

Use more response-generating essay questions rather than the typical "How do you rate the product questions?" It's hard to put this data into computers and analyze it, but that's your supplier's problem, not yours.

Make sure you're getting the reactions you're paying for. Your future success depends on it.

Look for Credibility Rather than Believability

Almost every research maven likes to ask if a premise for a product is believable. My answer is simple. Who cares? Moviegoers suspend belief if a movie grips them. Consumers will suspend belief if the product offers a solution to a problem.

There's a difference between *credibility* and *believability*. Managers and ad researchers—again misguided—test advertising premises to make sure they are believable. Believability is really not that important. Credibility is not the same as believeability. Good advertisers know that consumers will suspend belief when an ad or product strikes a psychological nerve.

Consumers believe what they want to believe. Perception is reality, even if it's wrong. It's the creative person's job to make the consumer *want to believe*.

Reducing Research Costs

Research can be expensive, but there are ways that even the smallest companies can get the same research results as bigger companies.

Do-It-Yourself Research

Do your research personally. Hang out at the local supermarket. Watch how a customer reads labels and makes buying decisions. Learn about your customers by talking to them. Learn how they speak, and more importantly, how they respond. Talk to them! It's a lot cheaper than getting a researcher to talk to them.

Research Before You Spend

DON'T scrimp or create prototypes too soon. Entrepreneurs spend thousands on packaging, equipment, and ingredients before they ever explain the product to consumer to make sure there's a purchase interest and a viable selling proposition. Your research will serve as your blueprint. It's easier to build a home from scratch the way the occupants want it than to tear down walls and renovate.

Conduct Your Own Focus Group

If you can't afford a moderator, moderate yourself. It's not rocket science. Show concepts—watch how your respondents react. If you can't afford a traditional focus group, be creative. For instance, if you have a product for kids, go to a local nursery school for sampling, or to local little league games or soccer games.

If you can't afford groups, approach strangers with products and ads. One software company wanted to develop a program for veterinarians. After he read my other books, he took his products out to veterinarians and gave them $20 for looking and talking about the product. Because of this he decided he would lose money if tried to develop and market the product. He figured handing out $20s saved him about $100,000 in money he would have lost creating the product.

The Business-to-Business Link

When you have a business product, talk to businesspeople in your industry. Most entrepreneurs don't believe ostensibly busy people will give up their time, gratis. They're wrong. Businesspeople are the easiest people to approach. If they know you're not trying to sell them something, they're usually thrilled to spend an hour or more talking about your product. People love to give advice and promote themselves as experts.

Don't Ask Friends or Colleagues

One major caveat though is DON'T ask friends or colleagues what they think. They'll either be polite and tell you it's a nice idea or they'll be brutal and say, "This is the stupidest thing I've ever seen." Keep away from the people you know; they're the worst people to talk to. When I wrote my recent book, I was reticent to the point of paranoia about letting friends read it. If they liked certain passages I would want to keep them even if I wasn't comfortable with them. If they didn't like it, my ego would take a hit and I would write the whole thing over. Be sure to keep your perspective.

CHAPTER FOUR

Strategies for Written Communications and Presentations

Earlier we talked about the one-sentence solution to developing a marketing strategy. Let's transfer that strategy to paper. We've seen that you and your product are, by default, reduced to one sentence in the minds of your prospective customers. But that's not the end of it.

Brevity is the watchword in all your marketing efforts. When you write, your entire selling premise is going to be reduced to a piece of paper or two. Lunch dates and personal appearances are going to grease the way to a successful sale but your hard copy document is going to clinch the deal.

A while back, I was teaching an MBA class in Marketing Strategies at the University of New Mexico. As part of their course work, students were to write a presentation for a mythical new product. They had worked long and hard for three solid months on the project, and some of the product ideas were excellent. They weren't thrilled when I asked them to write their papers over. The grammar was right, the MBA six-syllable words were used correctly, even their indexes were acceptable. They made one mistake. They forgot—or never knew—that they were writing a *selling* document.

Writing as a Marketing Tool

Every piece of paper you send out is a selling document and should be treated as such. To many people, you are the letter, or memo, you write.

Your letter or memo may be the only chance you'll get to attract someone's attention. When you present your case verbally, your words vanish into the air. But when you write, your work may be studied over and over.

You don't only use written material to sell to customers. A well-written memo is often the strategy you need to motivate your co-workers or management.

Never underestimate the power of a letter or memo. It cements relationships and serves as the basis of a super marketing program. Yes, letters and memos can also backfire. Written documents carry great force, but they also leave a paper trail back to you. That's why paper-shredding machines are so popular. Many people wait until a premise is in writing before taking action. Advance your goals by writing better and faster than anyone else does.

Pay Attention to the Details

Forceful writing is a strategic tool that allows you to button up what you've said personally and to reinforce your personal presentations. Ninety percent of a presentation is forgotten within one hour of a verbal presentation. Your letters and memos reinforce the strong points you've worked so hard to make. In addition to closing or opening a deal, your written communications say a lot about how you run your business, whether you're conservative or creative, detail-minded or sloppy.

When selling in a business-to-business situation, your letter will be handed through various management levels, to people waiting to nitpick with you on something. So our first strategic rule of writing is to avoid giving anyone anything to nitpick about. Make your letter and style perfect from the "Dear so and so" to the "Sincerely Yours." That also means, when revising a form letter on a computer, to always change the date. (I always forget that rule.)

Tips on Writing Style

Jargon is important. Assess your reader's level of expertise and USE JARGON that the person is familiar with. Yes, I know that most books on business writing say in bold type DON'T USE JARGON, but your prospects want to know that you are familiar with the buzzwords. Using jargon correctly shows that you are part of the prospect's club. Just don't overdo the jargon because it can obfuscate the message to even you.

Avoid generalities. Make sure you are specific. Generalities bore readers to tears. Specifics give people the ammunition they need to make a decision. If you say a certain strategy can help the reader, explain how. If you point out a specific feature of a product, give the benefit. Don't say "This new product can save you money." Say, "This product can save you X amount over a competing product."

Write the way your audience talks. Be conversational. Read the letter out loud to make sure that the letter is conversational. When you find that you're stumbling over a sentence, redo it. When you do stumble over a sentence, it is probably too long. Make two or even three sentences out of it.

Intermingle long and short sentences. Short sentences invite the reader to read more. The reader doesn't have to work too hard.

Vary the paragraph lengths. Long paragraphs look—and are—daunting to the reader. An ideal paragraph should have about four sentences of varying lengths. The perfect mix is a ratio of three short sentences (eight words or less) and a longer sentence of eight to twenty words.

Furnish only what the reader needs to know—then shut up. Making more points than is absolutely necessary gives more reasons for your prospect to react negatively.

Humor is VERBOTEN. Don't be humorous. The reader probably won't get the joke and you'll come off looking foolish and/or naive.

NEVER send out a letter the same day you write it. Look at it the next day and react to it as if you were the target of the letter.

If the letter is a follow-up to a meeting or a presentation, repeat what the prospect has told you as exactly as you can. Don't surprise the reader. If you give her what she wants in her own words, it's more difficult to turn you down.

Don't worry too much about length but try not to exceed two pages. When your writing has a strong reader benefit, you can write an encyclopedia and the reader will read it. The problem with a document that's more than two pages is that the material is perceived by the prospect as a tough read. The prospect will keep putting it off.

Take the time to personalize all written correspondence, if possible at the beginning of a letter. It helps develop an immediate rapport and relationship. You can bring up a business deal, a seminar you shared together, or a recent promotion. I once sent a letter to a former client congratulating her on a new promotion. She called me back immediately with a project. At a later meeting, I questioned her about how many people wrote to congratulate her. She told me I was the only one. That's why I had no competition for the project.

Relate to the reader's problems or their opportunity throughout the letter. Use the word YOU. It is the single most important word you can put into a letter or memo.

The Most Important Words You'll Ever Use

Free and *new* are the most important words in advertising and sales material. But there is one additional word you must know. That word is *you*. There is no greater interest than self-interest. Every time the word *you* is used, you are targeting a person's self-interest. Now, one might say that in communicating to a company like Xerox or IBM you are selling to a corporation. That is not true; you are selling to a person within a corporation who has the same goals as you.

Write with a Purpose

You don't send out a written communication because you want to. You send it out because it is necessary to achieve a goal or action. Your purpose should be totally clear. Each communication should focus on just one point. The best sales letters focus on getting the recipient to do just one thing. Clearly tell the reader what you expect him to do and how you want him to do it.

Take This Self-Test Before You Write Anything

Why are you writing this letter?

What action do you want this person to take?

What do you want this person to get out of this letter?

How is it going to advance your goals?

How do you want the reader to feel after receiving your missive?

Writing in Five Steps

There are five parts to every sales letter and most memos. While the order of the parts is not always constant, this guide can help you build your letter. Every letter should consist of a lead, a benefits statement, the deal, a credibility statement and a call to action.

The Lead

Begin your communication in an interesting way. Your lead must be interesting or catchy. The lead must sell and/or captivate the reader personally. Even the longest sales letter begins with a lead. The lead will make or break your letter because if you don't motivate the reader to read on, then the letter probably won't get read.

Ten Extraordinary Leads for Sales Letters

1. "Sally Jones (someone the prospect knows) thought you would be interested in this product." This is the best opening for a letter since you have immediately established a relationship and commonality.
2. "It was enjoyable speaking with you yesterday. As we discussed, we are looking to enter into a joint venture...." This is great for a follow-up after a meeting. Use the exact words your prospect said.
3. "I need your help...." (People love giving advice.)
4. "My name is Sally Jones and I can show you how to...."
5. "In the next few minutes, you're going to discover...."
6. "Congratulations!" (Don't forget the exclamation point.)
7. "I invite you...."
8. "I've enclosed...." (Don't forget to enclose something.)
9. "If/then" (i.e. If you're like me, then you'll appreciate...."
10. "Thanks...."

The Benefits Statement

In a sales letter, these are the benefits the people will get out of using your product. Make them clear and relate the benefits to the prospect as specifically as you can. Use bullets, if possible and back-up the benefits more fully in the body of the letter.

The Deal

This is the offer you want to make in a sales letter or the points you want to make in a memo. Explain what you are trying to sell to the reader. It could be yourself. Or it could be your ideas for a marketing strategy. Make your points clearly and succinctly. Again, using bullets makes it easy for the reader to assess what she's getting.

The Credibility Statement

In a sales letter you need to tell your reader why you (or your product) are qualified to do the task you are writing about. In a project memo, this is how you are uniquely qualified to reach your conclusions. If your letter is going to be passed on though various management strata, this can help make you an authority figure.

The Call to Action

The call to action is the key part of your letter. Without a specific call to action, you might as well toss the letter into the trash. You can learn more about specific response mechanisms in the chapter on direct marketing (Chapter 16). But for now, remember that you must ask for only one action—whether it's to make a phone call or to return a reply card—in every letter. In memos, recommendations or project status letters, you must always include next steps.

Writing Proposals That Work

Proposals should not be difficult for you if you've learned the essentials of writing effective letters. They're just a little bit more detailed and a bit longer. But the principals are the same.

Two Killer Mistakes That Marketers Make

1. Don't send out a letter or proposal before it is properly done. It's worse than not sending a letter at all.
2. Never fax the prospect an advance copy of a proposal, thinking it is for the prospect's eyes only. NEVER send anything to anyone in a

Sample letters for you to adapt

Illustration 4.1

An example of the five-point letter-writing strategy with call-outs

BARRY FEIG'S
CENTER FOR PRODUCT SUCCESS

Telephone 800-707-0739

6217 Antigua, Suite H
Sandia Mountains, New Mexico 87111

October 15, 1991

Ms. Fran Heller
AnyCompany Books
229 Westword Way
Cedar Crest, NM 87111

Dear Ms Heller:

{LEAD}
Bill Brown thought you would be interested in my book on developing new products that succeed.

[BENEFITS AND REASON}
My New Product Strategies column generates numerous calls for help from companies desperate for a "marketing flotation device"....and with good reason.

The marketing world is constantly evolving with new products and new ideas to satisfy changing tastes. One thing is definite, though. There is a 90% failure rate for new products. What worked five years ago may not work today. I see this book as a collection of the how to's and why's of successful, proven marketing with exciting case histories, marketing insights and controversial viewpoints.

Even in a recession (or especially in a recession), people dream of the one new product that will make them financially independent and able to control their own destiny.

And companies know that if they don't have successful new products to compete in ever-evolving markets, competitors will snatch their business in an eyeblink. That's why it's important to have new products constantly in the pipeline.

This is a how-to book to help both entrepreneurs and established marketers achieve their goals. It's a unique approach for developing and marketing new products (without going broke). Unlike other books in this category, it's as appropriate for the small company or novice marketer who wants to sell a new kind of beverage as it is for the mid-sized or larger company who wants to establish a successful new product program.

The book establishes several new principles that go beyond the scope of typical M.B.A./ business school mentality or competitive books. The method outlined in chapter 7 has proven itself time after time and is available no where else.

formerly New Products Workshop, Inc.
New York, New York

{MORE BENEFITS}
The potential market for this book is broad. Of course, there is the core, easily targeted market of standard businesses. An even larger market, though, is the "wannabee" marketer who really has no clue of where to begin....or the small business who is bogged down in any phase of new product development. I cringe when I attend industry trade shows and find that the people who can least afford it are making basic marketing mistakes. Management types, too (almost always closet entrepreneurs), usually lack any real knowledge of new product development outside of their own particular discipline.

The book can also be updated annually as new trends take place and new success stories (and failures) added. My contacts, resources and the hundreds of consumers I interview every year as part of my business keep me extremely current and aware.

{CREDIBILITY STATEMENT}
As background information, I am President and Creative Director of New Products Workshop, a company that specializes in new products and positionings. (Clients include American Express, Colgate-Palmolive, Church & Dwight, Pepsico and American Cyanamid). A more complete bio is enclosed.

I can have a finished manuscript ready in three months and am able to write continuing books with similar themes. I could also play a major role (if you desire) in promoting my book. The publishers of the popular trade magazine I write for have also offered to contribute promotional efforts.

{CALL TO ACTION}
Please call me to discuss it further.

Sincerely,

Barry Feig
President

Illustration 4.2

1. A typical (weak) sales letter "A" and major improvements "B."

BARRY FEIG'S
CENTER FOR PRODUCT SUCCESS

(A)

Telephone 800-707-0739

6200 Eubank, Suite 423
Sandia Mountains, New Mexico 87111

January 20, 1998

Mr. Fred Heller
AnyCompany, Inc.
229 Westword Way
Cedar Crest, NM 871111

Dear Mr. Heller:

This letter is in reference to our conversation yesterday regarding your company's interest in a European Distributorship.

We sell over $10 million dollars of gaskets every year. We think that your company can help us break into the competitive European market. We have made major inroads in the American market since our humble beginnings but we feel that there is a major potential to increase our business. There has to be a vast market in Europe that our advertising and sales attempts have missed. Your office in Zurich may be able to help us reach that market.

We feel the best method to proceed would be to have reciprocal meetings at our facility and yours to establish an agreement that would be mutually equitable.

Sincerely,

Jeremy Fox
Executive Vice President

formerly New Products Workshop, Inc.
New York, New York

BARRY FEIG'S
CENTER FOR PRODUCT SUCCESS

(B)

Telephone 800-707-0739

6200 Eubank, Suite 423
Sandia Mountains, New Mexico 87111

January 20, 1998

Mr. Fred Heller
AnyCompany, Inc.
229 Westward Way
Cedar Crest, NM 871111

Dear Mr. Heller:

Here is an opportunity, Mr. Heller.

As the exclusive distributorship of Del Ram Monorail Gaskets, you can expand your European sales markets. We offer you an extensive line of monorail gaskets whose reliability has been proven here in the United States and in the Pacific Rim.

Our reputation has been built by manufacturing the highest quality gaskets at competitive prices. You'll be handling a line of parts with a solid track record of sales and profits. We can ship your orders within a week or less — guaranteed. As I mentioned to you, some of our customers include Rockwell Monorail Systems, Hughes Aircraft, and Toyota Technologies (Japan).

We invite you to see our facility and our unique production process. We can discuss, in more detail, the benefits of an alliance between our companies at that time.

We'll make all the arrangements. I'll call you next week to set up a visit to our New Mexico plant.

Sincerely,

Barry Feig
President

formerly New Products Workshop, Inc.
New York, New York

2. My form letter. I customize each section after speaking with a prospect.

BARRY FEIG'S
CENTER FOR PRODUCT SUCCESS

Telephone 800-707-0739

6200 Eubank, Suite 423
Sandia Mountains, New Mexico 87111

January 20, 1998

Ms. Frieda Hella
AnyCompany, Inc.
229 Westward Way
Cedar Crest, NM 87111

Dear Ms. Hella:

John Hughes thought you would be interested in the work of my company and my unique and very successful) new product/positioning methods.

Time was when you could make a good product, sell it at a fair price and the world would come knocking at your door. As you know, it's become a lot more challenging and complicated today.

I'm considered an authority on product development and marketing — my work has been recognized worldwide. McGraw-Hill Business Books — extremely demanding when it comes to their publications — thought so highly of my skills and successes that they published my book, The New Products Workshop: Hands On Tools for Developing Winners. I've enclosed some information.

I also write on marketing and new product strategy for various trade magazines (including Food & Beverage Marketing). I've enclosed a complimentary collection for you.

If you desire:

- successful new "breakthrough" products or product concepts — or to be the first to capitalize on potential growth areas,
- a dramatic new positioning for an existing product,
- to translate new or existing R & D technology into motivating products,
- a selling, original NAME for a product or new brand,
- original, truly motivating ideation techniques,

then we can put you right on target with your goals. We can help you expedite a project faster, better and less expensively than any other source you can find.

This is the same proven approach to product development and marketing that successfully opened up new growth areas for Colgate-Palmolive (professional and consumer products), Kellogg's, Arm & Hammer, American Express, Ralston-Purina, Dorman-Roth, CIBA Vision, American Cyanamid and many other fine companies.

formerly New Products Workshop, Inc.
New York, New York

My unique approach uses "radical hypothization" as a part of a comprehensive program that spawns marketplace innovation in a unique way because it simultaneously identifies both new product/merchandising opportunities and consumer purchase triggers.

It's painstaking trial-and-error procedure that defines consumer purchasing behavior in terms of your specific equity versus the competition. Every product we recommend is an on-the-shelf self-salesperson with a superior, recognizable selling premise that takes full advantage of your resources.

That's how Union Carbide made a remarkable turnaround with its Glad Lock Bags. From a test-market failure prior to our ground-breaking strategy, it now regularly challenges Dow's Zip Lock for market dominance with a forty-percent share of market in key areas.

You'll receive a specific product profile that's immediately actionable. It includes:

- key features and benefits — consumer driven necessities with our exclusive "Share of Heart"
- key positioning strategy (and back-up strategies)
- marketing requisites
- suggested brand names (if desired)
- promotion and packaging recommendations
- pricing recommendations

Other products we have turned into household names are Colgate Junior, Colgate Toothpaste with baking soda, Deli Singles, Arm and Hammer Dryer Sheets, and many more. You'll find complete case histories in our Info-pac "How New Products Workshop Works for You" (we've changed our name but not our literature), which I've enclosed.

I'll call you to set up a meeting.

Sincerely,

Barry Feig
President

3. Proposal, sales letter and confirmation—all in one.

BARRY FEIG'S
CENTER FOR PRODUCT SUCCESS

January 20, 1998

Telephone 800-707-0739

6200 Eubank, Suite 423
Sandia Mountains, New Mexico 87111

Mr. Fred Heller
AnyCompany, Inc.
229 Westward Way
Cedar Crest, NM 87111

Dear Fred:

Thanks for giving me the opportunity to work with you to develop and implement the Public Relations program. I know we can make it a success. This formalizes our understanding.

1. **Press Kit:** Develop a press kit consisting of a biography on you, company backgrounder, case histories, reprints of relevant articles, photo of you, information on books, etc.

Cost = $1500.00 +$500.00 to develop the media list.

2. **Broadcast Media Relations:** Pitch your presence on relevant shows. Develop letter, survey findings release and mail with press kit; follow up.

Cost = $1,500.00 +/-

3. **Print Media Relations:** Pitch business publications and local editors in cities where you are working with clients. Effort could be specific to the product or service you are providing the client, and could involve a story using the client's product as an example.

(Since the book was published in 1993, we feel promotion of the book alone is limited. We recommend including the book as a secondary sell.)

Cost = $2,500.00 +/-

4. **Create News:** Position you as the leader in your field by releasing to the press your findings, trends, or predictions. We believe it is imperative to include this as a news hook to encourage the media to do something "now." For instance, topics could be the most popular new product names or categories in 1998, or the ten ways to revitalize a product in the 1990s or the ten keys to marketing success in 1998. You will do the research, and we will create the release and publicity for the findings.

We see this as the first priority, to mail with your press kit.

Cost = $1,500.00 per release.

formerly New Products Workshop, Inc.
New York, New York

5. **New Products:** Issue a press release to trade publications when you are instrumental in launching/repositioning a new product for a client. This will be in cooperation with the client, but the release would highlight your contribution and capabilities.

Cost = $1,500.00 per release

Fee for Above Services: Fee will not exceed $2,500.00/month including the above, unless specified by you. Term of agreement is from February, 1998 and will continue for one year six months, until January 31, 1999.

Out of pocket expenses (such as postage, long distance telephone calls, travel expenses) will be billed at cost.

Total project fee is $12,000.00 plus out of pocket expenses.

We also request authorization to engage professional services if needed (such as a designer for a brochure or newsletter) provided you approve their estimated fee in advance prior to incurring any cost.

Payment Schedule: Payment requested within thirty days of receipt of invoice. Invoices will be mailed at the beginning of each month.

If this meets with your approval, please sign where indicated, and return a copy to me.

We look forward to working with you and appreciate your confidence in us.

Sincerely,

Barry Feig
President

Approved and accepted, January 20, 1998

Fred Heller
AnyCompany, Inc.

4. How to integrate a proposal and a letter. Notice the use of the client's name in the last paragraph. It makes it a little more personal.

BARRY FEIG'S
CENTER FOR PRODUCT SUCCESS

Telephone 800-707-0739

6200 Eubank, Suite 423
Sandia Mountains, New Mexico 87111

January 20, 1998

To: Karen Heller
From: Barry Feig

Re: New Product Development — Contact Lens Care

Karen:

Here is our program to ideate successful new products in the lens-care area. It's based on our discussions Friday.

You'll start seeing concepts a week after start-up. As you suggested, this project will be on an accelerated schedule so you can present the ideas at your upcoming sales meeting.

I know the project will be a success. If you have any suggestions or if there are any additions you'd like me to make, please give me a call.

Barry Feig

NEW PRODUCT DEVELOPMENT PROGRAM FOR ANYCOMPANY, INC.

OBJECTIVE

- To ideate, optimize and evolve a range of actionable, new products and new product concepts for AnyCompany lens-care products. Products will fall into two categories — those that can be manufactured feasibly now; and those that may need FDA approval for future introductions.

BACKGROUND

- AnyCompany is a major manufacturer of contact lenses and lens-wear products. They wish to increase their market penetration and develop a greater consumer presence by developing and exploiting new opportunities in lens-care products. They wish to create new lens and eye-care products with proven consumer and professional appeal that will enhance and be enhanced by the AnyCompany name.
- Karen, all products will be specifically targeted to contact-lens wearers. Among areas we will consider are new formulations, promising lifestyle appeals, new uses for existing products, unique packaging and delivery systems. Additional fertile areas that come up in the ..... (continued)

formerly New Products Workshop, Inc.
New York, New York

5. How to get to the president of one of the largest financial companies in the world.

BARRY FEIG'S
CENTER FOR PRODUCT SUCCESS

Telephone 800-707-0739

6217 Antigua, Suite H
Sandia Mountains, New Mexico 87111

June 6, 1992

Mr. John Baum, President
National Financial Services
100 Fifth Avenue
New York, NY. 10285

Dear Mr. Baum:

We have a proven history of success working with National Financial Services on assignments developing new products and new business opportunity concepts.

I think you've hit the nail on the head with your remarks in the June 15 Business Week regarding National Financial Services' emotional appeal and what makes your company special.

We can help you turn around the National Financial Services business. That may sound audacious, but it isn't.

In fact, several of the new product and positioning concepts for your NWD and Altima divisions that evolved from our assignments have enormous profit potential for National Financial Services. They were overlooked in the departmental divisions of the previous management atmosphere.

I'd like to share these with you.

Our project assignments for your company have given us extraordinary insights into how you can motivate consumers and merchants to appreciate and retain loyalty to National.

With the need to differentiate the National Card from bank card competitors, our exclusive "enhanced value" principals provide National Financial Services with numerous exclusive competitive advantages.

Like you, I believe that the emotional benefits of a product are just as important as the physical (financial) benefits. That's why I'm also faxing a copy of an editorial about capturing consumer "Share of Heart" I wrote about for Advertising Age.

I'd like to come to your office and review the work we've done for National Financial Services and offer you concrete ways to build your business.

I'll call you to set up a meeting.

Sincerely,

Barry Feig

6. A letter introducing a new product and business opportunity. The venture was a huge success.

BARRY FEIG'S
CENTER FOR PRODUCT SUCCESS

Telephone 800-707-0739

6200 Eubank, Suite 423
Sandia Mountains, New Mexico 87111

January 20, 1998

Mr. Fred Heller
AnyCompany, Inc.
229 Westward Way
Cedar Crest, NM 87111

Dear Mr. Heller:

It was a pleasure speaking with you today. As we discussed, we are interested in entering into a joint venture with a baked goods manufacturer to develop a value-added product for supermarkets. We are currently developing specifications and prototypes as well as doing preliminary research.

As background information about my company, we develop new products, product positionings and marketing strategies for major companies. Our clients include Kellogg's, Pepsico, Colgate Palmolive, Ralston-Purina, Kraft and American Express.

We helped develop Glad Lock Storage Bags, Cocktail for Two for Schenley, Kibbles and Chunks and Lucky Dog dog food for Ralston-Purina. We opened a major new profit category for Colgate and were responsible for the worldwide positioning of a famous Pepsi soft drink. A new cereal we developed for Kellogg's has just hit the shelves to great success.

I also write regular features for marketing magazines about new products and marketing.

We should meet to discuss this joint opportunity.

I'll call you next week.

Sincerely,

Barry Feig
President

formerly New Products Workshop, Inc.
New York, New York

7. Short, strong sales letter to have products included in a catalog.

BARRY FEIG'S
CENTER FOR PRODUCT SUCCESS

Telephone 800-707-0739

6200 Eubank, Suite 423
Sandia Mountains, New Mexico 87111

January 20, 1997

Mr. Fred Heller
Any Company, Inc.
3200 Mountain Rd.
Cedar Crest, NM 87111

Dear Mr. Heller:

TURNKEY PROFITS! NOW!

We're very excited about our customers who have turned big profits with our mail order merchandise during the fifteen years we have been in business.

Mail order merchandise is our business. And we have it down to a science. We manufacture the product AND produce the ad too. Here is our catalog. All of the ads are available to you — **FREE.**

When you see our tested products, remember that:

- **Our products are individually packaged — ready to go in our own self mailer. Just add the shipping label.**
- **You get a category exclusive for your specialty catalog. Tell us when you plan to run the ad. No one else in your business category can use the same ad.**
- **You get 50% discounts off the list price**
- **Immediate delivery — even during the Christmas season.**

This could be the best year ever for mail order. Call me at 800-999-0000 and we'll send your product by two day Priority Mail.

Sincerely.

Barry Feig
President

formerly New Products Workshop, Inc.
New York, New York

8. Congratulatory notes can be a great help in building or rekindling a relationship. Don't sell too hard in your first letter.

BARRY FEIG'S
CENTER FOR PRODUCT SUCCESS

Telephone 800-707-0739

6200 Eubank, Suite 423
Sandia Mountains, New Mexico 87111

January 20, 1998

Mr. Fred Heller
AnyCompany, Inc.
229 Westward Way
Cedar Crest, NM 87111

Dear Mr. Heller:

Congratulations on your new position as head merchandiser of AnyCompany, Inc. I know you're going to bring in new ideas and innovations.

I extend my best wishes. If there is any way I can help you smooth your transition, please call. I know you're going to be busy for a while and so I'll call you in a month or so about how we can further your business goals.

Sincerely,

Barry Feig

formerly New Products Workshop, Inc.
New York, New York

9. Letter inviting a prospect to a trade show booth.

BARRY FEIG'S
CENTER FOR PRODUCT SUCCESS

Telephone 800-707-0739

6200 Eubank, Suite 423
Sandia Mountains, New Mexico 87111

January 20, 1998

Mr. Fred Heller
AnyCompany, Inc.
229 Westward Way
Cedar Crest, NM 87111

Dear Mr. Heller:

You're invited to our booth at the upcoming Housewares Show.

The New York Times just predicted a 20% growth in sales of storage containers. That's a sizable opportunity. If you've decided you want to get in on this product opportunity, we'd be delighted if you stop by our booth.

You'll find sixteen innovative storage solutions. And we've come up with a first — designer canisters that keep food as fresh as the day it was packed — for as long as six months.

You'll also find a complete display of our advertising and sales promotion programs. I'll be on hand to explain our dealer program and to answer your questions.

Mention this letter (or better yet, bring it) and we'll give you some free samples.

I hope to see you soon

Sincerely,

Barry Feig

formerly New Products Workshop, Inc.
New York, New York

10. Letter to respond to a trade show lead.

BARRY FEIG'S
CENTER FOR PRODUCT SUCCESS

Telephone 800-707-0739

6200 Eubank, Suite 423
Sandia Mountains, New Mexico 87111

January 20, 1998

Mr. Fred Heller
AnyCompany, Inc.
229 Westward Way
Cedar Crest, NM 8111

Dear Mr. Heller:

Thank you for visiting our trade booth at the Housewares Show. I hope your move was successful. Moving into new offices **{personal info from lead form}** offers a unique challenge to anyone's organizational abilities.

As you saw, we have many products that offer excellent merchandising and profit opportunities. The products we spoke about have strong growth potential for your business.

Enclosed is the information you requested.

Bob Jones will be following with a call to make sure your needs are satisfied and to answer any questions you may have.

Sincerely,

Barry Feig
President

formerly New Products Workshop, Inc.
New York, New York

11. Follow up to a phone call

BARRY FEIG'S
CENTER FOR PRODUCT SUCCESS

Telephone 800-707-0739

6217 Antigua, Suite H
Sandia Mountains, New Mexico 87111

July 12, 1991

Ms. Laura Meadows, Dir.
New Industries Marketing
Credit Card Division
National Financial Services
100 Fifth Avenue
New York, NY. 10285

Dear Laura:

I enjoyed talking with you today about the prospect of helping you develop new industries which would be a source of revenue for your Special Services division.

Our concept development work in the past for the Consumer Lending New Product Development Group at National Financial Services provided exceptionally successful results and earned the enthusiastic respect of Sharon Quan and the others who participated in your company's project with New Products Workshop.

Some assignments we worked on were --

. Members' Savings Program
. National Financial Services Gift Checks
. New Consumer Lending Opportunities
. Worldwide Card Services Assessment program.

I've enclosed a copy of Sharon's "recommendation" letter to us and a brochure describing the benefits you will receive working with our innovative group.

When you have a tough positioning problem or an "impossible" new product concept need, call us. We'll come through for you every time.

Sincerely,

Bob Bolton
Executive Vice President

formerly New Products Workshop, Inc.
New York, New York

12. Another follow-up to the same company

BARRY FEIG'S
CENTER FOR PRODUCT SUCCESS

Telephone 800-707-0739

6217 Antigua, Suite H
Sandia Mountains, New Mexico 87111

July 11, 1991

Mr. Robert Early, V.P. Marketing
Member Services
National Financial Services
100 Fifth Avenue
New York, NY. 10285

Dear Bob:

Following my phone conversation with you this morning, I plan to call Anita to set up a meeting so that you can personally meet Barry Feig, an extraordinary creative maverick who has made many marketing people at National Financial Services quite happy.

In advance of setting up a meeting with you, I've enclosed a brochure describing the benefits you will receive working with our very innovative group.

Concept development projects which New Products Workshop handled in the past for the Consumer Lending New Product Development Group at National Financial Services provided exceptionally successful results.

Some assignments we worked on were --
- . Members' Savings Program
- . National Financial Services Gift Checks
- . New Consumer Lending Opportunities
- . Worldwide Card Services Assessment program.

We earned the enthusiastic respect of Sharon Quan and the others who participated in the various assignments. I've enclosed a copy of Sharon's recommendation.

When you have a tough positioning problem or an "impossible" new product concept need, we'll come through with similar successes every time.

Our successful assignments with National Financial Services have given us excellent insights into effective procedures in working within your corporate structure comfortably.

Looking forward to seeing you again soon.

Cordially,

Bob Bolton
Executive Vice President

formerly New Products Workshop, Inc.
New York, New York

company unless the whole company will read it. They can and they usually will. Once that document is sent, it is set in stone. That goes for e-mail too.

Two Simple Ways to Get Positive Response from Your Proposals

1. Add a personal letter to the prospect on the same page as the proposal introduction. It keeps your relationship going.
2. Use the prospect's name in the proposal as often as possible, even if the proposal is mostly "boilerplate." This practice makes the proposal less object-oriented and more personal. (If you're using a computer to revise a proposal you sent to someone else, make sure you delete all references to the prior prospect, especially their name.)

A Strategy for Stirring the Creative Juices

Write the first draft of your proposal like a grade school primer. Remember the old Dick and Jane reader? It went something like this. "See Dick. See Dick and Jane. See Dick run." It was genius in its simplicity. Write your outline in this format, before you get to your well-crafted prose. It will help you track and make your ideas clear. For instance:

"Yesterday we had a meeting.

Joe loved the roast duck.

Joe also loved the proposal.

He might want to work with us.

He didn't like the whole proposal.

He wanted some changes.

He wanted the delivery date moved up.

We can do that."

Now, of course, you don't write your final copy like this! But it can help simplify your thinking. (And you thought you didn't learn anything in school. Forty years later, I still remember Dick and Jane.)

Your Proposal as a Sales Tool

When you venture into a store, there are all sorts of items to try out. Maybe you can't take that new fishing rod home with you, but you can inspect and play with the reel to try a few practice casts. You'll get a general feel of the product and how it would work for you.

That's what proposals do, too. Proposals allow customers to get a feeling of how you work, what methodologies you will use and how the process will work for them.

Sure, proposals are time consuming but they give prospects something to react to. As part of your sales plan, always offer to do a free proposal. The worst a prospect can say is, "If you really want to, then go ahead." By doing this you are furthering the relationship, and creating an excuse to call back.

A very effective trick in a standard proposal is to turn the entire proposal into a letter, complete with salutation. It adds a personal touch to the proposal. Sometimes, in RFPs (Request for Proposal) from large companies, institutions or the government, you are locked into a particular format. In these cases, use a cover letter for a personal message.

A Strong Cover Letter Can Sell Your Proposal

Instill the key points—especially the benefits—of a proposal into a strong cover letter.

A cover letter is a necessary addition to a proposal. Sometimes it carries more weight than the actual proposal document. People will read a short one- or two-page cover letter more readily than they will wade though an entire proposal. In my first book, my editor never bothered to do more than scan the entire proposal—she bought it solely on the basis of the strong cover letter.

Getting Your Customers to Write Their Own Proposals

When a prospect is interested in a project they will have many questions, and it's your job to solicit these questions. Ask, in simple language, what the prospect wants out of the project. Then, in the proposal, give the prospect what he wants and use the same language he does.

Use follow-up calls to the prospect to make sure of the correct language. You can read parts of the in-progress proposal to make sure you're giving him what he wants. But, don't fax him the proposal to look at. He'll conclude it's a done deal. I can't say this enough: Don't send ANYONE anything you don't want EVERYONE to read.

Prospects Don't Like Surprises!

Don't surprise the prospect by adding new services even if it's to his benefit. Give him exactly what you said you will give him. He will get leery of extraneous promises and copy and will usually rethink the project. You don't want him to do that.

Making Powerful Verbal Presentations

I've been writing presentations for myself and for others for more than twenty years. Since I'm on the supply side I usually start off by asking my audience what they're looking for in a consultant or in a supplier. They tell me what they're looking for, and that's how I slant my talk.

When you know what your audience wants, the presentation guides itself. In effect, you should never give a presentation, even a canned one, unless you know what the audience wants.

When you make a presentation, you are trying to attain a goal. You must go after that goal in a single-minded way in everything you say and do whether you're on stage or in a conference room.

You can even ask point-blank: "What would you like to come out of this meeting today?" or ask them to verbally fill in the blank at the beginning of the presentation: "I'm glad Barry came out today because ____________."

When you give a talk or a presentation you establish yourself as an expert in solving a client's problems or in making the client more profitable, efficient, etc. If your presentation is effective you establish your credibility and expertise.

Presenting Along Gender Lines

Surprisingly, you usually have to present differently to men and women. Men want the dog-and-pony show. They want to be dazzled. Women usually want a dialogue. Men usually want you to talk AT them; women want you to talk TO them. I don't know why this is so—or even if it's universal—but go with it. In a mixed-sex presentation, show the charts by looking at the males, then explain them to the women in the audience. It may take some on-your-feet choreography, but it works.

Three Steps to Making Winning Presentations

Think of your presentation as having three parts.

Part One: Attract. The first part is where you establish your rapport and credentials with your audience, and tell them the objective of your presentation and what you hope they will get out of it. Everyone in the room should already know the purpose of your meeting but there will always be some in the audience who have no clue. Establish your objectives early on and focus on them for the remainder of the show.

Part Two: Expand. Focus on the meat of your presentation. Discuss your topic and deliver the facts. While you may think this is the most important part of the presentation, it really isn't. Most people, in fact, don't remember the details of the mid-section.

Part Three: Close. This is the key to a successful presentation. It's where you focus on your final objectives and field questions. Like the final part of a sales letter, it's your call to action.

Your whole presentation strategy should be summed up in the following three line classic quote:

"Tell 'em what your gonna tell 'em.

Tell 'em.

Tell 'em, what you told them."

How to Command a Marketing or Sales Presentation

I find that the most important part of a small meeting comes before the meeting. It's the little chitchat that you start while putting up your charts and while people are entering the room. Your "small talk" questions should not only put people at ease, they should furnish the information you need to gear your talk to what your audience finds most important. At this time, you should pass around a sheet of paper and ask everyone to write down their names and job titles. Save these for follow-up calls.

I once presented a medical glove that I had invented to the CEO of a glove manufacturing company who knew nothing about the medical field.

On the way to getting coffee with him (a great maneuver for getting people to open up—everyone has the same rank at the coffeemaker), I asked him how his company was doing against the imports that were made in third-world countries with cheap overhead and labor. He admitted he couldn't compete. He complained that his prices were as low as he could go and that he was being hurt by the cheap imports. Knowing that, I tailored my pitch to how high he could price the glove and the difficulties that foreign companies would have knocking off this patented new product.

Take your cues from the people who try to sell you time shares in resorts. The salesperson spends the first part of the presentation asking about you, your lifestyles and desires. Your only chance to view the property comes at the very end. The salesperson knows what hot buttons to push because you already gave the salesperson the answers. You told the salesperson your dreams and the sales person is putting it in the contextual framwork you gave him.

Successful multilevel marketing organizations structure their presentations the same way—you should, too.

When you sell to a person's needs and wants you command center stage no matter what your speaking style or situation is.

Another way to command center stage is to name names and give as many case histories as you can. This makes you sound like you've been in the business a long time. People are fascinated by how other people market their products.

Strategies for Presenting Visuals

There are as many speaking styles as there are people in this world. Your speaking style and audience should dictate the kinds of visuals you use. According to the 3M Company, when visuals are used in a presentation, persuasiveness jumps 43 percent. A presenter who uses visuals is perceived as better prepared, more professional, more persuasive, more highly credible and more interesting.

Your choices for visuals include slides, charts, overhead projectors and film. Using computers and computer-generated art can also be helpful.

Overhead transparencies are the easiest to produce but they get mind-numbing really fast. Also, changing transparencies can take your mind too far from the material you want to present.

Film looks professional, but is expensive. A canned film presentation leaves little room for customizing your pitch to your audiences.

Twelve Commandments for Winning Sales Presentations

1. Always bring an extra bulb for the slide projector or overhead.
2. Actively solicit questions before, during and after the presentation. Be flexible. Play off the questions.
3. Keep it simple. Don't use one more slide, statistic or projector than you need to make your point.
4. In a one-on-one presentation, spend at least 75 percent of your time inquiring and listening and 25 percent talking.
5. Talk specifics, not generalities. Try to use real-world examples for every specific point you make.
6. Sell the dream. Back it up with facts.
7. Establish rapport with your audience early on. Your style should flow from the image you want to present. But don't be fake. Be yourself.
8. Remember, what you say is not always as important as how you say it. If you can fake sincerity, you've got it made.
9. Use real-life stories as often as possible. People want stories more than they want information.
10. Get your audience involved as often as possible.
11. Don't try to please everyone. You can't and you won't. If a presentation works great and you get people emotionally involved, you'll have your supporters and your detractors. If you polarize people, at least half will want your product.
12. Use audio-visual material as aids, not the reason for your presentation. It's not how cool your multimedia toys are, it's how you use them. Use visuals only when it's appropriate. Keep in mind though, that people retain only about 10 percent of what they hear, but 50 percent of what they see.

Slides are easy to show, relatively inexpensive and easy to customize.

Charts, when properly done (and not overdone), convey a feeling of professionalism and expertise. They are not always adequate for a large room, however.

Some Strategic Tips on Using Visuals

- Use visuals to grab the audience's attention, but be careful they don't detract from what you're trying to say.
- Use each visual to emphasize one idea, and only one.
- Use visuals to display data graphically.
- When preparing printed material for slides, use only five or six words per line, and no more than five lines per slide.
- Don't keep a slide on view for more than a few minutes. Change slides often to keep up interest. Make your audience wonder "What comes next?"

Ten Ways to Get Management on Your Side

The chances of you getting an order or a sale the first time out can be remote. Even if you're selling in-house, it will probably go through a formal or informal committee for review. If you're selling to a company, you might need as many as ten sign-offs for a sale. You can't afford to alienate anyone. Here are ten ways to get management on your side.

1. Understand who's in charge and who makes the final buying decision. You can usually do that in your preliminary small talk. Sometimes, however, it might take four or five presentations or telephone conversations until the "truth outs."
2. Make your presentation as often as you have to. Don't rely on others to sell your ideas for you. Sometimes (actually often) down-line managers will say "We'll present it to management for you." It doesn't work. No one knows you or your product better than you do. Instead of allowing others to pitch for you say something like this:

   "Research shows that about 90 percent of a presentation is forgotten about an hour after a meeting or presentation. I feel so strongly about how this product will work for you that I'd like the opportunity to present it personally to your management."
3. Know the background of the decision makers. If the final decision maker has an accounting or engineering background, she has a different "dream" than one who comes out of a product development background.

4. If you are working for yourself, deal with the CEO as president to president. That way you'll be speaking to him on a peer level.
5. Document your successes visibly. Show how your product (or a similar product) has led to the growth of a business.
6. Treat everyone as equals. Even the lowest-ranking person can come back to haunt you if you don't treat him respectfully or answer his questions.
7. Make sure you allocate your resources as efficiently as possible. Don't spend your time trying to persuade juniors when it's senior line managers who are going to make the decision.
8. Establish realistic goals but sell the dream. Always show top management how the program will increase the equities of the whole company and how it will fit in with their current strategies.
9. Suggest ways to implement the program (i.e. next steps). Management will be happier if the idea or program fits in with its current ways of doing business.
10. Build specific, concrete measuring sticks into the project so that everyone can track and see progress.

Presenting to Your Sales Force

Salespeople are interesting and so are the ways companies deal with them. When presenting to your sales force don't try to sell to them. They'll outfox you every time.

Salespeople can tell you how to sell to others, though, and they are great sources for research. Salespeople make their living communicating with buyers and have a sense of what buyers react or don't react to. Go to them and find out what their customers are looking for. When you ask for their input they get a vital sense of ownership.

If you ask for their advice, they will react positively and give even more advice. The purpose of pitching to sales is to make them act—and think.

Six Ways to Build Excitement Within Your Sales Force

1. Show how the product idea will work for the here and now, not the future. Salespeople are action-oriented. They live for today, not for

tomorrow. Salespeople want immediate gratification. Salespeople are generally paid commissions on sales. They have a vested interested in an immediate payback.

2. Salespeople, as a rule, like to sell what has always been selling. It's the easiest and most profitable kind of sell. Show them how easily the product or service fits in their current ways of doing business.
3. Listen and be open with the sales force. Take their suggestions to heart, even if you can't immediately implement them.
4. Make sure the sales force gets copies of the material you send to other managers. Don't allow them to feel left out.
5. Build a sense of common purpose. All members of the sales team should feel that they're participating in the success of the plan.
6. If salespeople give you a critique about something—say an ad—try to incorporate it (if it won't do any harm). Do this a few times and you will get a reputation as someone who listens. It's worth a couple of brownie points.

Four Strategies to Get People (Even Management) to Remember What You Say

1. People remember more when you are in motion. State your main points when you are reaching, demonstrating or pointing.
2. People remember even more when you are both in motion. "Tell your story walking" is not a putdown but a real communications strategy.
3. Relate your benefits to your listeners' core experiences, including where they work and where they live (and don't forget their families and loved ones).
4. Use specific emotion-laden language and mannerisms when stating the positives. Use neutral tones and language when discussing negatives.

CHAPTER FIVE

Strategies to Implement Marketing Programs and Advertising

It's great to think about a marketing program and to analyze every permutation and variable you can think of. And, it can be downright soul-stirring to plot a promotion while staring at a smudge on the ceiling at 4:00 in the morning.

The groundwork we laid out in the first four chapters has given you numerous strategies for your marketing plan. But programs don't usually go anywhere until they're put on paper.

Too often things tend to get lost when you translate a plan that looks great on paper into one that's truly executable. So there are two challenges we have to solve here: putting your plan on paper, and making sure that your paper plan actually works in the real world.

In order to create any business, it's imperative that your goals are realistic and that they fit into your current way of doing business.

Create a Strong Mission Statement

The best strategy for keeping your business and your marketing program on track is to to create a single mission (or strategy) statement and to make sure everything flows from that statement. This statement will eventually evolve into your marketing strategy.

Once your mission statement is in place it's relatively easy to develop a strong strategic marketing program that

- identifies your company's goals and objectives
- isolates your company's strengths and weaknesses
- clarifies where you have strengths over the competition
- identifies customers so you can you can help solve their problems
- keeps you flexible so you can maneuver in a changing marketplace

Strangely, many marketing divisions operate without a mission statement. They don't pry into their business and their potential customers but instead come up with grandiose plans. This is like building a house without a blueprint.

Types of Mission Statements

There are three basic kinds of mission statements; those that are driven by the *market* (consumer-driven mission statements), those that are driven by the *product* (product-driven mission statements) and those driven by the *competition*. Of these, the consumer-driven statement is the most useful.

The Consumer-Driven Statement

In a consumer driven statement, you adapt and adopt your products to your ultimate buyer's preferences. The consumer controls all. All your marketing plans flow from consumer wants and needs.

A short, succinct customer-oriented mission statement guides your growth and keeps you focused on your customer as it builds new opportunities.

Market Share vs. Market Creation Regis McKenna in his marketing book, *The Regis Touch* lists his three steps for a successful marketing strategy:

Know where you're going.

Know thyself.

Decide on a strategy.

McKenna likes to talk about the difference between the market share strategy and the market-creation strategy. They require different types of thinking. In the market share strategy, you hope to gain share by taking anyway someone's else's market. In the market-creation strategy, you bring new customers to your brands by solving a want and a need better than anyone else can.

The Product-Driven Statement

A product-driven statement makes sense when you have a certain product or certain technology that you want to sell and when you filter your product and selling strategy through various consumer segments.

A product-driven strategy is best used for a company with limited vision, a short product line and limited resources. It is strictly for the short term, since there is no flexibility or product-development scheme inherent in the statement.

The Competitive Matrix and Benchmarking

There is another alternative. In this strategy, you pretty much forget about a marketing plan and follow your competitions' movements. When they zig, you zag. You follow their introduction with knockoffs of their program and their products. While you stand small chance of becoming a strong number one, you can do well as the number two or three player in a market.

Similar to the competitive matrix, the mission of benchmarking is to go competition one better by making your product better than theirs. While this seems like an ideal market-plan strategy, it can be difficult. You can probably outdo the competition by reverse engineering the product, but your superior performance may be negated by having to persuade your customers that your system is somehow better.

Although Macintosh might be a better computer on the technical end of things, Apple found it too difficult to persuade people who were told about I.B.M compatibles by their friends.

Strategically Focusing Your Mission Statement

Base Your Mission Statement on Your Goals

Goals are the heart of the mission statement. Start by making sure that those goals are realistic and sound.

Your mission/strategy statement, which flows from those goals, is a one- or two-sentence declaration of your business desires. It's brief and pithy. The well-thought-out—and reviewed—mission statement makes sure your business strategy stays on target.

Sell It in a Sentence

There is always going to be a temptation to add new sentences and ideas to your mission statement. Resist the urge. The more succinctly and accurately you target your business to match your firm's capabilities, the more successful you are likely to be. It's important you satisfy your customer's needs as thoroughly as possible. Your whole marketing plan should focus on one consumer benefit. A short pithy business concept is enough to run even the most complicated business. Remember, the Ten Commandments were written on two plaques—and they've lasted for some time now.

Writing a Super-Charged Mission Statement

The success of the *Readers's Digest* is based on a simple rule. Deliver the goods—the gist of the articles—fast and furiously. The leads of the articles capture the reader instantaneously. The rest of the article is supporting material.

Use the *Reader's Digest* format. Embrace your audience with a pithy opening that will hook them. Then furnish everything else as support to the overall strategy. End with a call to action or reinforce the basic premise of the article. The *Reader's Digest* strategy can guide even the most complex marketing plan.

The Three E's Approach

The Three E's of marketing can also help focus your business mission:

Embrace your market with a strong up-front mission strategy that is totally consumer driven.

Expand on the major points of your mission strategy.

End with a specific call to action.

Four Tenets of a Sure-Fire Mission Statement

1. *Make it specific.* Many businesses make a mission statement sound like an advertising slogan but slogans come and go. A successful mission statement should have staying power.

2. *Make action be your buzzword.* Just as the Gideons put their bibles in hotel rooms for everyone to see, distributee your mission statement to everyone in the organization once a month. You should be able to act on your mission statement every day. Every employee should be able to act on the mission every day.

3. *Be flexible.* Market conditions change daily. What worked five years ago will probably not work today. Your mission statement should allow for eternal changes. It should be updated continually.

4 *Make sure your goals are attainable.* In Greek mythology, Sysiphus had to roll an enormous boulder up a steep incline. When he got to the top, the boulder would roll down. He was never able to attain his goals. The mission goal should always be within reach so that employees can take a look back and think "Look what I've accomplished (or have yet to accomplish)."

Six Steps to Strategic Implementation of Your Mission Statement

It's easy to come up with a mission statement while staying within the confines of your office walls and propping up your legs on a nearby desk. That's also the most misleading way to approach your business. The best way is to design your mission statement from the perspective of your customers and the people who are in contact with them. One way is to think of your marketing strategy as a five-step ladder and use your mission statement to guide everything you do.

1. Using your current product line as a base, hypothesize additional product lines. You can use your competitors' products, drawing board products or product ideas that come up through brainstorming sessions or meetings. Hypothesize reasons consumers might want your product.

2. From the above hypothezations, have an artist create catalog pages and mount them on large boards (11" x 14" is a good size). The headline

Four Strategic-Plan-Building Questions

1. *What business are you in?*

This is the very first question you should ask yourself as a marketer. Of course, you eat and breathe your business and go to bed at night to the lullaby of spread sheets but it's easy to lose sight of what brought you to the party to begin with. Deciding on your business means going to your customers and finding out what advantages (psychological or physical) your product or company holds over the competition. You need to develop a leadership positioning and a seminal focus for your business.

2. *What should your business be?*

Customers and their product choices are constantly changing to meet in this evolving marketplace. The mission statements that are most successful reflect this.

3. *Who is your customer?*

A key to a strong mission statement is knowing your customers intimately. Nabisco has a product mission for all of its divisions. For Snackwell's, the mission is to create low-fat knockoffs of popular products. Another division creates snack cookies, like Chips Ahoy, with no real healthy connotations. Both divisions are profitable because their marketing programs run with an eye on the mission statement and the bottom line.

4. *Who can your future customers be?*

Looking into the future can be daunting, but a strong mission statement should be flexible enough to change with evolving consumer needs.

on each page should be a proposed mission statement. One board should also have your current mission statement, if you have one.

3. Show these boards to your existing customers, prospects and your salespeople. Ask for their reactions. You can do this by setting up focus groups or one-on-ones as per suggestions in Chapter 3. If your respondents don't like your ideas, they'll hiss and boo (especially your salespeople). Or worse, they'll look numb. If they perceive disconnects, they'll let you know. Probe your interviewees for your perceived strengths and weaknesses in a

particular product area. Probe for your competitor's strengths and weaknesses.

4. Revise your boards based on what you've learned, Re-evaluate your corporate situation through the information you've obtained in this feedback. Change your headlines based on this feedback.

5. Go back to your prior respondents with your newly revised catalog pages and repeat the interviewing process. Seek out new respondents.

6. Refine, revise and add more pages until you gain strong acceptance of your premise from your respondents, and your management.

Implementing Your Marketing Plan

The perfect product has never been invented. For every product benefit there is an evil twin lurking about—a product negative. That twin can be neutralized when you identify it and deal with it creatively. I've seen marketers wallow in a morass of self-pity if their product has some kind of negative about it.

In truth, every product is a yin and yang tradeoff. None of us have the ideal product. Even so it's easy to sink in the morass of your problems. The grass is always brown on your side of the fence if that's the way you choose to see it.

Turn Negatives into Positives

You can make the negatives of your new product work for you. It's the magic of marketing. You can make the consumer believe you did it on purpose. You can build markets when you turn a negative into a positive.

Here's a quick case history. Dark meat is not the prime delight of the chicken industry. More people like white meat. But it's a fact of life that a chicken is born with both white and dark. Smart marketers started blending white and dark meats into patties that resemble white meat and chicken nuggets were born.

Here's another problem. How would you like to be the guy who has to market beef leavings? Beef leavings are the leftover parts of cattle. They are usually attached to bone after the good parts have been cut away. Gene Gagliardi, master meat cutter had a better idea. Instead of giving it away, why not compress it and shape into slivers of beef? Gagliardi and his team called them "Steak-Umms" and people all across American created a new kind of sandwich by frying the slivers for about 30 seconds.

You can't rest on your assets...because they are constantly changing. Your assets will give way as marketers target your company and learn how to do what you do even better. Even as you are reading this page, consumer tastes and markets are evolving.

Turning a negative into a positive can be as simple as changing the product placement in the store. When Ocean Spray's Cran-Orange drink was introduced, it was located in the store near orange juice. While consumer tests showed that it was liked better than orange juice, the fact that it had cranberries was perceived as negative. People liked their orange juice straight. The solution? Place it and position it near the other juices for a "change of pace" beverage.

Even if your product's recipe was derived from the hand-me-down recipe of your great Aunt Ethel, it's not etched in stone. Add or subtract an ingredient. It can often make the difference between a success and a failure. Rancher's Choice salad dressing (made with real mayonnaise) was disappointing in test markets. Kraft wanted to fix it. The answer, as usual, was deceptively simple. They changed the legend on the bottle. Instead of saying "made with real mayonnaise" they said "made with real buttermilk." It turned out that Kraft doesn't have a strong enough equity in mayonnaise (where Hellman's is the standard of identity) and Kraft was realistic enough to make this minor change even if it was at a loss of some small corporate vanity.

Fulfilling Your Mission Through Advertising

This section is in the chapter on mission plans because all advertising should flow from your mission.

We all know the story of the pet rock. Some guy got a bunch of rocks together, put them in little boxes with care instructions and made a fortune with the little devils. The unfortunate thing was that this wonderful idea spawned a host of imitaters who spent their life savings trying to duplicate this fad's success.

I mention this because a hot advertising agency may hit the creative jackpot once—and recruit new clients who want the same breakthrough results. It doesn't usually happen. We need more than a transient spark from an advertising agency.

We need to hit winners every time. We need advertising agencies to be a key part of the marketing strategy. But the strategy must come from you, not them.

Consistent winners come from your upfront research into the hearts and minds of your target market. It means that your agency must sell what the customer wants to buy in a way that the customer wants to buy it. We're going to get into advertising agencies in more detail in the next chapter but here are two strategies to make sure your advertising is on target.

Drawing Up the Creative Brief

Make sure your agency interviews consumers before full-scale production is started on a campaign. Constantly work with consumers on every part of the creative program to make sure you are delivering the right message.

You should develop the communications plan, not the agency. Just as a successful mission flows from a clearcut mission statement, the successful advertising strategy flows from a creative brief. This brief should be a page or two that highlights everything about the product. When all the background work is done, you'll be amazed that the commercial will almost write itself.

Your brief should include:

- Product
- Target market
- Positioning lifestyle and imagery
- Superlative statement (Why your product is better physically, emotionally or spiritually)
- Key point you want to get across
- Creative treatment that has been developed all along

Do Your Own Positioning

Do the upfront positioning (see Product Profile on the following page) work with your in-house people and researchers. Of course, you'll share the results with your advertising agency and make sure the strategy is executed exactly as written. Agencies are strong on executions but they are weak on marketing. Research costs them money and creative people tend to rebel against research, especially if it doesn't jive with the preconceived notions about how a campaign should be run.

Illustration 5.1
Product Profile

BARRY FEIG'S
CENTER FOR PRODUCT SUCCESS

Telephone 800-707-0739

6200 Eubank, Suite 423
Sandia Mountains, New Mexico 87111

PRODUCT PROFILE

Name: Top Blend, Chef's Blend, Second Nature, Nature's Fixins, The Natural Choice (more work can be done on names)

Descriptor: Complete nutrition for the life of your pet.

Positioning: Pet-store quality at its best now in your supermarket.

Key Communication Elements: Package should communicate:

- All natural — no fillers, no by-products. (Package back should explain this).
- New vacuum package locks in flavors and goodness (holds as much as one 4 lb. bag).
- Flavor names as per report
- 100% money back guarantee your pet will love it

Package Graphics: Show full body photo of hearty one-or two-year-old animal; cat should be in sitting position.

formerly New Products Workshop, Inc.
New York, New York

Illustration 5.2
Product Profile

BARRY FEIG'S
CENTER FOR PRODUCT SUCCESS

Telephone 800-707-0739

6200 Eubank, Suite 423
Sandia Mountains, New Mexico 87111

PRODUCT PROFILE

Name: Natural High, Sun Energy

Key Benefits: It provides the nutrients for a happy, healthy lifestyle.

Key Positioning Strategy: An energy cereal designed for people who want to stay fit and energized.

Key Elements/Communications: Show jogger running on beach with family in background. Superior taste should be mentioned.

Rationale/Appeal: The runner on the beach with the family hit a strong note with our focus groups and made for a strong selling concept. The runner is casual and intense, yet enjoying his run. The beach and water imply energy. The energy implication is strong and not overplayed. Both men and women saw themselves in the concept. While Natural High is a strong name, Sun Energy was also strong in this concept.

formerly New Products Workshop, Inc.
New York, New York

Marketing Trends Good and Bad

THE TEN BEST time-tested advertising strategies: (No, not all advertising is ineffective. There are some good trends out there that you can jump on.)

- Infomercials that create enthusiasm for your product.
- Commercials that use humor to make the client's point, yet still have a selling benefit.
- Commercials that meld physical and lifestyle benefits;it's a winning combination.
- Slice of life commercials.
- Slice of death commercials. Loss of control of fear of losing something valuable is a strong hot button.
- Commercials that use point of sale and attention getting devices.
- Commercials geared to businessperson that identify the entire person rather than picturing a businessperson as an automaton.
- Clear, unambiguous dramatic product demonstrations.
- More intermingling of minorities.
- Treatments of African-Americans as trendsetters.

THE TEN WORST trends in advertising today (Avoid them with all you've got!)

- MTV commercials with trick camera angles and quick-cut graphics. They are old hat now.
- Commercials that give the product name only at the end of the commercial.
- Endorsements that don't show the name of endorsee. Who are these guys anyway?
- Endorsers who have no connection to the product.
- Extreme games-type commercials, i.e., sky surfers, bungee jumpers. They're old hat and don't work anymore.
- Classic rock songs in commercials. It's old hat.

- Imagery commercials that offer no product benefit. Sometimes they don't show the product at all. They're cute, they entertain. They win awards. But they don't sell.
- The catch-all "10 reasons why" you should buy this product. It's used mainly when the agency can't think up a good campaign.
- God, motherhood, dogs and patriotism. Like the preceding one, it's used when the agency can't come up with a good idea.
- Any commercial that's a satire on talk shows. It was funny—once.

Repeating Your Message Again and Again

Reach and frequency are still the keys you need to attract people. As a rule of thumb, the more you focus on the creative presentation of your message, the less you will focus on repeating your message. But it's sort of a nice Catch-22. If your sales are good, you will have even more money to spend.

Too many companies change their advertising each year. I think that's a mistake. Management gets bored with the campaign long before consumers do. Just keep updating the creative and adding new graphics. A message is never boring if it solves a real need. People never, ever get tired of hearing about themselves.

At the time of this writing, Quaker Oats sold its Snapple business for about $300 million. This sounds like a lot, but it paid $1.7 billion for the franchise in the first place. Quaker's problem was that it could not carry through on Snapple's consumer equity. It didn't match its own.

Quaker ran into the same problem that Procter & Gamble did some years back when it acquired several soft drinks. P & G could not translate its business methods into what was a new quirky area.

Look at the BIC company, for example, and its throwaway products: razors, pens, lighters, and so on. You'd laugh if BIC tried to sell you a $500 fountain pen. The company would be ignoring its consumer franchise. But its mission is to develop inexpensive one-use products that fulfill our common everyday needs. That is the mission, and they don't deviate from it.

Ten Tested Advertising Strategies and When to Use Them

There are many advertising strategies that are put to good use every day, but consumers are bombarded with over 1200 sales messages every day. (It's probably more, but I got tired of counting.) It's important that you choose the right strategy for your particular marketing environment. This listing is obviously not meant to be exclusive and all-encompassing, but it can give you a good head start on your communications strategy.

1. *Product as hero*. In this strategy, your product is a godsend just waiting to happen. Your product should be a breakthrough product that is so devastatingly strong, the mere mention of the product and its benefits should have customers flocking. But, a caveat, if your product is not that strong, then this kind of advertising gets lost in the clutter of other products claiming "I'm the greatest."

2. *Imagery advertising*. All advertising, in one form or another is imagery advertising. However, imagery is wasted when it has no bearing on the lifestyle of the person you're trying to sell to. Imagery advertising should have a tie-in with product benefits. Imagery advertising is expensive, however. It works best with products that are going against other products with similar benefits—or when your product's imagery can offer psychic rewards to the user.

3. *Competitive advertising*. Naming the competition can be very helpful when you are an also-ran in the market. It can separate you from the other also-rans and link you in the mind of the consumer to the name brand. But there are a few caveats. For one, consumers don't always take to you treating the competition unfairly. And there is also the problem, that in naming the competition, you're giving them free publicity. Make sure your comparisons make sense. Several years ago Detroit compared a Mercury to a Mercedes SL in terms of comfort and luxury. Nobody bought it.

Also, when you're a market leader it usually doesn't make sense to bring your product down to the level of the riffraff. Choose another strategy that defines your superiority without naming names.

4. *Slice of life*. There's life in the classic slice of life commercial. This strategy works best when you can identify a specific lifestyle and you can solve a realistic problem that relates to a targetable segment of consumers.

5. *The announcer as hero.* While it's boring to some, a strong announcer carries weight with customers. The product, the appeal and the end benefit should be simple and direct. The announcer can be treated as an authority figure or as "just one of the folks." Another advantage is that commercials and ads of this type are relatively inexpensive, and great for small budgets.

6. *The dramatic demonstration.* A dramatic product demonstration is one of the best ways to show off a new product. Master Lock hyped sales when they showed a bullet piecing a lock—that stayed locked upon impact. Crazy Glue lifted up a worker by his hard hat to show how strong the glue was. Use this strategy when the product is simple and has one major benefit.

7. *Humor and whimsy.* Any product can gain interest when you instill it with a little fun. Unfortunately, it doesn't always translate into sales. Humor works best when you can solve a "little problem" or when you just want to separate your product from the other similar products in some small way. Humor wins awards, but not always sales.

8. *Warranty advertising.* On the surface, warranty advertising sounds good. In fact, in some product categories, a strong warranty is a necessity for entry into a product category, But look at it this way. Is your customer buying the product because she can't wait to take it back? Use the warranty hook when your product is expensive and/or complex. Use it to symbolize your product's integrity and reliability rather than as an "out" for the consumer.

9. *Just name names.* If you are entering a new market, just advertising your name, saying it as loud and often as possible can be very effective. It builds familiarity and can set the stage for more product-oriented advertising. This works best for products that are entering a saturated market and want a low-end or mid-priced positioning.

10. *Play to the heart.* Perhaps this is the strongest advertising technique of all. Build emotion into your product. Play it straight, but sappy. You'll think it's trite, but your customer can get a serious case of the warm fuzzies. Michelin Tires gets more mileage from its baby-sitting-in-a-tire commercials than larger tire manufacturers who douse us with a great many meaningless details and tire specifications. The heart overrules the head in almost

any purchase decision. This strategy is good for almost all products in almost any marketing situation.

Frequent User Strategies

Back in the 1800s an obscure economist came up with a theory that still holds true. Vilfredo Pareto came up with the famous *Pareto principle* that says 80 percent of your products will be bought by 20 percent of your customers. That's why marketers are always looking for frequent users.

The best frequent user programs were devised by the airlines who knew they were really selling a commodity product. The product has become so successful that frequent flier miles seem to be the new coin of the realm with airlines marketing their miles to other companies.

On the other hand, America Online tried to create a frequent user program for their subscribers. They were too successful. Everyone in America tried to sign up for their services. The irony of the AOL program was that they drove away their frequent users who grew frustrated trying to connect. There is a happy medium though.

Frequent user programs are a great way to stroke your customer's egos. People like being recognized as frequent users.

Eight Successful Frequent User Programs

1. Many successful supermarkets and retailers are developing frequent user programs. They offer discounts with frequent user cards. After a set volume of purchases bought within a specific time frame, customers receive a free gift.
2. Campbell's soup company has run a frequent user program for a long time. Parents of school kids pool their Campbell's labels and redeem them for audio-visual equipment for their schools.
3. Many retailers give out a punch card that can be redeemed for free merchandise or discounts.
4. Instant scratch cards can be given out after purchases. They work well as incentive bonuses.
5. M & M's created a promotion where customers get a prize for finding a grey "imposter" M & M.

6. With some charge cards, the more a customer charges can mean a lower interest rate.
7. The Discover card gives cash back after so many purchases.
8. Many companies give refunds or gifts for sending in UPC codes.

Key Tags Are Hot in Frequent User Programs

The most effective frequent user device is a humble key ring, used by Blockbuster Video and a host of supermarkets. Rather than dig out a card, voucher or sales slip, people use key rings with a bar code. People always have their keys handy.

The bar code allows marketers to instantly track their customers' responses to ads per frequency of visit and the items bought at each shopping trip.

Companies can also offer sales to the shopper which generate even more sales.

When developing your own key chain, make sure the printing and the bar code won't rub off in the consumer handling of keys. A plastic laminate can help. Also make sure the key rings are sturdy enough not to fall off with rough handling.

CHAPTER SIX

Strategies for Choosing Advertising Agencies and Other Suppliers

As a supplier of marketing services, I recently completed a presentation to a respected soup company, when I asked a simple question.

"What do you look for when you finally settle on a supplier?" I asked.

Their answer threw me.

"Well we don't like using them at all, but when we go outside, we want someone who can show us a good time when we're on the road together."

"Say what? I was incredulous (although they didn't know it). I had been pouring out my heart, my soul and my credentials and they wanted a supplier who knew where all the hot bars are located (I have since become the world's foremost expert on the subject).

Since then, I have started asking that same "What do you look for?" question at the beginning of all my presentations. Here are some of the answers I've received.

"Someone who can work with all divisions peacefully and smoothly."

"A person who can sell my ideas to management."

"They have to be responsive and return all my calls."

"They have to be neat and organized."

"I have to like them on a personal basis."

"They must have worked in my brand category."

All of these factors are important. But it is rare to receive an answer like "The work has to be first rate."

There is an old saying that I love. "When the gods want to punish you they give you what you want." And that's what happens to corporations when quality of work is judged less important than showing the client a good time.

Working with Outside Resources

One of the manager's or entrepreneur's toughest decisions is whether they should work with outside resources, and if so, who.

Compounding the issue is that consultants and advertising agencies keep coming out of the woodwork like so many industrious carpenter ants—all alleged miracle workers. Everybody with $19.95 for a handful of business cards or a cheesy business card software program is now an immediate expert.

How does one decide who to use? Many managers and companies have a bias against going outside for help on a particular project, except when they hire accepted disciplines like advertising agencies, public relations firms and promotion houses.

This fear of going outside happens in few other management disciplines. Engineers, for example, go outside their companies all the time.

For some reason, going outside seems emasculating to marketing managers. Then too, their bosses reason, "I have a marketing department that I pay a ton of money to, and an R & D department, why should I go outside?"

Why Go Outside?

Of course, there are a great many financial reasons for going outside; you usually can't afford to keep highly talented creative people on staff and your company may need some specialized knowledge for a short time. By going outside, you can keep this talent on-call and tap them whenever you want.

But there's an even better reason for getting outside marketing help. Specialized marketing professionals can offer more expertise and a larger perspective to the total business picture. They can bring in new ideas.

You're often too close to your own work. The day-to-day operations of business often make it difficult to generate ideas and look at marketing opportunities that may be "outside the box." But a strong outside marketer can show you what you've been missing.

Outside of economics, there are three main reasons for outsourcing a project.

1. To get this "outside the box" thinking
2. To solve a problem that requires specialized skills or knowledge
3. To get a second opinion

Marketers rarely even know they need an outside person until the last minute or until they realize they have problems with their existent sources. It is often only when a project has failed that a marketer realizes that a specific task is more difficult than it appears and special knowledge and skills are required to complete it.

I'm tempted to say that by then it's too late. But many fires have been extinguished without having too much damage done by choosing the right emergency repair crew.

In-house people are often stymied by too many rules. You can create opportunities and strategies by choosing a source who can go outside your business category and your usual way of doing business. In fact, if your consultants bring you ideas that you already have, can them fast.

A large financial company hired me to come up with ideas for new financial products. But when we came up with the ideas, they vetoed them saying it would be too hard to sell though the various divisions. I asked them "What's more important, developing new ways to make money and fix your business or following procedures?" They said following procedures. I resigned the account.

Do Your Homework Before You Begin

Before embarking on an advertising search you should have the marketing plan intact. You should determine the following:

1. *Your goals.* You should know what your advertising should accomplish. Specify the goals of the marketing program in terms of dollars

and market share, or in terms of consumer awareness (see sample objectives earlier in this chapter).

2. *The advertising message.* This is the core of your advertising. All advertising should flow from this central theme. It should contain the positioning, the product's reason for being and reasons why your customers would want the product.
3. *Your target audience.* Your market should have been chosen in your marketing plan and research. These are the key demographics your should shoot for.
4. *The tone of voice for your advertising.* What are the basics of your consumer strategy? In what manner should it reach the consumer? Using the research tools in Chapter 3 will supply your answer.

The Strategic Approach to Resolving Problems

You should definitely have a methodical approach for addressing the entire issue of calling in outside resouces, if you hope to achieve a speedy and effective resolution.

Choosing an outside source is as much an art as a science. For every gem you find, you're going to work with at least two duds—the kind of consultant that looks at your watch and then tells you what time it is.

What Do You Really Need?

To make a knowledgeable decision ask yourself two basic questions:

1. *What exactly do I need—a unique skill or knowledge?*

   This is the first decision you have to make. Knowledge is typically easier to obtain than skills.
2. *Am I dealing with a problem or a symptom?*

   It can be problematical just to define the problem itself. Problems and opportunities, rather than symptoms, should be recognized before outsourcing a project.

For instance, if an advertising strategy for a new kind of cheese does not appear to be working, is it because of the positioning? The product? The advertising? Do you hire an industry expert on cheese? Or do you hire someone with no food experience but who claims to be an expert on positionings?

Before you start your search, some paper work is in order. Write down the problems as you see them. Explain the challenge to yourself in your own words.

Getting Outside Help from Consultants

But what if you can't identify the problem? Are you stuck? No, because a properly chosen outside person can help you define the problem. Make it plain to the outside person that you know the symptoms but are not aware of what's causing them. Then ask for a proposal and see how the outside source goes about diagnosing the problem and finding the solution to the problem. The simple act of generating a proposal can give you strategic insights that you never thought of before.

More about the proposal in a few pages, but finding an outside person to even write a proposal takes some proactive thinking.

How to Find an Independent Consultant

Often, when looking for an outside person, you will be entering a sort of Twilight Zone, where consultants speak in mysterious tongues known to no one outside of the consulting community. Three of the best places to look for the right outside help, listed in order of effectiveness, are:

1. *Colleagues.* They are the first people you should ask.
2. *Books and journals in relevant fields.* You can often judge the effectiveness of consultants by the books and magazine articles they write. If you don't buy into their theories, they're not going to be the right choice for you.
3. *Trade magazine editors.* They use outside people as expert resources and often know who has been in the business for a given length of time and their reputations.

Here are other places to look that are not as productive as the three above, but helpful nonetheless:

- Relevant professional affinity groups
- Paid advertisements. You can place ads seeking a strong marketer or supplier

- Trade magazine ads placed by the consultants themselves
- Trade groups that specialize in helping consultants and clients find each other
- Home pages found over the Internet or the World Wide Web

Conducting the Strategic Interview with Consulting Prospects

Once you have found consulting prospects, it's time for the interview. Don't be dazzled by flash or three-piece suits.

The interviewees should demonstrate the following:

1. A thorough understanding of your problem and an ability to restate it. You don't want a parrot who's going to agree with everything you say. They should be able to speak of your problem in an extended conversation.
2. Genuine enthusiasm for the solving of the problem.
3. Sincerity in solving the problem (a judgment call on your part).
4. A track record of success. Prospects should present strong cases for their qualifications, resources and experience. But don't overdo the experience part. You can often get more productive work from "green" consultants who have knowledge and skill, but lack strong track records. The way a prospective consultant thinks is as important as the tangible skills the consultant demonstrates.
5. An overview of the skills they have and how they can use them to solve your problem.
6. Flexibility in solving the problem and the ability to deliver receivables on your timetable.
7. Flexibility in adapting methods to solving your problem. The prospect should be able to fit the work into your needs, not the other way around.
8. A competitive price.
9. A unique way of thinking, even if it is totally divergent from the way your company does business.

Stay away from any consultant who verbally sends the message: "I can do it too." You must come away with the feeling that the chosen consultant has the potential to do it better than anyone else.

Eleven Inside Tips on Choosing Outside Suppliers

1. Don't choose a company because it fits in with your current ways of doing business. You want an outside person who can stretch the limits of your organization.
2. Choose a company that looks creative, from its portfolio or face-to-face interview. Hire people who give added value to your job title.
3. Don't choose a consultant because he or she knows your business. It's more financially rewarding to transfer ideas from one industry to another.
4. Do break the rules. Make sure your outside source questions everything. If the consultant doesn't, you're not getting your money's worth.
5. Never use any advertising agency for anything more than advertising. They won't do it right and will charge you through the nose. When you're looking for outside help, even for positioning work, you need a specialist.
6. On the other hand, get rid of the bias that says an outside person can't help if his or her experience is outside a particular discipline. That's rubbish. You should actively cultivate people from outside your area and try to transfer this knowledge.
7. Don't work with juniors. Work ONLY with the principles.
8. Do use small boutique shops. You can usually get better thinking than at a large shop with a departmentalized chain of command.
9. Make sure the consultancy is established. Those weekend wonders who just got fired from jobs are more interested in finding a new job than building a client base. Consulting is hard work. Few people have the talent and the wherewithal to stick with it for any length of time.
10. Don't go with anyone who promises a "black box" for marketing or new product. One guy goes around, literally, with a black box with little holes. He tells clients that when all the pegs in the black box are put in, the product cannot fail. There is no black box. Marketing is not a science, it is an applied knowledge of human behavior.
11. Don't go crazy about references. Of course, references are important, and you should do some follow-up work on references, but is a consultant going to give out the name of a person or company who did not like him or her?

Getting a Proposal from the Consultant

Now, it's time to ask for the proposal. Don't work with anyone who balks at doing a thorough proposal or with a vender who gets the proposal in too late. That is a foreshadowing of the work you can expect.

The proposal should include:

- A thorough understanding of the problem
- Rationale and purposes of the consultant's methodology
- List of receivables
- Time frame that suits your needs
- Reinforcement of the points made in the personal presentation

Give the Consultant a Test Project

Of course, if you wait for a crisis to strike, you're up a creek without an oar. Your best approach is to keep your eyes open, even when you don't think you need to call in an outside expert.

The very best way to find out if a consultant or a shop is any good is to give them a small project. If they don't work out, you're out a little cash, but if they do work out, they'll pay for themselves many times over.

Choosing an Advertising Agency

Perhaps the most important outside marketing supplier you'll have a role in choosing is your advertising agency. Perhaps no other management choice is as chock full of pitfalls as choosing an advertising agency.

Potential Pitfalls When Working with Advertising Agencies

It may be hard to believe, with all the research tools at our disposal and with all the tomes written about consumer behavior, most advertising is a product of speculation, pure and simple. Advertising agencies are just guessing when it comes to developing their campaigns. They're hoping the client will buy the campaign, and secondarily that the consumer will buy the product.

It's the nature of the beast. In fact, in most campaings, the rationale is developed *after the campaing strategy is thought of.* I use the word strategy ironically. Agencies put together what looks best in the conference room, regardless of strategy. I have many friends in the advertising business (perhaps not after they read this) and I watch as they substitute boilerplate text in the strategy reviews and proposals they deliver to various clients. They all seem to say the same thing.

The reason is simple. There are many jobs at stake and much media to be bought. Agencies want to make an easy sell. They, like most businesses have learned to "sell what's selling." If MTV-type commercials are the rage, many agencies, with the approval of their clients will go to MTV production values— "the message be damned." That's why we as consumers have become befuddled by waves of singing, animated dogs, commercials that only give the name of the product at the very end, and commercials with sixties rock tunes.

I may seem a bit cynical, but here's an example:

A major advertising agency was forced to show a commercial to focus groups. The respondents loved the commercial. Everyone was ecstatic, until a key question was asked of the respondents.

"Would you buy this cereal?" asked the moderator. "Hell no" was the response. Despite the commercial being shown to over eighty people, only one respondent was motivated enough to say he would buy the product. The major problem was that half a million dollars was already spent producing the commercial. Wasn't anyone watching the store while the commercial was produced?

Advertising agencies are more interested in pleasing the client, rather than in selling a product. Glitzy production values are an easy sell to marketing management. Solid marketing skills are intangible, and thus, a harder sell.

And that's one of the things wrong with most advertising today—lots of flash, great production values but the quality of marketing expertise is not there.

This even shows itself in advertising agency presentation dog-and-pony shows. If the work was effective, agencies wouldn't have to work as hard selling it.

Bring Your Own Strategy

Advertising agencies, Regis Mackenna says, as a rule, focus on promotion. They attempt to sell a product for the here and now. Most advertising agencies miss the point. They try to reinforce market positions. They don't try to create them. For this reason, it's wise to go to your advertising only after your strategy is thought out.

Advertising agencies pride themselves as being providers of a full line of marketing services. They are far from it. The problem goes back to an advertising agency's reasons for being. In truth, agencies are really sellers of media space. Few agencies have the time, inclination or talent to be marketing agencies. For public record, they call themselves communicators or marketing firms but that is really just said to suck up to a client prospect.

We've all heard the axiom "I know that half my advertising is wasted—but I don't know which half." In no other business would a failure rate of 50 percent (and I'm a bit on the optimistic side) be acceptable. The reason for the inadequacies of advertising messages is that there is no testing for the message. Oh sure, visuals are checked, likeability tests are run and awards are won. But none of these is a test for salesmanship.

Most agencies can't produce a good ad because they get little guidance from a company who wants to be impressed more than be sold to.

The strategic solution is to have a goal. The goal should be specific, an extension of the mission statement strategy. Focus specifically on your communication objectives. Only then can you and your agency focus on your specific strategies and executions.

Most companies and organizations don't have specific goals. Even if they do, they don't always share them with the agencies. That is the "agency as adversary" syndrome. Once again, it's inherent in the system.

Set the Ground Rules for Effective Relationships

Your objectives when working with advertising agencies should be concrete, measurable and realistic. Strict measurements for ads should be part of your objectives statement. If the advertising doesn't work or the objectives aren't met you can make your campaign better or pull it fast. Realism is important too. If your widgets have had a 10 percent growth annually, it's unrealistic to ask an agency to triple that growth.

Here are some objectives to shoot for.

- To increase awareness of your company by 20 percent
- To increase sales of your product in certain regions by 25 percent
- To generate actionable leads by 30 percent

Marketing consultant Carolyn Hoskens adds these tips for setting your advertising objectives.

- Develop a specific number of sales that your advertising should generate from its target audience
- Translate this into a dollar amount
- Create a specific time frame for achieving these goals

What to Look for When Auditioning Advertising Agencies

When going through advertising agency pitches, don't grade the presentations. You're grading a dramatization. Rather, grade the quality of work and how the agency is going to find the answers to your problems.

Don't expect winning ideas during your agency presentation. Don't even ask for answers to your marketing questions. How can your agency prospect know the answer to a particular marketing problem if it hasn't even gotten the job yet? You want tested winners. You don't want speculation or guesswork.

Strategic Selection Based on Size

Large Agency Most large marketers choose the larger advertising agencies because they think more people are needed to handle their account. They choose large agencies because they want a full range of marketing services. Companies like to think of their agencies as marketing partners. No way.

A large agency should be chosen only when your product or product advertising is so varied and the product has so may appeals that it has to be advertised to many different markets.

A problem with a large agency is that you can get lost in the shuffle and trapped in a labyrinthine bureaucracy. Or there is so much bureaucracy that a creative idea has to jump through so many hoops that it is watered down through every step of the management maze. A large bureaucracy creates its own form of censorship. A large bureaucracy also hinders agency/client communication.

I have heard many marketers complain bitterly that they can't even get one coupon ad produced. Only the largest accounts are served reasonably well by large agencies. The others get lost in the shuffle.

Midsized Agency A midsized agency should be chosen when it has strong marketing and research facilities and you're sure it has the marketing wherewithal to put these facilities to use. Choose a midsized agency when you're sure your account will be large enough to merit all the best people and the entire range of services.

A midsized agency can be chosen when:

- The agency's capabilities are fully researched
- The product positioning is nailed—by them or by you
- All the strategic work is done—by them or by you

Small Agency Smaller advertisers usually should choose smaller agencies because of the big fish in a small pond syndrome. But larger companies can gain immeasurably from a small agency provided that all the groundwork (research, positioning, and so on) has been done. A small agency should be chosen when:

- You're looking for the big idea
- You have the time and resources to test the agency on a small project
- The agency's credits have been thoroughly researched

Five Steps for Selecting Your Advertising Agency

1. *Find the contenders.*

The first task is (as Rick said in the movie *Casablanca*) to round up the usual suspects. These can come from advertising trade magazines, industry sources, trade groups, even from solicitations that come in over the transom.

2. *Develop the agency questionnaire.*

Refer to the sample questionnaire on page 124. The answers, while helpful, should not play a deciding part in the selection process. They are merely résumés about who is out there. Some agencies are just too small or too creative to answer the questionnaire the way you think it should be answered, but it can be used to eliminate red flags and get a feeling for the advertising agency market.

Notice that our questionnaire is highly focused on creative capabilities. This is because the effectiveness of the creative product outweighs most other factors. Most questions are also open-ended to give you a feeling of how the agency thinks and writes.

3. *The briefing.*

All prospective agencies should be given a briefing from the product profile you have created (see Chapter 5) as well as the specific goals you have developed.

This can be done either personally or through a letter of transmittal. I prefer to do it personally because you can find out a great deal about the thinking that goes into the campaign by the questions that are asked. The briefing should not occur over lunch or at a social event because it's easy to get misled by the personalities of the contenders and the excitement of the event.

You can run the briefings en masse, with all the contenders present or you can brief each agency individually. I prefer to hold the briefings en masse because everyone has the same level playing field.

Create a somewhat unrealistic time frame for the agency to complete the presentation. In the real world, you're going to want plenty of things fast. You don't want excuses. If the agency refuses, cut them from your list.

4. *The interim.*

The time between the briefing and the actual presentation is very important. The smart agency will call you with questions to get your directional guidance and to clear up gaps in your briefing. Don't schluff them off. You want an agency that questions you. Don't be afraid of giving out too much information on the grounds that the other agencies will not be up to speed. The way an agency obtains information is one of the keys to doing a sound job.

By the same token, make sure the questions are relevant and not a ploy to "keep in contact."

5. *The presentation.*

The purpose of the presentation is not to dazzle you with graphics. Most advertising agencies are very capable of creating strong graphics and commercials. You don't want a slick, canned presentation. You want honest marketers who can respond to your questions and demands.

Illustration 6.1
Advertising Agency Questionnaire

Ownership and Employees

1. What is the history of your agency including date of start-up and first account?
2. Who are the principals? What are their roles?
3. What is your management structure? Formal? Informal? How does it benefit the advertiser?
4. Who makes the business decisions for your agency? Who makes your creative and media decisions? What are their background?
5. Who would be handling our account? Why were these people chosen?
6. Who would be our direct contact?

Creative Strategy and Development

1. Describe three creative strategies for specific advertisers that you were extremely proud of. What made you proud? How did you arrive at the strategy and creative product? (We are not interested in awards.)
2. How would you characterize the creative character of your agency?
3. If you have not handled products similar to ours, how would your experience and talents carry over to our product line?
4. What is your philosophy about effective advertising? How do you put it to use?

Accounts

1. What new accounts have you obtained in the past three years?
2. What accounts have you lost?
3. Why did you obtain (or lose) these accounts?
4. Please furnish a list of your accounts and key contacts. May we speak to them?

Illustration 6.1
Continued

Organization and Structure

1. Explain how your agency provides service to a client. What is your formal and informal business structure? How would it affect us?
2. How are creative decisions reached?
3. How many people are in your creative department? What percentage are juniors? What access would your creative people have to us?
4. How are media decisions reached? What is the smallest media you would deal with in buying time and space? Why?
5. How are research decisions reached? What role does research have in your creative and media strategies? Give three concrete examples of how research played a role in three separate creative strategies.

Financial Data

1. How would you characterize your agency's balance sheet?
2. What is the length of time you take to pay media bills?
3. What is your account billing system?
4. As of approximately six months ago, what were your estimated gross billings?

The presentations should consist of four steps.

1. What they have done in the past.
2. Why they have done it (the thinking behind it).
3. How successful the project was.
4. How they will handle your project.

Limit your agency to three commercials or ads of past or current clients. The presentation itself should be limited to flip charts and boards. Resist the urge to make the presentation exciting or to have your agency artificially stimulate the board room with unnecessary dramatics. You should be interested in the thinking behind fulfilling the strategy that you have created. Keep the process as informal as possible. No critiquing allowed.

If you notice, we are not asking the agency to solve your marketing problems at this point. How can they solve the problem if they haven't worked on it yet? When choosing an advertising agency, you should be looking for people who have the *potential* for solving the problem.

When you see a smooth, canned presentation, it is wise to take them out of autopilot by asking a question they are not familiar with. Once again, you are not looking for a definitive answer as much as trying to get into the thought processes of the contenders. For instance, if you are selling business machinery for offices, ask them how this might translate into the small business or home office market.

6. *Give the players a project.*

Farm out a small section of the campaign to the leading candidates—and pay for it. If the agency is too proud to accept this trial project, it is their loss. Choose an agency that is prepared to work with you for the long haul. Your marketing program doesn't have room for prima donnas. There are a great many good agencies to choose from.

In this project you will want to see:

1. Specific marketing strategies to accomplish your goals.
2. A variance of advertising strategies. If these are not totally consistent with your original thinking, that's good. You want an agency that can bring added value to your thinking.
3. The core advertising message.
4. Insight into the target audience.
5. A determination as to how the target audience and the message will be brought together.
6. A tone of voice for the advertising.
7. Specifics on how the agency came to its conclusions or how it will come to conclusions.

You can often find out about your marketing merits of your agency even before the creative is produced. Listen to the questions they've asked along the way. Are they germane or infantile. If an agency doesn't ask questions or does not listen to the clients, than it is not an agency you want to entrust to your account. The questions should deal with all facets of the campaign. They may know the basics of advertising better than you do, but you certainly know your business better than they do.

While the following agency rating sheet is not a be all and end all, it can help you decide on the creative group that's right for you.

Two Simple Strategies to Maximize Your Advertising Dollar

1. A wise choice is to choose a creative shop (or consultant) for the creative product and use another source for media buying. The advertising agency should help choose the media, but not do the buying. Isn't it silly to have the person with his hand in the cookie jar buying the cookies? Advertising agencies are paid to buy media. They will almost always choose more than is needed because that's where the money is spent.
2. Develop your own strategy. The work of the advertising agency should be limited to the communications and positionings you decide on before hand. Now I realize this is radical thinking but look at how agencies try to sell you. They usually develop three strategies:
    - One that they like
    - One that they think you want
    - One because three is a nice number

Let the agency do only what they do best—to develop strong creative materials. There's more than enough strategies in this book to develop your own marketing and creative plan.

Work WITH Your Outside Resources

Once you choose a consultant, or an advertising agency, you should be able to turn to him (or her) as a colleague rather than as a vender or subordinate. Treat your consultant, your advertising agency and all your outside agents as a equal partners in solving your problems. Never withhold key information from them.

Of course, you'll want to stay on top of the people you hire. But remember, your suppliers are only as good as the direction you give them.

At the same time, the secret is to stay stay flexible. Make changes as you go along and let the project evolve naturally.

Illustration 6.2
Agency rating worksheet

	Strongly agree (3-5)	Agree (1-2)	Unsure 0	Disagree (-1, -2)	Stongly Disagree (-3, -4, -5)
Agency Management					
Sound strategic thinking.					
Come across as very professional.					
Our people would enjoy working with them.					
Knowledge seems strong.					
Seem flexible.					
Seem intelligent.					
Creative Work					
Quality of strategic thinking is excellent.					
Creative work is excellent.					
Strong initiative apparent.					
Thinks outside the box.					
Their advertising has been effective before.					
Willing to accept our input.					

Goal Orientation

The know our target audience.

Thinking is, or could be, on strategy.

Tone of voice consistent and effective.

Strong insight into our market.

The Presentation

Spent a great deal of time on the presentation.

One campaign can be used immediately.

Ideas and strategy were germane to our business intentions.

Did not try to con us or impress us.

Overall Feeling
(bonus points)

We should speak further with them—0 points

More trial work needed —+2 points

It should be our agency —+5 points

CHAPTER SEVEN

Strategies for Point-of-Sale, Impulse Items, and Trade Shows

Companies are committing more of their marketing dollars to trade promotions then ever before. In fact, at least two Fortune 500 companies have eliminated their advertising completely in favor of on-site and trade promotion. While I don't agree with such drastic measures as utterly decimating an advertising budget, putting money in media used where customers actually make the decision on buying your product has strong merit.

Point-of-Sale Promotion

On-site promotion is traditionally called P.O.S. (point-of-sale) or P.O.P (point-of-purchase). As the use of P.O.S. evolves, it will play a greater motivating role in the final sale of goods. It is estimated that in 75 percent of all purchases, the decision to buy the product is made at the purchasing venue. This figure has been rising steadily. An effective P.O.S. display reminds potential customers of their need or momentary want for your product and works with your product to do the ultimate selling.

Used strategically, P.O.S. advertising is much less wasteful than media advertising. Sales can be tracked easily and your target consumers see the product and selling proposition neatly laid out in front of them.

But P.O.S. budgets can be wasted too, if you don't have a clear-cut strategy. With other media, you pay for a certain amount of space and time and you know you're going to reach your audience. But with P.O.S, you can't even be 100 percent sure that you can get your display in the store.

Ten Strategic Questions on P.O.S.

Answer these ten key questions before you commit to point-of-sale promotion:

1. Does the idea tie in well with your advertising?
2. Does it fit the overall mission goal?
3. Can you fit it in your budget?
4. Is it practical from a construction standpoint?
5. Does it capture attention?
6. Can it physically deliver the goods?
7. Does it get your brand message across quickly?
8. Is it convenient for the retailer or display people to set up?
9. Is it motivating enough to create impulse sales?
10. Does it add something unique to your product?

Seven Goals P.O.S. Must Meet

Here are some strategic musts for choosing and implementing P.O.S. The unit or units must:

- Cajole, persuade and invite your customer to take the product home.
- Be memorable and distinctive.
- Command your customer's attention. In a brief matter of seconds you must capture the buyers interest completely, almost so the buyer forgets there are other products in the store.
- Function with the effectiveness of a giant banner headline in a magazine or newspaper.

- Be simple, grabbing your customer like the hook in old-time talent shows.
- Attract the customer's interest big time and invite your customer to learn more about your product.
- Should be a key part of an entire dealer program, not just to fill space.

Strategic Uses of P.O.S.

A P.O.S. piece does more than just sell a product on the floor. It can be a cornerstone of your program to find more distributors and a persuasive way to get merchants to stock your products.

Ten functions of strategic P.O.S. deployment are:

1. Secure more, and more effective display space for your products.
2. Sell merchandise through impulse sales.
3. Remind people of your product and your advertising.
4. Preempt the consumer's mind and heart over other products in an aisle, and in the store.
5. Create store traffic.
6. Keep retailers happy by showing them you care about their business.
7. Keep distributors and wholesalers happy by encouraging "self-shopping."
8. Help keep salespeople (distributor and retail) knowledgeable about your product.
9. Tie in your national advertising at the point-of-sale to reinforce the key message.
10. Identify stores as outlets for your product.

Test P.O.S. in Regional Markets

When a marketer thinks of P.O.S., he usually thinks of one basic P.O.S. piece covering a whole nation. The best strategy, though, is to think regionally and adapt your P.O.S. program to your particular market peculiarities.

Before you commit big dollars, test your idea in a variety of markets and in a variety of retail outlets. Don't look at a display in terms of attractiveness. Make sure it works. Station researchers at the P.O.S. and see how the display pulls shoppers into your web. Start with a limited number of displays. If you have too few, you can always reorder.

Four Times Sell Strategy Redux

Back in Chapter 1, we talked about the four times sell. Nowhere is this more important than on the retail sales floor where your P.O.S. has to act as a silent salesperson, persuading and cajoling the prospect to buy, buy, buy.

To review the point, here is the four times sell strategy. A product should sell:

1. on the shelf
2. at the checkout counter
3. in use
4. after use

What You Need at Each Point of Sale

On the shelf. We're going to get into packaging in a few chapters, but one of the most important parts of point-of-sale is the attraction of the package. Your display has to preempt the competition by calling to the customer.

At the checkout counter. Your product's packaging and your "deal" must be so strong it makes the customer's cut list.

At home. Your product has to work as promised.

After use. It should work so well, it should call to the consumer to look for the display again.

Using Interactive P.O.S.—The Hands-on Approach

More and more displays are becoming interactive—with good reason. When you get a person to interact with a display, he or she develops a personal interest in the product. Your P.O.S. objective is to forcefully grab the consumer so your prospect physically picks up your product, almost without realizing it.

Take a lesson from the people who sell you trinkets and clothes on the beach at tourist spots—human P.O.S. so to speak. Venders will do anything to get you to hold their product in your hands. Once you're holding it, it's hard to put it down. When that happens, the vender has gone a long way towards making a sale. One salesperson actually dressed my wife in a sarong over her bathing suit. She bought the sarong.

Picking up the product is one way to get consumers involved. Another is to do it electronically. Here's an example.

Tomoma Edmark invented a device for shaping hair. She knew she couldn't sell the device without some explaining on her part. Figuring that more information would help both retailers and customers, she produced a video of the product. Then she provided a VCR to Accessory Lady, a chain of women's fashion stores. (Who could say no to a free VCR?) The strategy was so successful, Accessory Lady put a VCR with the tape in all their stores. It was the most successful single item in the store's history.

Other Interactive Strategies

1. Use computers to selectively inform your customers about your product. For instance, if you sell shampoos that are designed for different kinds or hair, allow consumers to choose the shampoo that's right for them by feeding their particular hair characteristics into a computer. Maybe the right shampoo is a combination of two products. That's one more sale than you expected to make.
2. Use computers to tell consumers what products are available. Bookstores and music shops now have computers to help consumers "thumb through" thousands of buying alternatives. It's cheaper than stocking a million or so CDs. In a twist on this strategy, many stores now offer computer coupon dispensers which may be the impetus a shopper needs to choose your product.
3. Clearly illustrated flip charts show consumers how products will look and work in advance of the purchase. If you sell paint, a flip chart can be used to help consumers coordinate paint tints with colors that exist in their homes.
4. Thumb through books or computer displays to uncomplicate a purchase. Computer chips are sold on the retail level with clear diagrams that guide computer owners to products or add-ons they need.
5. Use good/better/best charts to list the features of a particular gadget.
6. Use portable VCR/TV combos to demonstrate the uses or installation of a complicated product.

7. Programed slide projectors capture attention at trade shows and in a selling aisle.
8. Use touch-and-smell devices in an aisle to get olfactory senses involved in a purchase. The more senses are involved, the easier it is to make a sale.
9. If you have an electronic product, create demos that start when a prospect presses a button.
10. Use tear-off rebate coupons good on the next purchase of an item or a tie-in item.
11. Create tear-off entries to sweepstakes or other promotions.
12. Use vending machines to get your product into stores without a great deal of space or staff.
13. Use in-store demos to create and hand out food or sauce samples.
14. Hold a party for some of your client's stores' better customers. You'll sell your product and gain strong word-of-mouth. The store will love the free publicity and word-of-mouth.

P.O.S. Makes Your Advertising Work Harder

Because P.O.S. is the actual "salesperson," it has the opportunity to supply the final closing argument for a sale. All media advertising should be fully integrated with your displays. P.O.S. is so flexible that almost any campaign can be translated into a results-gathering display. P.O.S. allows you to evolve your campaign's seasonality, regionality and publicity.

Seasonal P.O.S. Strategies

Timing is of the essence, especially in terms of seasonal appeals. Create P.O.S. for yearly events like Christmas, Easter and the arrival of summer. Create P.O.S. for traditional buying times, like September back-to-school sales, June weddings and January white sales. Combine your products with a new summertime movie. Batteries can be displayed near Christmas gifts. Chocolates and candy can be effective tie-ins to weddings.

Regional P.O.S. Strategies

Don't rely on one sales piece. Design several for different markets. The liquor industry, for example, creates varying P.O.S. units for urban markets and for more upscale markets. In urban markets they will often use giant cutouts of people enjoying their beverages.

Building Your Client's Business

Used creatively, P.O.S. can bring a client's business (or your business, if you're a retailer) to new heights.

Consider Best Plumbing. A plumbing supply store in Yorktown Heights, NY, it sold the traditional pipes, fittings, toilets and other items that you'd expect. At the bequest of a bathroom fixture manufacturer, Best Plumbing's owner installed a complete bath ensemble in his warehouse. The display featured a designer tub, matching toilet and vanity. Then something strange happened.

Instead of drawing just the tradesmen this P.O.S. was designed for, consumers started coming in and ordering the bathroom as a unit. Since bathrooms commanded a higher margin than plumbing supplies, he built a brand new showroom consisting of what was basically P.O.S. units. The concept was so strong, the owner is now franchising the idea.

P.O.S. Advertising

All P.O.S. is interactive in a sense. You are requesting the consumer to do something, usually to pick up a brand or to tear off a coupon. But there are other kinds of P.O.S. pieces that function as ads in the store.

1. *Signs and posters.* Use them for in-store sales or as banners for outside the store. They can direct the consumer where to go for the product. Just as importantly, signs can remind consumers of the need for a product. Strategies for signs include small banners on shelves (shelf talkers), even self-adhesive booklets or sales stickers attached to your product.

2. *Three-dimensional displays.* Since advertising liquor on TV is still mostly taboo, liquor companies simulate an entire commercial through vivid P.O.S. materials. You can use three-dimensional displays in windows, at the counter, even as table tents. Adding motion to a unit makes a display even more compelling to passersby.

3. *Specialty racks.* Racks made of metal, plastic or cardboard can help you stake out your own little section of the store. You can create custom stock bins for many kinds of products, including batteries, small food items, nuts and bolts. The uses are only limited by your imagination—and your goals.

4. *Checkout counter pieces.* These help keep the product name at the checkout counter where it counts most. They can help you get counter placement for impulse type products, remind consumers of products or direct consumers to the location of your product in the store. The best counter units perform some service to consumers, like calendars or take-a-penny-leave-a-penny trays.

5. *Odors.* One of the more effective additions to a display is a unique scent. Scents work because they are unexpected in a scentless retail environment. You can create special scents with machines that spray a scent every few minutes. You can also use "scratch and sniff" cards on a display. For instance, a great chocolate scent just might be what a customer needs to motivate her to seek out a special candy.

6. *Sweepstakes or scratch-off games.* These can help you differentiate yourself from the competition. If a customer is looking for a particular brand of sugar or a similar commodity type product, she might pick up your offering if it offers an "instant winner game" or a chance for an all-expenses paid trip somewhere.

7. *Sounds.* Add a sound to your display. It may involve the same music you use in your commercial or a sound that's unique to your product. Sound can be very intrusive. Not all retail stores are enamored of this intrusiveness.

Strategic Rules for Developing Your P.O.S. Program

1. The unit should never be more important than the product. Don't get caught-up in "gee whiz" production techniques at the expense of the product.
2. The display should sell, rather than merely advertise your product.
3. Make it easy for people to take your product from the display.
4. The display should be simple for distributors and retailers to set up. A display is worthless unless it's used.
5. The display should be field-tested for effectiveness (see Concepts in Context, Chapter 2).

8. *Pole units*. As space becomes harder and harder to procure, companies are getting back to the old pole unit. For instance, create a tree out of a pole, or a faux metro district complete with street signs. The advantage of poles is that they use very little floor space.

9. *Baskets*. Just throw sample-sized products into a basket and watch consumers come running. There is a large candy retailer called Mr. Bulky's whose gimmick is that almost everything comes in a basket. The customer chooses the items and pays for them by weight. Brach Candy Company and various cookie manufactures are using this simple merchandising idea to great success in supermarkets.

Illustration 7.1
Checklist for rating point of sale

Consumer Features
Does it zero in on a customer's needs?
Does the display show off your product in a way your competitors miss?
Does the display bring added value to you product?
Does it offer an additional service for the consumer?
Does it tell consumers how to respond?

Store and Merchandising Features
Is the display easy to put up?
Does it add something of value to the store or showroom?
Can it sell other products for the store (besides your own)?
Have you seen features on other displays that you should incorporate?
Would a store want the display or service item?
If it's a window piece, would it inspire a consumer to enter the store?

Appearance and Selling Factors
Are the graphics colorful and striking?
Is your display large enough to be seen from across an aisle or a window?
Does it zero in on your product's benefits?
Does it project the proper corporate image?
Does it ask for the sale?
Can it communicate an entire sales message in 10 seconds when consumers are just passing by?

Value-Added P.O.S.

One of the more effective ways of getting your point-of-sale in the store is creating counter units with high intrinsic value. Many companies have become successful by buying coolers or cooking units for their goods and giving them free to retailers in return for buying a large quantity of goods. Marketers love them because they are almost getting a free ride. Here's a caveat though. Many stores, after a short time, use these units for goods other than those intended. Your units should always be monitored for compliance with your terms.

Intrinsic value point-of sale examples:

- Coolers
- Ice makers and storage bins
- Single or multi-use ovens or cooking implements (products are cooked up fresh for each customer)
- Hot food dispensers
- Juice or frozen dessert dispensers

Retailer Incentive Displays

Some marketers develop displays with incentives that retailers get to take home after the display is used. For instance, a display that uses a fishing motif might contain a real fishing rod. A baseball display might pay off with a real baseball glove, bat or ball. It's sort of a bribe and illegal in some states and in some categories; research this before your commit.

Low Budget P.O.S. Displays

The most cost-effective form of P.O.S. is a simple display of your goods. The Orville-Kent company created a big hit in supermarkets with their potato salad, cole slaw and other salad type items. These "Signature Salads" as they were called traveled from store to store creating special displays that were more attractive than the competitors' in each store's deli department. They got premium prices for what was called a commodity product.

Choosing Venues for Point-Of-Sale Promotions

Getting placement in stores is as much a function of the store as it is of the strength of your P.O.S. unit.

The store will be more interested in bringing in traffic than selling your product. The retailer, of course, is God. Offer a complete program, partner with the retailer and she may treat you kindly. Your job is to convey to management that you are going to make them money—that your display will generate more money than any other use of that space could possibly generate.

According to Barry Lipsy, Promotions Manager at CPC Foods, chain stores have different rules than independents. Home-improvement stores have different rules than either of them. All stores have their virtues and drawbacks. The important thing to remember is that store space is expensive. Every square foot in the store is accounted for. If your P.O.S. promotion can't assure a predetermined amount of dollars (usually set forth by store management), then they won't let you in.

Lipsy's advice is to buy your way in. But it doesn't mean you have to pay for space. You may be able to barter with deals on flanking products or you can offer to deliver private label products.

Another strong way of getting in is to cross-promote with other established companies. We'll be getting into cross-promotions later in the book, but most stores drool when you can sell two products in one store space. Lipsy says the bigger the brand, the more likely to get a product display in. The program should be good for both parties.

Lipsy suggests you let your sales force play a major role in getting displays into stores. They are a major part of your frontline forces and should know the ins and outs of a store's policies. More importantly, they have day-to-day contact with the store's managers.

Robert Kovalesky, Divisional Vice President of Sales for Act 1 Media, a major developer of in-store promotions, avers Lipsy's thoughts. He maintains that there is only a finite amount of space in a store. To break through the clutter of manufacturers wanting to get store space often takes big dollars.

He points out that the difficulty of finding space is so acute that supermarkets are routinely breaking apart display pieces and selling the products separately.

The Cube Strategy

One strong strategy for getting into stores is to make your package and display in such a way that it is "cube efficient." Cubes take up the least amount of space; they are displayed compactly and efficiently.

Other P.O.S. Strategies

Here are some other strategies to get your display used:

1. Try the bin-dumping strategy. Make smaller sizes of your product and dump them in reusable wire or plastic bins.
2. Use handsome wicker baskets to get your products near the counter. This is particularly effective for C-stores and mom-and-pop delis. Well Bred Loaf, a manufacturer of cakes and muffins, built a multi-million dollar business on this simple strategy.
3. Tie in your items with other products in the store.
4. Tailor your P.O.S. around the store's image.
5. Create a value-added display by providing VCRs, freezers and ovens that add value to the store.
6. When selling a quantity of items to mass merchandisers, make the rack or P.O.S. unit an integral part of your program.
7. Scrounge around stores and look for any underused space. Tell the store how you can turn it into dollars.
8. On service pieces (counter units, and so on), make your product an integral part of the display.
9. Sponsor in-store demonstrations using the display.
10. Turn your shipping carton into a display piece by making the outside of the box as special as the inside. Use product stackings to call attention to a special sale.
11. Create seasonal units that decorate the store as well as sell goods.
12. Create a unit that's useful to the store. For instance, if you're selling shoes, create a sizing display. If it's good enough the store will keep it up all year.
13. Buy your way in. (Bet you didn't need me to tell you THAT strategy.)
14. Give out product samples, not only in the store but around the store. That simple ploy was the heart of Debbie Fields' (of Mrs. Fields Cookies fame) strategies.
15. Do multiple tie-ins of products with a similar nature. Dissimilar or complimentary products can also be banded together for joint sales.

Impulse Items

Impulse items are included in this chapter because they are the ultimate P.O.S. units. Impulse products should cause the consumer to react and open up their wallets even without thinking.

The first true impulse product was Life Savers candies. When it was first invented, the candy sold poorly. The breakthrough came when Life Savers' owner persuaded cigar and candy vendors to place the product near the cash register. Consumers would pick up a roll instead of taking a nickel in change. Life Savers caught on in a big way and spawned the myriad of impulse products we see crowding cash registers today.

Emotion: The Key to Impulse Sales

In the case of impulse products the whole rationality of the purchase decision is short-circuited. The consumer has no time to think, only to react. You have to do everything you can to trigger that reaction. That's how L'eggs pantyhose, with its cute plastic egg-shape container became the dominant force in the women's hosiery markets.

A successful impulse product conquers the information overload we talk about by substituting images and feelings for words.

Instead of four times, an impulse product must sell itself once, but in a big way. You have to grab the browser with a searing emotional hook.

Three strategic contributors to a successful impulse product are:

- A strong name
- A great package
- Clear-cut positioning

These must get across the product concept and cut through the repetitive blather of other products on the shelf. The name should trigger an emotion with consumers.

An impulse product is not the place to be subtle. The package should act like a beacon on the shelf. The name and package should hit consumers like a brick.

Your positioning should call out the consumer's name and lifestyle. Your product sell should flow from this positioning. If a product connects with consumers' lives at the key moment of decision, they're interested.

Eleven Tactics to Make Impulse Sales Soar

1. Make your graphics short and catchy.
2. Put your product close to the cashier by making it a key component of service items (as mentioned above).
3. If it's a food product, provide a clear plastic window to show the contents.
4. Price it just under a whole dollar amount (for example, $3.95).
5. Say "new" on the package boldly and brightly.
6. Put large price spots on the package.
7. Highlight "instant win" contests on the package.
8. Use scratch-and-sniff stickers on the package.
9. Use foil to catch the eye.
10. Use special bottles (such as "Collectors Editions") or containers to celebrate a season or a company milestone.
11. Use "As seen on TV" labels or put up a press clipping of a flattering newspaper story.

Trade Show Selling

Trade shows are the Rodney Dangerfields of marketing. They get no respect. They're looked upon as something one has to do. They're also a bit like a dog chasing a car. Once he catches it what does he do with it? Once you agree to display at a show, what do you do?

Trade shows are important because they are a gathering of buyers and sellers with mutual interests. Although running a booth can get tiring after the third day or so, trade show participation is a very efficient way of meeting potential clients and reinforcing relationships with existing customers.

Trade shows are outstanding research tools, too. Besides checking out your competitor's wares, you can get a feeling for the attitudes of buyers in general.

Advantages of Trade Show Marketing

1. Sellers and buyers finally get a chance to meet face-to-face. This is very different from the facelessness of telephone calls and faxes. Trade

shows are also more informal than sales meetings and power lunches. They allow you to let your hair down a bit and to bond with customers.

2. Potential buyers get a chance to see product demos and can even handle the product. It's your opportunity to show your products to people you haven't been able to connect with.
3. Buyers are in a purchasing mood. They are there because they want to see what you have to offer.
4. Buyers have the ability to compare your products with those your competitors offer. (Admittedly, this is not always an advantage.)
5. Customers get to discuss their particular problems with you.
6. Trade shows are an economic use of your time and resources. They cost a fraction of the price you'd pay for personal meetings at the prospects' places of business.

Difficulties with trade shows occur because many companies participate with no basic game plan other than the nebulous phrase "to get customers." With trade show lag times, it is often necessary to establish objectives a year before the show.

Profile of Typical Show Visitors

Although thousands of people may attend a trade show, prospects can be conveniently lumped into three categories:

1. Those actively seeking information to buy a product for the first time.
2. Those considering changing vendors if they find a product that meets their needs.
3. "Trollers," those not buying now but seeing what's available. (They might never have the budget or inclination to actually buy. But you can get a better sense of your market from them, too.)

They all want cogent reasons they should buy from you.

Strategies to Use Before the Trade Show

Trade shows can help you to move specials and trade packs as well as to introduce new products. They can also move regular merchandise. Trade shows help you fine-tune in-store promotions by educating retailers about brand names and suggested uses. This info eventually filters down to your eventual consumers.

A Dozen "Mission Goals" for Trade Show Participation

1. Reinforce your image and visibility.
2. Keep in contact with your customers (even those you only see at trade shows once a year or so).
3. Introduce new products.
4. Introduce refinements to existing products.
5. Identify new applications for existing products.
6. Research new products or selling ideas through interaction with potential buyers.
7. Build the morale of your sales force and dealers.
8. Recruit personnel or attract new dealers.
9. Evaluate the competition first hand.
10. Generate leads.
11. Close deals.
12. Train new sales people.

Promote Thyself

Trade show strategies actually begin many months before the trade show date. You should be promoting your show to your customers far ahead of time. If you don't maximize your efforts before and after the show you may be sorely disappointed, not to mention pulling your hair out over all the money you spent. It doesn't take much effort. Here are a few of the ways you can publicize your show appearance:

- Create and mail a direct-mail letter and brochure six weeks before the show.

- Follow up with phone calls to selected prospects to announce your show.
- Set up times and dates to meet personally.
- Use your exhibit booth number and a banner touting your booth in all advertising prior to a show.
- If you have a sales office where you receive customers, create signs advertising your presence at the trade show.
- Give free admission tickets to your best customers.
- Advertise in trade magazines and in your exhibitor's handouts.
- Advertise special show discounts.
- Run "teaser ads" for a new product you will be exhibiting.
- Send publicity to all media.
- Distribute literature to all convention hotels.

Handle Leads Systematically

All sales reps must be prepared to follow up on qualified leads. A simple rating system can help you filter the slag from the gold. Sorry, business cards do not count as leads. Lead forms should be designed to qualify leads for follow-ups. Lead forms should have follow-up information including names, titles and particular interests. (See Illustration 7.2.)

Lights—Action—You're On

Obviously all people who stop by your booth are possible leads. But many people won't approach your booth unless you offer them a little doodad or gizmo. These promotional items can be a pain to create and give out. And they can be expensive. But the expense and time is worth it if it brings you good qualified customers.

The way that you handle your appearance at trade shows and the graphics and props you use while there, will significantly impact your ultimate sales.

Tried-and-True Sales Boosters for Trade Shows

1. Give away unique advertising specialties. But be careful, they can be wasteful if they have little tie-in to your products. Put some effort

Illustration 7.2
Trade Show Sales Lead Generator

Name ____________________________ Title ____________________________

Company __________________________ Phone ___________________________

Strength of interest: Strong ___ Good ___ Slight ___ None ___

When to contact __________________ How to contact __________________

Hot button (or product interest—be specific) ______________________

Any objections to be overcome? _______________________________

____

Did you talk price? _______________Interested in show special? _______

Other people in organization to contact ________________________

Follow-up desired (i.e., call, literature, samples) __________________

Personal comments of prospect's likes, dislikes, and interests* _________

____

Your name ____

* This should be of a personal nature for follow-up letters and conversations to add a personal touch.

into selecting give away items that encapsulate your entire sales story.

2. Create and schedule product demonstrations at regular intervals throughout the show (see specifics next section).
3. Create hands-on exhibits that get prospects involved.
4. Create sweepstakes or contests at regular intervals.
5. Furnish press kits at the booth for customers as well as the media.
6. Avoid any graphics which might detract from your main message. You're there to sell, not to look good. The average scan time is 12-15 seconds—hit 'em hard, hit 'em fast.

7. Display your main benefit points high and large, so you and your staff don't block views.
8. Create a one- or two-sentence verbal "differentiated benefit" to grab passersby. Create a banner or poster with the benefit and post it conspicuously. Prove your benefits with specifics, not generalities. This will attract visitors and make them stay longer.
9. Offer real-life examples (three is a nice number). Use third-party endorsements and testimonials. These endorsements should cover a wide range of product uses and categories. Display these on the booth and in promotional materials. Use graphics, artwork and colors to set off these quotes from the rest of the booth.
10. Make your pitch interesting and brief. Try to make the attendees feel like they're in charge. In that way they'll feel free to ask questions so you can recognize their needs, their decision tree and their hot buttons.

    The sales staff of Imaging Solutions creates a list of questions to ask prospects so they can focus their pitch quickly. Before the show, they attend a role-playing seminar on how to get information from potential customers without seeming pushy. (You might want to consider adapting this practice.)
11. Create a "conference offer" or "limited show deal" to move prospects closer to a deal.
12. Stand on the side of your prospects rather than in front of them (in relation to the booth). People are more comfortable in this position and stay longer (trust me on this one).

A Dozen Ways to Bring in Customers

Before you finalize your market strategy you have to decide who you want to come to your booth and how you want to sell to them. Large high-profile companies are content to bring masses of people to their booths using some gimmick or other to get visibility. Smaller companies may be content to lure just a few visitors and discuss their products in a quiet corner. No matter which approach you choose, be clear about your objectives and tailor your efforts to accomplish them.

1. Show your product in action. The reason a trade meeting is called a show is that it is a show, not an ad. Create drama. Stationary displays are

boring. If your product works better or differently than the competition, show it, don't tell it. If your product is smaller, lighter, more colorful, tastier—show it. Any product can be demonstrated.

2. Build drama around your product, even if the product is inherently dull.

Baird, in Bedford Ma, is a company that manufactures instruments that are used to perform chemical analyses on metals. This is one topic that is not particularly thrilling to talk about and one that is challenging to create drama with. If you've seen one analyzing machine, you've basically seen them all. But Baird wanted to introduce this technology to a new market. While searching through customer files one day, Baird's sales and marketing team discovered that clients used the equipment to test cosmetics, jewelry and children's toys—just for fun. Baird ordered giant toothpaste tubes, watches and crayons for the booth. Booth traffic increased 400 percent. But, ah, here comes the rub...and another strategy.

3. One of Baird's competitors watched jealously as people flocked to the booth. So, just about the time the Baird's team was about to make a presentation, they scheduled a raffle for 25 wristwatches. This simple tactic stole half of Baird's crowd. The moral (and the strategy) is to watch for rival presentations or shows and schedule a proven audience getter at the same time to usurp traffic. Yes, trade shows are a jungle.

4. Build your exhibit around your product, not vice versa. A trade function is show-and-sell time—most companies need a lot more than image to build sales. Image displays look fine to management, and they can be effective, but they bore visitors to tears.

5. Show as many products as you can. Prospects like to pick through an entire product line.

6. Use three-dimensional cutaways to show how a product is made. Show your customers why your product is as good as you say it is.

7. Encourage audience participation. Get prospects personally involved in your product as much as possible. Let them play with your product. You can even make up some sort of game with your product—say as a playing piece in a bingo game. This gives prospects a hands-on opportunity to prove to themselves that your product is special.

8. Make your demonstration visible from an aisle. Make sure that people in your peripheral vision have just as much chance to see your demonstration as immediate passersby.

9. Use a live demonstrator rather than a taped voice. A live person is much more compelling and pulls people in like the old carnival barkers.

10. Use drama and keep it simple. If you want to show how strong a product is, drop heavy blocks on it. If your product is lighter than the competition's, let passersby feel the difference.

11. If you use a celebrity in your ads, employ him or her at the exhibit to reinforce your sales message.

12. Create a slide show or video.

Beyond Introducing New Products

Admittedly, the best way to get attendance at trade shows is to introduce a new product. New products are big news to prospects. That's why the attendees are there. But there are other ways to create traffic for your booth.

- Offer services (i.e., message centers, free luggage tags)
- Celebrities
- Caricature artists
- Magicians and other performers
- Giant blowup of photographs or transparencies
- Polaroids of people taken at the booth
- Water. You can use recyclable waterfalls and other water-type tricks like perpetual motion faucets
- Robots. They're always fun. People want to see who is controlling it (It's done using radio waves)
- Costumed mascots with your logo who walk around the show
- Free shopping bags ALWAYS bring in people

While there is no limit on the number of activities that can be carried out, remember the purpose is to show and sell, not just to entertain.

Select Your Best People to Run Your Booth

The most important element of the trade shows is not the creative exhibits or stunning graphics. It's the people manning the booth. A trade show exhibition can be bewildering to many marketing people even if they're seasoned sales people who are used to going to the prospect's place of business.

Choose gregarious, seasoned people who don't get overwhelmed by meeting hundreds of people (at least 50 percent of whom are going to be of little value). They should be able to separate the strong prospects from the others.

All selected booth staffers should be totally briefed on your program with tune-up meetings the day before the show starts.

Motivation is very important. Sales reps should be convinced that participation is not only good for the company, but good for the rep.

Make sure that you have enough people staffing your exhibit. It's best to rotate your people every few hours. Remember, dealing with this many people effectively is an energy-draining activity. You want to keep energy levels high to the very end and prevent burnout.

Follow-Up Is Critical

All qualified leads should be followed up with personal sales calls and letters. Since prospects have been to your booth and met your people, you have now started a relationship with them.

I/O Data Systems sends booth visitors regular broadcast faxes of sale prices. They figure they spend about a $1000 on follow-ups which include the faxes and personal phone calls. Their sales are more than twenty times that annually.

Generating Sales Without a Booth

A trade show can be fertile territory even if you don't have a booth. People are in a festive frame of mind. They're there to meet people and have fun. You can capitalize on this and generate sales even if you're not an exhibitor:

- Leave literature in the press sections and at the various seminars. Also, give out your brochures to people manning and visiting booths. (Yes, sellers are buyers, too.)

- Network at parties and cocktail hours.
- Rent a hotel room and advertise your presence.
- Use a hotel room for cocktail parties and solicit guests and prospects.
- Walk around and look at the name tags and companies they represent. Keep your eyes and ears wide open for prospects.
- If you know that your customers will be attending the show, set up luncheons and meetings. After all, they are attending the show to meet people who sell what you sell. And that's what a trade show is all about.

CHAPTER EIGHT

Strategies for Pricing and Adding Value

Okay MBAs. It's time to price your goods.

Bring up your spread sheet on the computer like you've been taught and access your P & Ls. Your product and marketing costs have been factored in, as have your five-year business forecasts. You've gone over the cost of your raw materials and labor so you know your break-even points where you can amortize your capital equipment and take-in costs such as light bulb replacement and employee coffee breaks.

Of course you've incorporated the standard industry markup and have prepared a worksheet of pricing differentials. Now you know exactly how to price your product. You've even asked the focus groups for a suggested price. (I can't believe you would really do that but many marketers do).

I'm proud of you.

Now, after you get your computer printout, you can toss the whole complicated mass into the circular file and go back to playing Sim City or Space Invaders.

You've missed something.

You forgot that your prospects have the ultimate say in what your product is going to sell for. They're only interested in what's in it for them. So all effective pricing strategies have to do with buyers, not manufacturers.

There are about a zillion books on the shelves about pricing formulas. I know, because I read them all while preparing this chapter. The most effective pricing strategies stem from consumer buying behavior rather than algebraic equations. Pricing is a tool, and a bit of an art.

Consumers want to buy a product at a "fair" price. But what does "a fair price" mean?

A fair price has to do with convenience, quality and how important the product is to the consumer. A fair price has to do more with a consumer's perception of the deal than with any hard realities. It also has to do with how you perceive your company. Do you want to be considered a low-price provider or a maker of high-profile and high-price goods? It's back to your mission statement...again!

Sound Pricing Strategies

Pricing is more a function of intuitive judgement and Psychology 101 than it is a function of cost of materials. Pricing should be done backwards. It should flow from consumers rather than toward consumers.

You should be using your cost of goods to give you bottom-line numbers only. Don't use them to decide how much you should charge. Consumers don't give a damn about what it costs you to make a product as long as they can reasonably afford it and that it's worth the money (to the consumer, not you).

Most published price strategies are a function of paybacks, lifecyles and theoretical costing schemata. Of course you have to make money on your product, but pricing is a single element of the marketing proposition.

Sound pricing strategies are a key factor in producing sales. This may sound obvious, but in too many companies pricing is seen as the determining factor in investment paybacks. If your price is too high or too low for a market you're not going to get a good return on your investment so you might as well do it right.

People dislike spending more money then they have to on some goods rather than on others. These attitudes change from one category to another and even from one store to another. It also depends on how far the consumer is willing to go to buy your product.

But I digress.

Get What You Can...

In the wilds of the Southwest where I now more or less permanently reside, there's a health-food megastore called Wild Oats. They sell alternatives to supermarket foods and health-care items. The place is always mobbed with customers from all economic stratospheres. In some cases, consumers pay double for the identical products they can find in their supermarkets.

...And What the Market Will Bear

Akio Morita was president of Sony when the Walkman was developed. He was told by R & D the consumer cost would be about $200. Morita balked. He knew that his target audience was young adults 18-30 and they could afford around $100 without a great deal of price resistance. He ordered R & D to bring it in for that price. They followed his directions and the rest is, as they say, marketing history. Morita built his costs backward, with his eye always on the final selling price, even in the developmental stages.

Both Wild Oats and Sony followed a key marketing dictum. Price by perceived value, rather than spreadsheets. I call it *Power pricing*.

Pricing 101

Of all the skills in the marketer's repertoire, none is as elastic as pricing. You can actually compare pricing to a rubber band. When a rubber band is in its original form, like a commodity product, it's powerless. When you stretch it taut, like a value added product, it does the most good. If you stretch it too far, it breaks; but the more you stretch it, the better it works.

Pricing by Category

A product can be priced one of three ways relative to a category:

Low-Price Range—the unused rubber band

Mid-price range—the taut rubber band

High-price range—stretching the pricing elasticity of the marketplace to its fullest extent without breaking

All three of these price ranges have their advantages and drawbacks.

The high-price range is tough, but often profitable. You won't get the volume you look for, but you may win with heady product margins. To make this range work you usually have to have a demonstrably better product or imbue your product with luxury cues. Godiva Chocolate, with its glitzy packaging, is an example of greater perceived value being added to a product to make it more glamorous than its competitors.

The mid-price range is where the bulk of new products live. It leaves room for merchandising, deals and value-added appeals. The drawback is that it is highly competitive and there is a large potential for brand shifting.

Products at the low end of the spectrum are usually staples, with little value-added glamour. Volume is key to these products, but like our unused rubber band, a low price has drawbacks too. If it's too low in relation to the competition, the consumer often tends not to believe they are good products. It's also the pricing category with the least flexibility. You can always be hit with higher raw materials cost and lose the price advantage. Because there is little opportunity for an emotional consumer wedge, you risk being undercut by a stronger competitor.

Pricing from the Consumer's Perspective

To understand the consumer marketplace, you have to remember that it is always evolving. It is made up of four categories:

1. Poorly conceived or mispositioned products—these are not going to sell well no matter how you price them.
2. Staples—our survival needs, like milk or bread, electricity and even batteries. These are almost always price shopped and people resist price increases like the devil.
3. Things that would be nice to have, like a Walkman—discretionary goods that are *actively* sought out by the consumers. A "thing" can be an experience, like a movie or an amusement park. It can be a service, like a special beauty salon. It can even be a store like Wild Oats.
4. Killer products we ABSOLUTELY MUST HAVE! These items require an emotional commitment on the part of the consumer. It usually exceeds the physical worth of the product by a wide margin. These are, ironically, usually well-considered purchases and impulse items where the usual purchase decision arguments are short circuited, like the single-use camera or the tube of Rembrandt whitening toothpaste.

High-ticket items are almost always rationalized. For instance, an expensive house might be rationalized as having a good school district. The toothpaste is rationalized as a little luxury, a chance to be the best looking that one can be.

Finding the Most Effective Price Point

The best way to find the right prices is to let your customers choose them.

An easy way to determine a consumer-friendly price point is to test it in context with your product. But here's a caveat: Don't ask a consumer what a fair price is. Consumers will almost always say something ridiculously low. Instead, in focus groups, or whatever research form you use, put price bullets or price ranges on your product or concept and wait for your respondent's reaction. Change your prices one at time until you get acceptance from most people.

Another strategy is to set up displays in stores as tests. Use varying price points to see which price point consumers are most receptive to.

Straightforward Research Strategy

Here's the best way to determine what price is ideal for your item:

1. Develop positioning concepts and take them to your focus groups.
2. Prepare a range of price stickers of varying pricing levels and stick them on your concepts. Show prices that are even higher than you expect to charge and wait for your respondents to flinch. Do the same with competing products.
3. Probe respondents on their purchase intent at each of the price points. How often they would buy the product? What product would it replace? Where is the money going to come from? NEVER ask a consumer what he or she would pay for the product without a direct reactive price like a price sticker.

Learn from the Chocolate-Chip-Cookie Controversy

A while back, the great chocolate-chip-cookie controversy took hold. Famous Amos, David's Chocolate Chip Cookies and others created fresh-baked cookies and sold them for the then outlandish price of $1.25. Marketers laughed. Who would spend $1.25 for a single cookie? Many consumers did and it spawned the "little luxury" category.

The $1.25 cookie changed the consumer reference point for comparing prices. Consumer reference points come from their purchase experience and is based on what others charge for a product.

If you're priced too low from a point of reference, consumers will think your product doesn't work as well as similar products. You cannot become a market leader by giving your product away at the lowest prices.

Charge too much and don't offer the consumer an apparent benefit, then consumers will think you're ripping them off. You can't become a market leader by charging more than the traffic will bear.

No one is saying that you should abandon costing procedures in determining a price—that is ludicrous. But your production costs will come down as you continue to sell more products.

But there are other strategies for pricing, almost as many as there are products. Here are some of the better ones.

Keep Tabs on the Consumer's Pockets

Here's a major factor in considering a pricing strategy that is never mentioned in marketing textbooks. Where is the consumer's money coming from? I don't mean drug money, or lottery winnings, but in what pocket is the consumer going to reach to pay for your product? If it's from the family money, chances are she's not going to lay out a bundle for a "prestige product." If it's from her discretionary funds or mad money, she's more apt to go for the little luxury.

How do we find out where the money is coming from? Simple. Ask. Use focus groups to pry into buying habits. If consumers want your product, ask them where they will get the money to pay for it. We asked a moderate-income female prospect recently where she would get the money for a proposed high-ticket item which she and her husband would supposedly appreciate equally. She said she would steal it from her husband's bowling fund, so I hope he likes the product.

Power Pricing 101

Power Pricing takes all of these factors into account, and more. The Power-Pricing Strategy strives to achieve a win/win point for your retailers and distributors, for your consumers and for you. Power pricing strives to identify that unique point where:

1. Retailers and distributors will handle your product and give it the attention it deserves. There's a weird paradox at work here. If you ask their opinion, retailers and distributors will invariably say you should price at the lowest price point to make it easy for them to sell. But if it's too low, there usually is less profit for them and they will loathe carrying and selling your product. Also, if you charge too little, you're not leaving any room to excite the market with price promotions.
2. The consumer will perceive your price as reasonable for the value received and will continue to buy your product.
3. And, most importantly, you can make money. Because if you don't, no pricing strategy in the world is going to help you.

Three Examples of Power Pricing

1. At one time it would have been obscene to pay $10 for a tube of toothpaste that claims (somewhat spuriously) to whiten teeth, but Rembrandt Toothpaste created a super-upscale niche market product.
2. If you have a camera, like most of us, you can have your film developed for $7.00 or less. If you buy a single-use camera, the price (camera and film) can be $21.00 or more. It's the hottest photographic product today, even though the basic concept is almost ninety years old! (With the first primitive cameras, you actually sent the entire camera in to get the pictures processed.)
3. A shampoo that costs $7.50 has the same active ingredients as a product selling for 99 cents, but the $7.50 product sells better.

Is the consumer being taken for a ride? Not really. To a consumer, all are worth the money at the time of purchase.

Consumers often create mental price ranges that dictate what they will or won't pay for a product. The range is based on past experiences, lifestyles and how customers feel at given moments. The range of prices varies from category to category and from store to store. It solely depends on your customers' frame of reference.

Guidelines for Implementing Power-Pricing Strategies

Price High (in relation to other products in category) when:

- There's no competition.
- Consumers have no frame of reference to establish a value in their own minds.
- You're targeting consumers who consider themselves "on the cutting edge" and will pay top dollar.
- You have a steady customer base that is willing to pay more for your products.
- You need a strong profit margin (but remember, consumers don't care if you make or lose money).

Price Medium when:

- You are entering a category in which a manufacturer has already staked a claim.
- You don't have a major new benefit to offer.
- Your consumer has many choices.
- Your product is new to your business but is firmly established in the consumer's mind by comparison with others.
- You have mid-priced consumer equity like Kraft Macaroni and Cheese or any of the Golden Grain rice entries.

Price Low when:

- You can make a product cheaper than anyone else and still make money.
- Your consumer equity is in a low-priced position, such as Arm & Hammer or Michelina's.
- You can obtain a major advantage by selling a no-frills product (or generic) or want to fill out a product line with high, low and medium price points.
- Consumers are not willing to accept a high price in a given category.

Forward-Looking Backwards Pricing

Just as Sony did with their Walkman, you can too. Try pricing your product backwards. Figure out a selling price that will be effective for your market and build your product around the selling price rather than vice versa.

The Euphoria Principle

Products that make people feel better and identify an area that gives them enjoyment, luxury or status, command higher prices than products that satisfy basic needs. Sell dreams, not necessities. People do not begrudge the money so much. Go for the markets where there are marked differences in quality. Your high quality differences should be obvious to everyone, and not hidden. You may have to highlight them artificially in some way. If your quality difference is intangible, then promote the difference heavily. Use the high price to "prove" the existence of your mythical quality.

Pricing for Prestige

This is another backwards strategy. You attack the top end of the market and focus your marketing dollars on people with money to spend on your product. Then you market your products strictly to them. People without money may want your product badly, or they may have an obvious glaring need for your product. But they will give you a hard time over your selling price.

Product Loyalty and Pricing

Loyalty is another factor which affects price sensitivity. Where a market's loyalty can be secured, those customers are not too sensitive about prices. As a product area becomes more familiar to consumers through greater competition, you either drop your prices or take advantage of segmentation possibilities.

The Dislike Factor

Also related to pricing for the consumer is the dislike factor. There are certain products that consumers hate spending money on. The person resents the expense. This can be a quart of milk, a doctor's bill or pantyhose. The dislike factor is often related to staple products, products that consumers must buy (as opposed to products consumers "must have").

You want to keep this dislike factor in mind when pricing your product. But remember that the customer who balks at spending too much for a loaf of bread might actually look forward to spending more money on good steaks, rock concerts or traveling.

Linking Budget to Power Pricing

Arm & Hammer has pricing down to a science. They also add an interesting twist to the cause of low-end Power Pricing. They offer products that perform as well as leading brand-name products in their particular categories. But Arm & Hammer charges less. In short, they don't substitute quality for lower prices. And they're right. A low price should always be treated as a bonus, not an excuse for hawking an inferior product.

Contrast this against another company that charges less for a BIG BRAND NAME but in the process cheapened the product. The brand name is now forced to labor as a subject of marketing trivia, while Arm & Hammer continues to roll along profitably.

In the same vein, Michelina's, a relatively new name in the frozen-food entree section of the supermarket, also does it well. The company offers a superior product at a lower price. It's pretty much a win/win situation for everyone concerned. Michelina's is paying its bills and making money; the consumer gets a superior product.

It doesn't take much high-level thinking, does it?

Both Arm & Hammer and Michelina's successes are somewhat unique. Arm & Hammer has a powerful reputation that allows consumers to believe that they are getting more for less money. Michelina's products are demonstrably better than other frozen entrees.

If you can't vividly show that your product is better, then consumers will think they are getting an inferior product.

One of the best product names in the nineties was Budget Gourmet. The Gourmet part of the name gave consumers a psychic reward. And the Budget part of the name showed that they were saving money.

Pricing Impulse Sales

Impulse products have their own set of rules. You can usually charge more for your product because its purchase is predicated on an impulse decision, and all of the brain wave decision-making electronics are short-circuited. That's why there's always room for the buck-fifty brownie. The high price adds to the self-reward factor.

Promotional Pricing

Several years ago Procter & Gamble came up with something call EDLP (everyday low pricing). There were to be no special deals for anyone and no promotional pricing. P & G would sell its products at the same cost every day. They ran into the same problems others do with inflexible pricing schemes; it left no room to create pricing excitement and it didn't allow retailers to create excitement with their own promotional pricing.

Promotional pricing can fill up slack demand and fill in slow sales gaps. Hotels time their promotions seasonally, when they have excessive empty beds. Promotional pricing can also be used effectively when many people are interested in your product or service and your volume can make up for the lower prices.

When you know a competing product is about to be offered in your market, offer volume discounts, say three of an item for the price of two. This strategy can cause consumers to stock up on your item so they won't be motivated to try the new product. It's a strong defensive measure.

Promotional pricing can be used by retailers and manufacturers to force the market to sell more or to hold a market position. It can be used to clear special problems of excess stocks and slow selling lines.

Everyone involved in distribution should be involved in the promotional price deal to elicit their cooperation.

Pricing Points for Everyone

Many businesses use this simple pricing formula, especially in the packaged goods industry. If you want to sell toothpaste for example, price it so the distributor and retailers are given a profit margin. This can be tricky if you want to promote your product at a certain selling price. You will have to make sure the distributor gets his cut and leaves you with a profit.

Don't Go Crazy with Discounts

Many sellers misuse the promotional pricing strategy. They run price deals during the peak selling season, thereby providing a price discount at a time when demand is higher and relatively less elastic. Other sellers run frequent price deals and then find it is difficult to sell the product at its "regular" price because the buyers have either stocked up or are waiting for the next deal.

Here are five strategic guidelines for choosing a promotional pricing strategy.

1. Off-season price reductions are more profitable.
2. Too-frequent price promotions make the consumers more price conscious.
3. Deals are not usually very effective in countering new competitive brands nor are they necessarily more effective when accompanied by product or package innovations.
4. Price deals are more effective for new brands.
5. Price deals are not cures for generally "sick" products.

Like all pricing strategies, promotional pricing has its disadvantages. If you succeed with promotional pricing, your competitors will follow. Soon, no one will make money. Also, when promotional pricing is used too often, neither manufacturers nor consumers are inclined to pay regular prices.

Force-Your-Way-In Pricing

Commonly called *wedge pricing*, in this strategy, you force your market share by undercutting a category. Use this pricing when you want to get in a market by any means possible or if you can make your products for dramatically less than anyone else can because of better technology.

The Bic company created its ballpoint pen market using this strategy. The owners of Bic acquired a huge factory for building ballpoint pens. Instead of asking for higher prices, Bic undercut every competitor significantly. Distribution followed rapidly.

The "We're Number One" Pricing Strategy

Market leaders often make the most money. On average, the price is better, the volume is greater and unit costs are lower. This pricing strategy sets the tone of the market. In this strategy you get whatever the market will bear and control the prices to a great extent. The drawback is that you leave the market open for price leaders and companies who want to one-up you in terms of more product benefits. Also, advertising costs tend to be higher for market leaders.

The "We're Not Number One, But We're Close" Strategy

You can do extremely well by being number two, or number three. Set your prices slightly less then the market leader but about 10 percent over the market average. This will help position you as a leading brand in the consumer's mind.

Pricing for Low Price

If people understand that the quality can be taken for granted, as in staple goods, then price promotions and discounts will help to move the product. Price promotions on milk will always move more milk.

The Lowest Price/Everyone Wins Strategy

We've all seen the ads: Get the lowest price or we'll refund the difference. The problem with it is that it takes so much work on the consumers' part. First they have to buy the item, than keep a steady eye on the ads. Then, if they do find a lower price, they need a face-to-face confrontation with the store's salesperson or manager.

Sun Television & Appliance out of Dayton Ohio, found a better way, which helped turn the business around. They tracked prices for the consumer. They hired an outside marketing firm to track all the prices in their selling area. If a store beat Sun's price within thirty days, they would mail the customer a refund. No work was needed on the consumer's part at all. The strategy created a lot of very contented customers who sent slews of word-of-mouth referrals.

The Mythical List Price

Some companies prefer to list their prices high and immediately mark them down. There are strong arguments for, and against, this policy. The pro groups say that it establishes a prestige price point in the consumer's mind and allows the company to give the appearance of large discounts.

The con group argues that the manufacturer's image will eventually suffer because it has become too promotion-oriented. People will see

Illustration 8.1
Pricing Strategies Based on Objectives

Objective: High, short-term profits
Strategy: High price, market leader, upscale niche
How to do it: Determine consumer acceptance, charge premium prices for tangible and emotional product differences
Advantages: Protects against rising costs; heavy, immediate ROI; suggests higher value, enables you to control demand
Disadvantages: Attracts competition; likely to lose share as category develops with mid-price range entrants; can often keep buying demand artificially low

Objective: To obtain a reasonable volume at above-average prices
Strategy: Upscale positioning to allow steady, high-profit sales
How to do it: Start at parity with high-priced brand and slowly lower your price below the market leader; stay flexible in response to deals, production, competition, etc.
Advantages: Provides rapid return on investment and cushions against cost variances; basis for becoming market leader
Disadvantages: Need to stay extremely aware of competition, expecially in regard to product enhancement, costs and pricing strategies

Objective: To fulfill exisiting product demand
Strategy: Competitive, standard market pricing
How to do it: Start with ultimate price and work backwards to control costs. Keep eye on market and competition's pricing; steady flow of product enhancements to retain market share against competition
Advantages: Meet customer demands; steady flow of sales
Disadvantages: Will almost never become a market leader; at the mercy of competition and changing consumer prefences; great competition with mid-priced goods; must rely on product differences, heavy promotion or a me-too sales strategy

Objective: Stimulate market and capture a reasonable market share
Strategy: Market penetration
How to do it: Charge low prices and create a mass market, review past, current and future competition's prices and react to them quickly
Advantages: Discourages competition because of low-profit margins; maximum exposure and penetration in a relatively short time frame

Disadvantages: May not get volume wanted and justify the low price; always at the mercy of costs, small pricing errors may result in large losses

Objective: Fill low-end price niche
Strategy: Price at low levels to keep competition out; set prices as low as possible in relation to actual cost; create further low prices through buying and manufacturing economies
Advantages: Discourages potential competition; gets rid of excess product and overruns
Disadvantages: Extremely difficult niche to crawl out of, negative consumer equities hard to build on; needs very high costs control; long-term payback period

through your pricing and it will eventually hurt the manufacturer's image. They also say that distributors and consumers will become aware of your ploy rather quickly and wait for your markdowns before buying. But it is an option that you should consider.

Avoiding Bottom Feeders

Bottom feeders are those consumers who are "waiting for the price to come down." But these people are not just looking for lower prices, they're looking for "supercharged" products at lower prices. This usually happens in a slow-growth marketing category. When business is good, few people have to look at the bottom line. When business is bad, people have to work harder because the bottom feeders are preying. By constantly evolving your products and updating your pricing strategy you can ease your bottom lines, even in a slow-growth area.

Establishing Value

Since I've been out of school, I've heard companies speak about one magic word: VALUE. Value is supposed to conquer all sorts of marketing ills.

In the seventies, it was "Consumers want more value."

In the eighties, we heard "All the focus groups point to a need for greater value."

Value-mania continues to run rampant. Almost every large company I've worked with talks about offering value, like it's a new concept. If you don't offer consumers a value, they won't buy your product, at least not the second time. Value should be a given, not a marketing concept.

Value positioning is the mark of a lazy marketer who can't think of a more creative way to market his, or her, goods. A true value should offer consumers something special.

Value isn't what you put in a product, it's what your customer takes out of it. A value does not always correlate with a low price. Only a very low percentage of consumers say price is the determining factor in a purchase. But long after the price is forgotten, the consumer's memories of your product's effectiveness (or ineffectiveness) will remain.

Remember, we said that consumers usually have a range of acceptable prices in mind that they're willing to pay for a product. A little luxury like a pint of premium-priced ice cream, or even a premium-priced bottled water can be the Holy Grail to someone who's had a tough day at home or in the office. Yet the same people who pay $30 for a steak in a fancy restaurant may get pretty annoyed when a container of milk jumps a dime. The steak was a value at the time of purchase, the milk was no value at all...it's a necessity.

Pricing for Quality

If you run a blindfold test with users of certain products, like liquor or chocolate, consumers cannot select their own favorite brand from close competitors with any significant success rate. If you conduct blind taste tests and you tell consumers that one product is cheap, one is expensive and one is normal, then they will report on the quality in line with the price.

For many products, the price is the most significant indicator of quality (items such as cosmetics, liquor, and so on). In the upper ranges only a small increase in quality is necessary to make your product acceptable. Paradoxically, in the lower pricing ranges, a large difference is usually expected.

Add Quality When Raising Prices

In certain product areas, consumers are sensitive to changes in price, while in other areas they are less so. For certain goods, only a small increase in quality is expected to justify a higher price. In other areas the increase in product performance must be great.

The consumer might expect to pay $50 for a bottle of wine, and even try other higher-priced brands without complaining about price. But that same consumer might complain bitterly about a 2-cent-per-gallon rise in gas prices.

Adding Convenience

Adding convenience to a product does not necessarily increase its value. Consumers won't pay more for convenience unless it manifests itself in a product that is more effective than other products or has other reinforcing cues. Consumers know that they are being charged extra for an aerosol or pump and won't pay extra for the convenience. But you can help the consumer rationalize the purchase with extras wanted by the consumer, such as extra richness in a product, fancy packaging or a new fragrance.

Twelve Ways to Add Value Without Breaking the Bank

1. *Add more uses for the product* (this can be done with graphics) so that it does the work of an additional product. A toilet-paper gadget that deodorizes the bathroom while it dispenses toilet paper conquers two problems for the price of one. Campbell's soups has created incremental sales by selling their soups as tasty recipe ingredients.

2. *Make life easier for your customer.* It can be a new package that's easier to open, or even a reinforcement of your advertising message.

American Express spends a great deal on quarterly management summaries it sends to all cardmembers. The summeries help their customers track their expenses. Glad Lock bags with the color-change seal showed women how it could help keep food fresher by making it easier for kids and husbands to close the storage bags correctly.

3. *Process your product a little more.* Cheese is a value- added product from milk. With a little work you can turn a commodity product into something the consumer wants. For instance, microwave popcorn added great value to plain popcorn. Prepared Rice Krispy Treats were simply an added-value form of Rice Krispies. Of course, people could make the snacks by themselves, but why bother? All commodity producers can add value if they have imagination and a modicum of marketing skills.

4. *Slim your product down—especially the packaging.* People got very tired of paying high prices for cereal packed in conventional boxes. Malt-O-Meal, a small cereal producer and Quaker, a large cereal producer, each packaged large amounts of their product in cellophane bags. Consumers flipped over the money they saved on products that had previously been packaged in wasteful boxes.

When you use this tactic, make sure you compare your products to the highly advertised and familiar ones.

5. *Offer coupons or additional products* from you or from other manufacturers.

6. *Create frequent-user programs.* This is great for parity products and commodity items. It gives the consumer another reason for choosing your brand.

7. *Show how your product or service is better.* In service situations, show how your service can bring in new business. In product situations, show how your product will satisfy several members of a family instead of just the buyers.

8. *Make your product so aesthetically appealing that the buyer uses it as decoration.* Designer paper towels, and even answering machines offered by Conair, are good examples of these.

9. *Create a container with multiple uses* (people claim they never have enough storage space).

10. *Add additional time to a product warranty.* Add a guarantee if you don't already have one. By offering a guarantee that's better than competing products you are creating a product with great value because it gives the consumer piece of mind. Often the life a product—particularly an expensive or complicated product—has components that need to be replaced periodically. Offer lower prices on disposable aspects of your product or offer free replacement parts.

11. *Send your customer a free magazine or newsletter.* Here's a way to reinforce the fact that you care about your customer and to precondition the person to buy your product again because of excellent customer support.

12. *Increase the size.* Add an extra portion of an item or make it bigger for the same price.

Give Away the Sizzle—Sell the Steak

Pricing is an important part of your marketing mix. Sometimes you can actually give your product away to create an opportunity.

The classic example is Gillette, which learned long ago that it can make more money on razor blades than razors. So the company prices its razors low and factors in high margins for its blades.

Another example is the cell phone industry. For a long time, providers kept their rates high for their business customers. They now give away the phone and price their basic rate at $19.95, placing the product within reach of the average consumer who, now, gets the phone for security measures. This new pricing created a brand new market.

For another example, a new home security company is giving its expensive alarms away free, and is making money on the monthly fees charged to connect the buyer's home to the central monitoring location.

When to Offer Your Product Free

When you're looking to become a standard in a market and you have other revenue streams. A good example is the net browsers that Microsoft and Netscape give away.

When you expect to have a continuing relationship with your customers and can sell them other things.

When your costs per unit are low. It doesn't cost much to clone a computer disk or program. That's why software companies and shareware (programs that you try before you buy) producers are eager to send out free demos or even full programs for free.

When you can reach invaluable, key decision makers. Giving away a product, or even hundreds of products at trade shows can spread word-of-mouth about your product.

When you can get something better in return. For example, if you have a website, you may give away a page or so to a prospect in return for setting up a sales meeting.

CHAPTER NINE

Selling and Marketing Strategies That Create Record Sales

As I was researching this chapter and exploring the selling strategies of experts, I noticed a backlash against relationship selling. Relationship selling is out, the articles and books suggested. It takes too long. People want high-tech answers quickly. Customers don't have time to build relationships. They want answers to their questions fast. Customers are only out for themselves.

I thought all this was interesting, because relationship selling has always been at the heart of my consulting practice.

Strategic Relationship Selling

Strategic relationship selling is exactly right because it supports all these new demands and adds the factor of trust and business respect into sales. But it's a new kind of relationship. It's a sort of hybrid between the spit-shined shoes of the old masters who took pains to learn about a prospect's children and hobbies to the avant-garde sales artist of today who spends the same time learning more about the prospect's business.

If you can learn about what makes the prospect's heart beat faster and also earn the person's respect, you've got it made.

BUILD RELATIONSHIPS, EARN RESPECT AND GET MORE FROM YOUR SALES PROGRAM

Building relationships with your customers, your associates and the company you're trying to sell to is still the key to marketing.

On a project one day, I asked about a certain executive who seemed to keep to himself in his corner office. "He may be good," my contact said, "but nobody here listens to him because in the few years he's been here, he hasn't been able to earn management's respect. They don't care about his ideas. They won't entrust him with a project."

I had occasion to have lunch with the downtrodden executive. He seemed bright and personable. But he was totally into himself. Now, that's not totally bad, but he was unable to understand the complete mission of his division's business. He had no business acumen. He was unable to package his ideas in a way that management would buy into. He never bonded.

Most people can sell a product once, but it's the building of respect and relationships that builds businesses:

1. You relate with your customers and retailers through packaging, promotion, the product itself and your sheer personality.
2. Bond with your sales people and your distributors by sharing your ideas on increasing their businesses and proving to them that you're on their side.
3. Connect with outside companies by dealing with key people on a relationship type basis rather than "those people I sell to."
4. Sell your ideas to management by packaging yourself as an expert and proving your ideas' worth to the business.

SELF-INTEREST IS THE OVERRIDING FACTOR IN EVERY SALE

There's an overriding factor that permeates every sales call and presentation, whether it's to an outside customer or your own management: "What's in it for me?"

Every decision maker is interested in two things—making money and success. In fact, to most people, making money *is* success. If you can show them how to achieve these and earn their trust at the same time, they will be very interested.

A business sale is a combination of these elements:

1. Solutions that help customers achieve their business objectives.
2. Solutions that help customers achieve their personal objectives.
3. Relationships that move the decision making process toward closure.
4. A compelling personal reason to make a decision.

NO RISK IS THE SECOND OVERRIDING FACTOR

People don't like to take risks. They want a win/win situation at all times. They won't risk anything for you. When my esteemed editor Tom Power pitched this book to management, he wanted a no-risk done deal. He looked at my previous works, my proposal and spoke with my agent. Only when he was reasonably assured that I would do a competent job did he pitch the book to his people. Whether or not it met his expectations, only Tom can decide.

MAKE ME A HERO

Everyone wants to be a hero. When you pitch to people, keep everyone excited about the role they are going to play. The successful marketer subordinates his ego to give credit to all the players.

Once, a friend of mine got an invitation to pitch a product through a lawyer friend. The lawyer said, "I'm giving you this 'in' but I don't want any risks. Don't embarrass me. If it goes over well, I want to be the hero. If it embarrasses me, I'll never talk to you again." This statement pretty much sums up selling through the marketing maze. It's the marketer as Hercules syndrome.

Three Key Strategic Rules For Selling to Anyone

1. *Don't pitch to anyone unless you are fully prepared.* Make sure you can answer all questions before they are put forth. A misguided off-the-cuff answer can be a death knell to the most diligent marketer.

Rehearse your pitch and hone your skills with dress rehearsals to "long shot" companies. These are companies that, for whatever reasons, are not likely to buy your product. Make your mistakes with them before going after real prospects.

2. *Don't make a pitch unless you know you are talking with the decision maker or with someone who can get you to that decision maker.* Often entrepreneurs are so thrilled by being allowed to make any presentation at all that they focus on a person in a wrong department or one who has no decision-making capabilities. Just obtaining the meeting is an emotional high to the seller. I call it the "professional guest syndrome."

Don't set up a presentation unless it can help you achieve your goal. If the person invites you to make your presentation saying he or she will relay the information to another department, decline courteously. It usually doesn't happen. Or if it does, that person will be a lot less effective than you would be.

3. *Refer to the Hot Button List in this chapter.* Whether you're making a sale to an individual or presenting a formal sales presentation in a corporate structure, people typically buy based on emotion and rationalize the purchase with facts.

Bonding with the Biggies

Many entrepreneurs, particularly smaller ones, are intimidated by the idea of selling to upper management or to large companies. That's a mistake. You aren't selling to Xerox, for example, but to a person who works at Xerox, who has the same hopes and dreams as you do. When dealing with your own upper management, you're not dealing with the Vice President of International Sales and Global Implementation. You're dealing with a person who wants to be president and increase profits.

Intercompany and Intracompany Selling

There is not a great deal of difference between the intercompany (outside) sell and the intracompany (inside) sell. A case can be made that it is easier to sell to people outside your own company, because they don't know you on an everyday basis. The people you work with every day are familiar with your characteristics and foibles. When you sell to another company, you create your own persona.

Pitching to Your Own People

If you sell in-house, the good news is that you can probably buttonhole enough people to set up a meeting. The bad news is that each person attending your meeting will have his or her personal agenda.

This is like the fairly recent phenomena of having a medical specialist for every ailment. If you have a headache and go to a doctor who is a gastrointestinal specialist, the doctor may tell you the problem is in your digestive system. A chiropractor may tell you your spinal alignment is poor. An endocrine specialist may tell you that it's strictly glandular. The problem is that each of these specialists have a narrow focal area which they know quite well.

People tend to fit problems into areas they know best. And that's how it works in in-house meetings.

As the marketer, you are in a unique position. You are the general practitioner who knows a great deal about the whole picture. Translate your story into how the product or marketing specialty will benefit each and every one.

Here's a real-world example covering both the intercompany and intracompany sell.

I developed a product which I was pitching to a large baked goods manufacturer. The marketing manager who had seen the product's potential and the whole profit picture was the middle man. He had to broker the idea to people who only dealt in the narrow world of their job titles.

Here was the initial feedback I got from the marketing manager.

The marketer, my contact, loved the product but found it was a tough sell to his in-house people.

R & D wasn't excited by the taste. It thought it could do better.

Research said it had no budget to pretest the product. The financial specialist worried that the profit turnaround for this heretofore untried product might be weak initially.

The plant manager said they might have difficulty getting it into containers.

The marketer's boss didn't see how it would fit into a five-year plan.

Game Plan for Intracompany Selling

Prelims:

- Before the meeting, whet the appetite of the team members through informal chats and memos. But be careful not to divulge too much until they can see the whole story.
- Find out what projects the team members are working on. If the projects are doing well, then they will probably be in an accepting mood. If not, your project will give them a chance to look good.
- Create an agenda that spells out your objectives clearly and succinctly.
- If you're bringing in an outside vender, send the vender's qualifications to everyone before the meeting.
- Book a conference room where there will be absolutely no interruptions. Choose an early meeting time that is acceptable to all.
- Make sure everything is 100 percent ready. Make sure the charts are first-rate and the product will work as promised. People will say that they can fill in the gaps on an uncompleted proposal, product or project. They really can't. Don't ask people to think. Show them how they should think.

During the meeting:

- Follow your agenda.
- Start with an overview of objectives.
- Speak only of the benefits for the company and the attendees.
- Listen actively to everything that is said.
- Keep moving during your presentation. People follow a moving target more closely.
- Elicit objections.
- Closure. Make sure that it is concrete. Summarize what was covered. If a decision was made, decide who is to do what.
- If no decision was made, set a time and place for the next meeting. If you don't know what you want them to do next, neither will they.

Follow-ups:

- Send a memo about the meeting, summing it up with next steps—what was decided, timetables, responsibilities, and so on.

And so it went down the line. Then I told the marketer "Tell you what...invite me back and we'll make the sale."

I structured a presentation that included benefits for everyone. Every discipline was targeted. We left no holes uncovered. Every discipline would be able to claim "ownership" of the winning idea.

We suggested that R & D tinker with the taste profile that had been favored by consumers in focus groups. They were now intrigued by the product. They were emotionally vested. They could be heroes.

We created mock packaging that excited the packaging department. We asked them to improve on our packaging ideas but leave the basic selling and positioning premise. They could be heroes.

For the financial manager, we created the entire profit picture based on projections and sales of similar products. He could be a hero.

For the VP and the entire project team, we created mock ads with the company's name to show them how well they fit the company's product line. Yes, they all could be heroes.

The project moved forward beautifully. By the way, you never tell the people they could be heroes. That concept is implied.

Pitching on the Outside

When you pitch to an outside company, you are going to face a wall of skepticism. It may not come from the person who brought you in, perhaps, but from the people at the meeting with whom you have not yet built a relationship.

Strategies for First-Rate Sales Presentations

1. Go easy on the overheads. They tend to bore people.
2. Don't *read* your speech, and be sure you make your presentation enthusiastically
3. Answer questions as they come up. Then you can tailor your answers to your presentation flow. If you are going to answer the question later in your presentation, acknowledge the questions and politely say you'll be covering that in a few minutes.
4. Be as helpful as you can, moving the attendees forward to accomplish their missions on the product. Guide them to next steps. All attendees

Game Plan for Intercompany Selling

Prelims:

- Build credibility through articles you've written, speeches you've delivered and case histories of clients you've helped. Try to get them circulated to all the attendees.
- Get a list of all the job titles of those who will be attending the meeting. Shape your pitch for men and women. Remember, women want to be talked to, they do NOT want to be talked at.
- Choose a time in the early morning when everyone's fresh.
- Make sure everything is 100 percent ready. Make sure the charts are first-rate and the product will work as promised. People will say that they can mentally fill in the gaps on an uncompleted proposal, product or project, but they really can't. Don't ask people to think. Show them how they should think.

During the meeting:

- Speak only of the attendees' needs, not yours. At the moment, you have no needs other than the obvious.
- Use as many case histories showing the success of the product or your work that you can. While name dropping may not be polite, it is effective.
- Keep asking questions until all objections come out.
- One of the most important things you will have to do is show them where to get the money. I don't mean you have to be an accountant but when they complain about budget issues, suggest ways to fund the program, such as through a research department budget, through an advertising budget, etc.
- Imply that everyone can be a hero by going forward and claiming ownership of the idea.
- Sum up with next steps.

Follow-ups:

- Call your contact to review the meeting and implementation of next steps.

will appreciate your help and your guidance. People want to work with managers who are helpful. Button down all to dos.

5. If there are objections or if people say they can't do something, brainstorm with your attendees as to how they CAN do it. The simple act of brainstorming can add emotional excitement as people come up with ways to fix the problem.

What to Do If They Bite But Won't Close

The best way to get managers or upper management to become enthusiastic is by encouraging them to buy into a project in small pieces. For example, if you are considering a new product, invite all to focus groups, or test market the project in a small regional area where costs are relatively small and finite.

Get everyone involved in the planning process. The more input you get from other managers, the more effective the project will be.

Build measurements into every phase. Establish realistic goals for continuing further. Management may give in if you have an effective plan to cut its losses if things don't go as promised. Don't overpromise. Be honest about what you hope to achieve.

Make everyone look good. The more successful you make everyone look, the more open they will be. The carrot-and-stick approach works particularly well with most managers.

Remember Murphy's Law

Between the time your presentation is made and the time when contracts and checks are signed, something is going to happen that has the potential to wreck the deal. This is going to happen. And you have nothing to do with it. Expect it. Try to manage the circumstances following the sale with constant callbacks, questioning of key people and contingencies.

Here's an axiom you have to deal with:

You won't get the accounts you think are locked up, but you will get the accounts that you have no business (or thoughts of) getting.

Seventeen Hot Buttons That Can Work Sales Magic

1. *Achievement and the desire to be thought of as a hero.*

Personal growth is important to everyone. Show how your product can add to a person's goals and self-image. Even a mundane product like

Hot-Button Selling

The key to building relationships is to know your customer's hot buttons. A *hot button* is a cue that triggers the emotion in a prospect which causes that person to buy something. This can be a company sell or a consumer pitch. Hot buttons work for business-to-business pitches as well as consumer selling. They work for services as well as for products. No matter what the selling venue, you're dealing with humans who buy more on emotion than any kind of "logical" thought process.

deodorant can take on new meaning when you show how the deodorant will keep an executive "cool" during tense business meetings.

2. *Status.*

Chickens do it. Orangutans do it. Even managers do it. Do what? Establish a pecking order and try to be number one in the psychological mind-set called status. This is related to the achievement factor and is really a subset of being a hero. The desire for status is an overwhelming drive. It is one of the key components of any selling strategy because when you sell your product on a status appeal, you are implying that other products are weak and that only the "riff-raff" will buy them. And who wants to be considered "riff-raff"?

3. *Saving money.*

Everyone wants to save money. But saving money on a product that gives little personal enjoyment is no savings at all. A money-savings approach should always tell consumers that they are saving money and getting a good product. Prove to buyers that they are being smart for buying your product, even if that product is you or your ideas.

Money itself has a different value for different people. If you don't have much, then spending it hurts you more than if you have a lot of it. This sounds self-evident but if you want to charge more, then create a product that offers a little more. Add a premium hook through intrinsic product benefits or create an "artificial" benefit like new packaging for an expensive wine. The people who want your product will actually think the product tastes better than a low-priced product.

In a business-to-business situation, it is more important to build trust than to come up with the absolute lowest price. If your price is much lower than your competitors, tell why it is lower in a way that doesn't look like you're compromising quality (for example, point to greater efficiency, your purchasing savvy, and so on).

4. *Self-help.*

There's a seemingly endless collection of self-help books in libraries and bookstores. There are audiotapes, videotapes and all sorts of gimmicky products that are designed to create "a new you." Use this hot button to create an instant affinity with your product. Remember and build onto the old proverb "Give a person a fish and he'll eat for a day. Teach a person to fish and he'll eat forever."

Even companies are into self-help. Companies are contracting with training firms that promise to instill the psychological traits of leaders into their employees.

5. *Power and dominance.*

"Power may corrupt" as the saying goes, and "absolute power may corrupt absolutely," but it makes a hell of a marketing hook. Instill your product with power that the consumer can harness to get more power. Or show your customer how your product can make her more powerful in controlling daily circumstances.

6. *Family relations.*

"Children are out of control. They continue to defy their elders and to rebel." No, this didn't come from a parenting magazine or some right-wing conservative. It was paraphrased from Aristotle over 2000 years ago. Adults want to rekindle their relationships with their family. If your product can help bring the family together, then you have a strong hot-button strategy.

When you want to bond or build a relationship with a prospect, talk about his or her kids. Prospects never get tired of the subject.

7. *Health.*

When we're old enough to think about health, it's often too late. Show how your product can contribute to health in some shape or form. Health maintenance is an important subset of this hot button. As this is being written, neutraceuticals are a big trend in the health-care industry. These are products that claim to be dietary supplements and purport (but never actually say directly) that they can turn even the sickliest among us into healthy Greek gods and goddesses. They used to call these potions snake oil but there has always been a market for them, and there always will be.

8. *Security and risk lessening.*

Security means that something you have will NOT be taken away from you. But security products are usually sold, not bought. So if you use this hot button, try to tie it into a tangible benefit.

Risk lessening should really be risk removing, but every product has some sort of risk involved, whether it's losing money or losing face with co-workers. Show how the risk of buying your product is small, and how the benefits vastly overpower the risks. If you think about it, most religions are founded on the premise of lessening risks—in the afterworld.

9. *Sex.*

We're going to be talking about love in a bit. Sex is not the same thing. You can create strong positioning by building on hedonism and lust. It may be our lowest common denominator, but it works.

10. *Love.*

The desire to love and be loved is a strong hot button. Show how your product will make a person be loved a bit more or show how love can be given.

11. *Wish fulfillment.*

When I start a project for a client, I usually start with an ideation process. My first brainstorming stimulus is to wish for the ideal product. In every product category, there is an ideal. In a travel category, for example, the wish may be for a deserted isle, surrounded by pristine beaches, all expenses paid. Of course, on this isle will be a four-star hotel with room service and the requisite jet skis and motorboats. You probably can't deliver wishes, but in most dreams, the anticipation is better than the reality. Sell the dream.

12. *The desire for control.*

Many people think their lives are out of control. They don't know where they're going or how they're going to get there. People equate loss of control with loss of power over one's own destiny, or of the destiny of one's loved ones. Show, through your product, your ads and your presentations, how to exert control over one's life.

In a business-to-business pitch, build control through strict measurements, accountability and detailed scheduling.

13. *Fun.*

Simple and strong. It's relatively easy to enhance your product when you add fun to it. You can do it through your ads and your product. Cereal manufacturers have been doing it for years with cute graphics and inexpensive premiums.

The whole reason for adding fun to a product is to lighten up the consumer for a brief moment. When your product is fun, it will be bought again and again. When your product is fun it will be remembered.

14. *Getting something for nothing.*

"Free" is still one of the most powerful words in the marketer's repertoire. Adding an inexpensive gift or two-for-one offers can triple your response rates in promotions and direct mail. Free trips through frequent travel promotions dramatically increased brand loyalty for the airlines.

15. *Time savings.*

What most marketers see as a convenience product is actually a tool to solve "poverty of time." It's a strong motivator for men and women 25-45. This is particularly true with women who have children.

But saving time is more than just putting cheese in an aerosol can. Your product has to perform as well, or even better, than products that don't save the prospect time.

16. *Reinvent yourself.*

One of the biggest features of America Online and the on-line services is the chat room. People who have not met before get to choose the personal scenario that they want to act out. They relieve themselves of personal baggage because nobody knows them except as blips on the computer. Find a way that your product or service can help buyers create a "new you."

17. *Hope.*

This is key in many products, particularly in the cosmetic and lottery arenas. People thrive on hope and look to build better lives. Cosmetic companies, plastic surgeons and neutraceuticals play on hope in a big way.

How to Get Consumers to Tell You Their Hot Buttons Instantly

The best way to get customers to tell you their hot buttons is to use the checklist and to create concept ads or even headlines around the particular hot button. Take your ads out to consumers and wait for their reactions. You can also use one-on-ones and read prospects your headlines. When they say, "I'll buy that," you know you have a winner.

Eight Ways to Destroy a Sale

I've offered a number of ways to build a sale in this chapter. I think it's only fair to list sales traps that even the best marketers occasionally fall into.

1. *Don't talk strictly about yourself without giving benefits to the company.* The prospect doesn't want to know anything about you other than why you are the best person to do the job. Any information you give about yourself beyond credibility can actually make the prospect think twice about giving you the sale.
2. *Don't talk price often without giving reasons for the high, or low, price.* Consumers will thumb their nose at a price that's too high, and so will companies. Prices and costs should not even be mentioned until you get approval on everything else.
3. *Don't confine yourself to a sales script without tailoring your presentation.* As an advertising manager, I learned to despise canned presentations. They weren't offering anything to improve my business. They just wanted to sell theirs. When you're in a meeting, everyone knows you're there to sell something. Tailor your presentation to fit the prospect's needs.
4. *Don't show up late for a meeting.* The customer can. You can't. It's that simple.
5. *Don't neglect to build credibility.* There's a funny dynamic about credibility. The more you have, the more you'll earn. Think of a sales pitch as a series of mirrors. Everything you say reflects back to you. But every mistake you make and every time you seem insincere, cracks that mirror (I thank supermarketer Bob Berman for the analogy).
6. *Don't fail to follow up.* Never make a promise that you can't or don't have the time to live up to. One company president cries about blowing a major deal by not filling out a simple vender form. That single piece of paper cost her $30,000.
7. *Don't speak disparagingly of the client.* Bad mouthing is verboten, because it always seems to get back to the person who signs the contract.
8. *Don't forget to listen.* Revere a prospect who finally trusts you enough to open up her business life to you or perhaps gets you on the inner track to a sale. She doesn't not want to repeat herself.

Making a sale might also depend on your willingness to learn a thing or too. A good marketer spends most of his time listening, and then acting.

Ten Strategies to Keep Your Personal Relations Growing

Staying in contact is just as important after the sale as your presentation in the making of a sale. One service-company president I know of became horribly upset when he heard that a particular company tried to contact him for more than a year. The prospect eventually hired a competitor.

Here are ten ways to stay in touch and keep your relationships going:

1. Send mailings on a regular basis. Newsletters are great for this. If a note comes back that so-and-so has left the company, find out through personnel where the person has gone. The person's new company could be another important contact for you.
2. Do "How am I doing?" telephone surveys. Follow up and ask for advice on how you can make your pitch better.
3. Write articles regularly for trade magazines.
4. Send out regular broadcast faxes listing successful new account acquisitions and additions to your staff.
5. Call just to say "hello." You'll be surprised at how fast a call is returned when you're not trying to sell something. This usually works only once though. Then prospects quickly learn your ploy.
6. Birthday cards and Christmas cards are always welcome. They don't come off as insincere as you think they do.
7. Mail, or fax, items of interest to the prospect—say about a new technology that might affect his or her business.
8. Attend conventions and trade shows to renew old friendships. There may be a certain backlash against relationship selling, but people still like to buy from friends or people they like.
9. Send congratulatory notes for a promotion or to a manager whose underling got promoted.
10. Take on as many speaking engagements and seminars as you can. One company holds free seminars for its clients. The resulting sales usually more than pay for the event. It runs a dozen seminars a year and have created a huge mailing list that achieves upwards of a 12 percent response rate.

CHAPTER TEN

Strategies for Speeding Up New Product Development

Just when you think you have it, you really don't. That's what the new product development process is like in the nineties. The hot new product you've spent more than a year trying to create is "always around the bend."

The path to developing a successful new product is never straight despite what alleged experts will tell you.

New product success will mean following many twists in your road toward Eureka. Each twist means an update of your plan. That's why rigid approaches to product achievement usually lead to failure.

There are as many alleged systems for developing new products as there are marketers. As I've mentioned earlier, I've even seen a case where a "new products expert" created a box with holes and pegs. "When all the holes were filled with pegs," he said, "the product will be ready for market." I don't know what happened to that fellow, but I bet he left a trail of angry clients.

In this chapter, we're going to talk about two kinds of new products:

1. Those that are market (or consumer) driven.
2. Those that are driven by corporate wants and needs.

Though both kinds of products can achieve success, the market-driven product has much better odds.

Build What Your Customers Want

The new product failure rate is about 90 percent. The main reason is that most products are built backwards. Managers develop products and hope someone will buy them. You can change the failure rate if you find out what people want to buy and build your product around this key finding.

Your First Customer Is Your Management

However your new product efforts are driven, a crucial element of new development is winning the hearts and minds of top management. The surest way to do this is to create products that are a perfect fit with your company's current products, technologies and goals. When you create the basic product idea and keep your management positive and upbeat, you'll be surprised how the technology needed to deliver the product falls right into place. New ideas, new research, prior and ongoing failures, even serendipitous events can be managed, planned and built upon when you foster an open, creative atmosphere that allows changes to happen.

Your Customers Are Never, Ever Wrong

Suppose you got in a taxicab and you told the driver you wanted to go to Manhattan. Suppose the driver then said, "Nah, I'll take you to the Bronx instead." You really wouldn't want that. It is the same thing in marketing. When the consumers tell you they want a certain item made a certain way, don't try to outthink them. Make the product they want. And sell it to them the way they want to buy it.

Get More D and Less R in Your R & D Program

Many companies seal their own fates when they put the brunt of new product development in the hands of R & D.

But R & D is supposed to come up with a breakthrough technology that will set the world on its ear, you say. Yes. This *seems* to make sense.

The fact of life, though, is that most R & D departments live for the R. There just isn't enough D. R & D should be guided by marketing, for marketing knows—or should know anyway—the pulse of the market. When you develop your basic product profile, R & D will rise to the task of meeting your demands, provided you enlist its help early in the process.

Ideas are needed from the beginning and throughout the project. Creative people know that ideas rarely occur between 9:00 A.M. and 5:00 P.M. Enlist your team early on so it will have time to think about the upcoming mission. The goal is to foster a vested interest in the project as a whole, rather than in its parts.

Start your project with a general orientation to get everyone on board. Include key members of R & D, engineering, research, operations and sales management. You might want to include possible vendors and your advertising agency. Your target customers should also be key parts of your team. Ideally, all team members should remain on the project until the end. This team approach is the one that companies have found to be the most effective. But every team needs a leader.

The Team Leader

You are the team leader. It's your responsibility to implement the effort.

You must know:

- The strategic directions management wants to pursue
- The dollar impact upon the business
- How to strategically manage innovation
- How to make it all work

Your information transfer should include long- and short-range goals, initial product directions, past products from your archives and competitive products. You should also review technical capabilities, your marketing and sales channels and capabilities.

Once you understand this you're ready for ideation.

Strategic Brainstorming

Just as wood is the building block of a new house, ideas are the building blocks of new products. At the beginning of the book, we talked about creativity and how to turn loose jangles of synapse output called mind chatter into great new ideas.

Now we're going to formalize the structure somewhat. It's hard to create in a void. Your mind simply has nothing to react to. That's why brainstorming was invented. A good brainstorming session offers the participants stimuli to get at the big idea. *Brainstorming*, for some reason, is now called *ideation*. Whatever you call it, it is simply the facilitating of ideas. The goal of all brainstorming sessions is to transform your respondents into an idea-generating train. When your train picks up speed, get out of the way.

A great many brainstorming companies have come about lately, offering a variety of methods with an equal variety of success rates. You can conduct your own brainstorming sessions. Here's what you'll need:

At least two hours, preferably in the morning. In the afternoon, people tend to have letdowns from lunch.

A room away from phone calls and other distractions. Feel free to go off site.

Easel and a large 22" x 28" pad.

Some markers and tape.

Some props that you can create:

— Two signs: One that says "No Negativity" and another that says "Everyone's Right"

— A third sign that states the mission goal of the session. Keep it short and terse.

— A little chart called "Scammper." Scammper is an idea exchange acronym invented by Robert Eberle. He called it "Scamper," but I've revised it and changed some of the categories. Each letter of the first category reading down spells SCAMMPER. These are new ways of looking at a product:

Substitute, Simplify

Change, Combine

Adapt, Adopt

Magnify, Minify

Modify, Multiply

Package, Purloin (no, it's not a sin to steal from the competition)

Elevate, Eliminate

Reverse, Rearrange

The categories are not carved in stone. Change any of them to fit your needs.

The idea is to write down on the easel every idea your team generates and to tape the filled pages to the walls. You want to wallpaper your room with pages and pages of ideas. One of them, with a little work and editing on your part, may be the big idea you're looking for.

Three Keys to a Great Brainstorming Session

1. *No negativity and no criticism.* The free flow of ideas can be stifled immediately by any rejection. You are in the position of power. Use it wisely.

2. *The more ideas the better.* You're looking for a variety of ideas. As you write the ideas down, and tape the giant sheets of paper to the wall, your people will feel a sense of satisfaction knowing that you are taking their ideas seriously. This approach is much like the gold and silver stars you got when you did something good in grade school. These ideas will also serve as additional stimuli. People will react to what you write down and come up with more ideas.

By the way, I find it hard to lead a session and write the ideas down at the same time. It's okay to ask one of your fellow brainstormers or to recruit someone special to help.

3. *Constantly restate the mission goal.* Restatement of the mission goal will furnish more ways of looking at the problem. For instance, let's say the goal is to come up with a new variety of sauce.

The Mission Statement: "Come up with a new variety of sauce."

Restatement: What kind of foods would a new sauce enhance?

Restatement: Why would a person want a new kind of sauce?

Restatement: What kind of people would be experimenting with new foods?

You're on your way. You'll find that each group takes on its own identity. Some people will volunteer their answers readily. Some people will take some prodding. But the most important attribute of the facilitator (that's you) is to listen and stay focused. Remember, it's physically impossible to listen and talk at the same time, so if the ideas keep coming, shut up and write.

In all groups there will be a lull. Sometimes you can just stand there and wait. At other times, you may need more stimuli. The following are some tested brainstorming tools that I use.

Wish Number One—the Ideal

This is usually my opening tactic. For instance, if you were developing a sauce, you might ask "What would be your ideal sauce? How would it benefit a consumer?" You'll get some wild, far out ideas. Not to worry. You'll later edit out or tame the wilder notions.

Wish Number Two—Reinventing the Product

Make believe the product doesn't exist. If you could create it again, what would it be? What would it look like? What would make it best? Perfect? What would it replace? Refer to the Scammper chart. Why is it better than...? What makes it better? ALWAYS ask, "Can anyone build on this?"

Personalization

If the product were a person, what kind of person would it be? How would you describe it? What would it be like—strong, docile, feminine, or masculine? Relate it to the problem. Create a product around the character.

Embellishments and Builds

Continue asking people to embellish and build on the previous ideas. They can build in any order they choose. Ask your brainstormers to combine ideas.

Other Viewpoints

Think of how other people would react to your problem. Perhaps your boss, your spouse, your secretary. The trick is to get the respondents to come out of their own heads and into some other person's. We want our brainstormers to look at things from someone else's point of view. An alternate of this is to use famous people, such as Bill Clinton, Thomas Edison, or Jerry Seinfeld.

Change the Rules

Rules and policies are excuses not to make decisions. Assumptions are limitations we bring to situations. Here's an example of how we follow past assumptions. Follow this track:

Do you know why our cars are as wide as they are?

Because they had to fit on horse and wagon roads...

which were developed from old Roman chariot measurements...

which were the width of two horse's behinds.

And no one since that time has rethought the process.

Have respondents forget their assumptions. Go beyond rules. Don't be afraid to break rules, not matter how sacrosanct they seem to be.

Metaphors I/Forced Associations

Looking at other situations as metaphors can help to both clarify the situation and give you some alternative avenues to pursue. Some examples:

"How is a new sauce like a kite?"

"How is developing a new sauce like writing a book?" (You'll have to figure out these yourself.)

The forced-association technique can be used in other ways. I frequently ask respondents to pick out two key words from our idea inventory— for instance, "thick." Then I ask someone to free associate with "thick." Then I go around the room asking brainstormers to free associate from the previous respondent's word. Finally, I ask them to build a completed idea around any two of the words that have come up.

Metaphors II

Choose a word that seems to be coming up—say, freshness. (Go for images.) Freshness is like __________. How can we relate this to our problem? How can we build on it?

Word/Concept Association

Have the most active person in the room choose a word. Have each person freely associate from that word. (Write words on board.) Have each person choose one of the words you've just written down and create a mental picture. Now implement these word pictures into solving the problem.

Transform Ideas into Solutions

But the process doesn't stop there. Now you have to edit down your ideas and build on the best idea seeds until you have the answer you're looking for.

The Role of Research in Product Development

All products start and end with the consumer buying something he or she wants or needs, right? Though obvious, marketers tend to forget this as they strive uphill to create a market-ready product. It is the marketer's main reason for committing to the time constraints and the many resources needed. It's up to your task force and you to develop a product that's consistent with the consumer's wants and desires. It's your responsibility to make sure the project stays on track.

Make use of your research department. Use it often. But make sure your research is actionable and consumer driven. A competent researcher should provide the consumer pipeline that the task force (of which the researcher is a key part) will tap into to develop the product strategy. The researcher should play an important role at every stage of the new product development process.

Speed Your Product to Market

As I mentioned at the beginning of this chapter, there are a great many methods (but no black box) for developing new products. This is one of them and it is the most successful. You may find it helpful to use one or more of its parts or to use the program as a whole (highly recommended).

However you decide to use the methodology, the positioning and the product benefits should be determined at the initial project stages. The positioning should determine the features and benefits of your product. The positioning of the product should be developed even before the product prototype. Identifying and fulfilling a consumer need is a great deal quicker than taking the time to develop a product and hoping someone will buy it. The positioning functions as the heartbeat of your product strategy and provides an ongoing checklist to make sure your product stays focused so each member of the team can work on fulfilling his or her part of the puzzle.

In this consumer-oriented method, the consumer panel, or focus group is your research lab. Your main tools are full-color hypothetical ads designed to communicate your product to potential buyers. Don't take shortcuts or you can be sure the information you get will be cut short, too. The goal of your product research is to develop the future of your new product.

Developing Your Product Strategy

Once you have your ideation done, here are the six steps you need to develop the product plan so that it's ready to be brought into play.

1. *Inventory hypothetical product superiority objectives.*

Guess at possible product superiority objectives positionings and hypothetical consumer problems that you can solve. (This is the only time guesswork in marketing is encouraged.) These can come from your brainstorming sessions, your advertising agency, or outside specialists. These will be added, modified and refined through the course of your project.

2. *Develop the concept.*

Create rough advertising layouts, complete with packaging, product benefits and, of course, the product. Relevant competitive products should also be rendered. Make each concept board read like a mini-ad. If you can't create an ad for your product, you won't have a way of getting the message across that will sell it. That means you don't have a viable product.

The concept board is the ideal way to experiment with ideas and to give each department the freedom to test the merits of their own personal biases. Each division should have the freedom to develop its own concepts. Don't create white card concept boards which merely state product benefits. They are horribly misleading. Also, don't limit yourself to a set number of concepts. The amount of promising ideas will be whittled down by the consumer.

3. *Set Up One-On-One Interviews.*

Have your researcher set up a series of brief one-on-one interviews with consumers. All members of the task force group should interview consumers, armed only with the concept boards and note pad. Resist the urge to provide interviewing guidelines.

4. *Expose the revised concepts to interactive consumer panels.*

These are the focus groups we talked about in Chapter 3. Stock your groups with consumers who you think will represent your potential target market. Also set up at least one group of consumers who regularly uses a competing product. The objectives of the stimuli/response format of the groups is to gain new and actionable insights into your products and to uncover triggers to consumer purchase. This can also be done in business-to-business scenarios.

5. *Build on your winners and losers.*

After each group (and after the one-on-ones) add to, delete and modify your boards based on consumer reaction. Continue the process until you identify the most persuasive motivations and the best features to put in your product.

6. *Develop prototype models and products from the most promising concepts.*

These, too, should be shared with consumers to make sure you can deliver on the concept. Our goal is always to develop ACTIONABLE insights.

At the project's conclusion, the concepts will have gone through a comprehensive set of consumer tests to confirm their excitement quotient and their impact.

A typical project will take three to four rounds of groups, each round consisting of two to three groups.

Conduct your focus groups in various geographic areas—wherever you expect to sell your product. If your products aren't faring too well, you can experiment with groups of different demographic make-ups.

Let Your Consumer Segments Drive You

By now, you have developed your product concepts and they have elicited cries of joy from your target market. You have gained the support of your task force. Your management has agreed that the new product investment is in sync with the wants and desires of your company. Of course you now know your competition's strengths and weaknesses and know how to exploit these weaknesses. You know why consumers want it, and even what they would pay for it.

And since all departments have participated in the early stages they're now gung ho. What's missing here?

Once you get the go-ahead, it's time to change your concept into a real live product. While the actual physical development is largely a task handled by others, this is not the time to drop the project. Your new goal is to guide R & D in making the product the consumer wants at a price he or she can afford.

When to Add Bells and Whistles and When to Leave Them Off

The KISS (Keep It Simple Strategy) usually works best in transferring your ideas into a marketable product. The more features your product has, the more something can go wrong. Complexity breeds complications. An extra bell and whistle, while loved by engineers and product-development types, will reap havoc when the consumer finds it doesn't work.

Keep these ideas in your back pocket until you need them—until your competition catches up with you and you need new features fast.

Also, don't allow anyone to make unnecessary changes that add cost. Keep running additional reality checks by returning to new interactive groups as new prototypes are developed. This, coupled with reviews of your overall strategy, will make sure you stay tracked.

By this stage, a working (if somewhat rough) prototype will have been developed and evolved through your consumer work.

The Make or Buy Question

The key factors that will help you decide whether or not to make the product in-house are cost and quality. But there's one more variable—speed—because we must assume your competition is already trying to fulfill similar consumer needs.

In a completely new product, you may be considering the use of technology that you don't currently have. Unless the product is simple to manufacture, you will find it more economical to purchase existing technology from outside sources. Don't force your current technology into new applications, just because you can do it. Keep your machines producing proven winners until you know you have a new cash cow. You might even venture into rival territory and have your competitors make it for you. It happens more often that you think. They don't like production downtime any more than you do.

When buying from the outside you will be dealing very closely with vendors. They can help you fine-tune your preliminary model. Have your vendors attend focus groups and grant access to your research material. Don't forget a nondisclosure agreement.

Some other sources of technology:

- Colleges and universities
- Research papers and grants from related companies
- Your archives
- Small entrepreneurial companies
- Your competitors
- The Internet and the World Wide Web
- Publications like the *Thomas Register*
- Other trade magazines

Later, when your product has been launched and has a somewhat predictable track record, you can bring the technology inside.

On the other hand, your machinery may be fully operational and may be modified to keep your product idea inside. Of course, this might be much quicker and easier to coordinate since less people are involved.

A good operations manager should be your best guide.

Drawing Up a Market Viability Outline

In developing new market products, it's important to remember that you still have to sell your ultimate product to someone. Here is a floor plan to help you establish your new product goals and guidelines.

1. Product Innovation Goals

   Define the general area of opportunity

   a. What is your service area?

   b. What is your market niche?

   c. What is your time frame or window of opportunity?

2. The Actionable Opportunity

   a. What is the specific product to be developed?

Strategy Worksheet to Keep You on Target

These are strategic questions you must answer to assess the level of consumer appeal.(But, don't spend the really big bucks unless you're reasonably sure your product will be a hit.)

1. *Product positioning.* What is the optimum positioning for this product? What are the key elements needed for generating consumer interest and trial including brand names?
2. *Key product benefits.* What is the key product benefit? Can its appeal be communicated instantly via mass media, point-of-sale or packaging? What are the user expectations—both sensory and in terms of performance? What sensory cues will be expected by the consumer to reinforce the basic product benefit and positioning?
3. *Brand names/packaging/delivery systems.* What are the optimum names and packaging configurations needed to drive the product? How can the convenience aspect of the product be rationalized by the consumer? Can leveraging an existing brand name inspire trial and purchase?
4. *Target market.* Who is the target consumer? When is the product expected to be used? What current products will be replaced? What is the main benefit to the user? What is the emotional appeal?
5. *Key communication.* What are the key communication elements necessary to support the strategy?

   b. What is the technology to deliver the product ?
   c. Who is the prime target?
   d. What is the volume goal?
   e. What is the profit goal?

3. Marketplace Position Sought
   a. What is your market share goal?
   b. What is your relevance in the category?
   c. What image do you want to attain or redefine through the product?
   d. What is an acceptable ROI and payback time?
   e. Is it diversifying?

4. Asset Leveraging
   Strengths to capitalize on:
   a. R & D performance
   b. Manufacturing skills
   c. Marketing
   d. Current image
   e. Financial resources
5. Nonself-developed Product Strategies
   a. Acquisition of companies
   b. Acquisition of licenses
   c. Joint venturing
6. Degree of Innovation
   a. Inventive—technological leadership.
   b. Innovative—use established technology in new ways.
7. Adaptive/economic—others lead, but be the low-cost producer.

Special Considerations

1. Acceptable risk level
2. Patentability
3. Market size or growth factors
4. Line completeness
5. Avoiding certain competitors
6. Avoiding regulatory or other legal/social pressures

Other New Product Strategies

Not all new product strategies live and die by consumer feedback. Some are developed haphazardly, and in some cases by out-and-out guesswork. Here are a few strategies that have occasionally proved successful.

Technology-Driven Strategy

Basically R & D runs the show and you can hope for the best. For more than 100 years, AT & T embraced that strategy to little success. Only when they took their new product development out of R & D did they really become innovative. While it may be successful some of the time, the lack of market focus results in poor profitability.

The Technology-Plus Strategy

In this strategy, you balance a technology and marketing orientation. In this hybrid, technology-driven accomplishments are balanced with consumer research and an eye always on the market.

The Me-Too Strategy

Surprisingly, this can be highly profitable. In this strategy, you develop your new products by mimicking the other guy after he has tested the waters. With this strategy, you'll never be number one, but if you care more for profits than for market share, this strategy can meet your goals.

The "Eureka" Strategy

You would think that companies who say "we'll innovate at any price" would be successful. Far from it. The new product odds gradually come into play, like the odds at a poker table. In this strategy, companies innovate for the sake of innovation. It's great for morale, but not wonderful for profits.

The "New Brand" Strategy

You can create a new brand in a category that's running wild. Use the strength of your existing brands to launch a brand in a new area. One caveat is to make sure your imagery and equity carries over to your new product.

Building Brands with Line Extensions

This is a conservative strategy, but it works. New products consist of line extensions and me-too products. There is little new technology or consumer motivation work. Sales of these products are steady, if not spectacular.

Line extensions are the surest way to enter a new arena. Line extensions are being pursued by an increasing number of firms. Some line extensions are associated with more consumer benefits than others.

Why Line Extensions Work

Line extension development offers a number of benefits versus traditional new products.

The major one is that it capitalizes on the company's most valuable assets, its brand names. The company moves into a new category from a position of strength, the immediate consumer awareness and impressions communicated by the brand.

Line extensions are a valuable method for a company to enter a new business. They are a great way to achieve significant growth, even if sales of a company, or a particular product, are stagnating.

A further benefit is that financial investments typically necessary to establish a new brand are dramatically reduced. An important related payoff is that introduction of a franchise extension can increase sales for the parent brand.

If you introduce a new brand into a category where you already have a market position, you are flanking the mother brand. When you flank a brand, you create a fortress of a sort on the shelf because there is literally no room on the shelf for a competitive market introduction.

To test your brand equity you must go to consumers to see what your brand stands for. Discerning your brand equity through research is a little like sculpting an elephant. You simply carve away at anything that doesn't look like an elephant. Adapt the protocol discussed earlier in this chapter for the best results. Take all the brand names your company owns and rate the appropriateness for inclusion in each product area.

Leverage your most valuable assets (consumer awareness, good will) and the impressions conveyed by your brand name. The process of exploring line extensions represents a disciplined approach for selecting new categories a company might enter. Inherent in this process is the ability to redefine the business you are in.

Investigating line extensions will likely result in uncovering new ways of looking at one's business.

Bic defines its business, not by pens, but instead, of disposability.

Clairol offers a head care (rather than just hair) definition of its business.

Sunkist has limited its extensions to products which have a Vitamin C or orange orientation.

When to Line-Extend

1. When the mother brand provides leverage in the new category. There must be a rub-off of perceived superior know-how, effectiveness or imagery.
2. When a benefit of the parent brand is the same benefit offered in the line extension.
3. When the consumer would perceive the new item to be consistent with the mother product.
4. When the company can leverage a new name and enter the new category with superior production, distribution and merchandising resources.

CHAPTER ELEVEN

Strategies for Making Distributors and Merchants Ecstatic

I remember watching the old Abbott and Costello TV show. Costello (he was the short, fat one) would advise his friend Stinky in "voce appassionato" (sensitive and passionate voice) that "Policemen are your friends." Then his "pal," Mike the Cop, would bop Costello on the head with his nightstick. That pretty much sums up the feeling companies have when they talk about their distributors.

Here's the dilemma. You are trying to get your product into a selling outlet the quickest and most efficient way possible. But your distributors treat you like the townspeople treated Godzilla when the monster tried to flambé Tokyo.

It's funny, but in developing a new product or business, distribution is the last thing novice entrepreneurs, or sometimes even more experienced entrepreneurs, think of. They simply get caught up in the excitement of their products. The common thinking is if you build a product that makes the earth move for someone, buyers will come knocking at your door. But in reality it works the opposite way—you'll get swollen knuckles from knocking at the door of potential buyers.

Choosing a Distribution Path

Deciding on the optimum distribution path is one of your most important decisions. The astute marketer puts as much research into learning about selling into a particular channel as in learning how to make the product itself.

To make distributors work for you—and that is always the ultimate goal—it's important to know where opportunities lie and the specific requisites of each particular channel. For instance, you may lie awake at night and fantasize about getting your product on a home shopping network. But if you were going to take that route, the minimum requisites are:

- You have 10,000 units on hand ready for immediate shipment
- The product demonstrates well on TV
- You have a targetable audience
- The product is telegenic

Making Your Distributor Relationships Work

Supplier/distributor relationships work best when each is important to the other. There are strong advantages in concentrating your distributor relationships by using a few strong distributors.

The rapport and communications can also help in many ways. Distributors can help with the filling of orders and testing new merchandise. Distributors may help you get rid of poorly timed merchandise as well. They are more likely to give a new product some time to grow.

Your relationship with a distributor can significantly reduce your costs of distribution. Plus, streamline your ordering and processing of goods, too.

Look for a Void

When you research distributors and merchants you can fill a void where another company has departed. For instance, when Eagle Snacks was broken up because of a divestiture by Budweiser, Granny Goose, a snack-food manufacturer, attacked Southern California to fill newly empty supermarket space.

Focus, Focus, Focus

Target areas that you can easily service without causing stress to your entire organization. It's better to have regions actively seeking your product than to try to cover the world and dilute your resources—offering shoddy or helter-skelter service. Don't attempt to cover the country and be all things to all distributor channels.

Create Excitement

It's important to get distributors caught up in the excitement of your new product.

Proctor & Gamble introduced a policy called everyday low pricing (EDLP) that seemed great on the surface. The company would always sell the same product for the same price. No deals. No promotions.

EDLP offered little incentive to distributors and stores who insisted on Le Grande Promotion. They didn't factor in the excitement that promotions create.

Cultivate Your Relationships

P & G also made a key mistake some time ago when it acquired two soda brands. It tried to bypass independent bottlers for its own warehousing system. Procter & Gamble seems to make a lot of mistakes for a company of its size and expertise. But at least it can afford it. You probably can't.

While Procter & Gamble made its giant mistakes, a little-known regional root-beer maker from Louisiana, Barq's, entered the hotly contested New York market by playing footsie with regional bottlers. It took seven years of relationship selling but it paid off in a big way. Barq's is now the number two root beer in the country, even surpassing Pepsico.

Build a Distribution Tree

Many companies live and die by their distribution systems. Why be at the mercy of a single system?

Let's not talk about distribution channels and distribution chains. This nomenclature is self-defeating because if you break one link in a chain, your marketing opportunity is also broken.

Let's talk, instead, about a distribution TREE, sprouting branches in all directions. If one limb fails to branch out, you can either fertilize it or leap to another limb to make sure your marketing program stays in full bloom.

Compaq Computers once masochistically supported a few dealers who wouldn't sell other brands. Than Compaq thought of a better idea. They grafted another branch onto their distribution tree. They sold to all stores including mass merchandisers. Now they are the number one (or at least the number two) computer manufacturer in the country and they sell through different chains simultaneously.

Be Willing to Walk Away From a Distributor

If your product is really good, distributors and stores of many different kinds will want you as much as you want them. Some distributors, like some stores, may not be right for your product. It doesn't help, for example, if a distributor carries your product and makes no real attempt to sell it. Plant your seeds where they are sure to bear the most fruit. Don't jump at the first offer. Make sure the distributor is right for you.

When you introduce a new product into a distribution channel, set a target volume to be reached by a certain time. That way, if you fall short of the target, you can always add another channel.

Developing a Distribution Strategy

Most entrepreneurs enter their particular distribution system through trial and error. Usually there's a lot more error than trial. The best way to develop your distribution is to take a look at your competitors and work backwards. Find out how the successful companies distribute their products and follow their trail. A few simple phone calls to store personnel and some well thought-out questions will show how these chains got their products in the stores.

Use the Five-Point Star Distribution Strategy

Once you identify your target customer's shopping habits and needs and you've learned the existing structure of distribution, you can arrive at a distribution strategy that is most appropriate for your product.

Think in terms of a five-pointed star:

1. Who are your final customers? Where do they buy? How often can you expect sales? If you expect high volume, you'll need broad distribution.
2. If your product is priced high relative to an industry, you'll need more highly focused specialty store distribution.
3. In terms of your timing, if you're under high ROI pressure and must meet stringent sales goals, you'll need to get aggressive distribution through national chain stores.
4. For market share, if you want dominance in the market or market segment, you'll attack and remove competitors. For a highly positioned product, carve out a niche with selected retailers.
5. If you have a high-tech, state-of-the-art product, consider limiting distribution to specialty stores until the general public catches up with the new technology.

Ten Ways to Make Distributors Love You

Here are some tips on greasing distributor wheels and making the initial distributor pitch. They're all contingent on the fact that your product is a strong fit with a given retailer.

1. Show that your product is easy to sell, even by unknowledgable sales staff.
2. Show how your product can create in weekly cash flow. Fast turnover is nirvana to distributors. Work within the store's profit margins, not yours. Make sure your final selling margins are within the standards for a particular industry.
3. Show how your product is a variant on a successful seller, but with a new twist.
4. Create three varieties of your product. It's easier to sell choices than a single product. But be careful, four or five products in a line is too much investment for a retailer or middleman.
5. Choose your product promotions to be consistent with each store's image and customer base. Store segmentations are becoming more

and more the norm. This goes for pricing too. Don't expect to get a high-end product in a store whose positioning is budget-oriented.

6. Sell *with* the buyer, not *to* the buyer. Review retailers one by one to determine how each buys. Do they want deals, or do they want consistent prices? Learn the individual company's buying strategies and customize your strategy accordingly. Learn the attributes of their selling chain. For example, if using a direct-mail channel, show how durable your product is or how easily and inexpensively it ships.
7. Promote region-by-region to coincide with a retailer's activities. Most retailers are oriented seasonally. You can easily predict when their selling thrusts will be. Create your programs to coincide with theirs.
8. Become involved in the retailer's business. Learn the type of promotions stores run and assist them. If a retailer is running a contest, participate in the promotion. Offer promotional ideas to the retailer as well as price reductions.
9. Create a strong advertising program for your product that dealers can use, and show stores how to use it. Also, consider offering factory displays such as special counter displays, bins, and the like. These can stimulate sales to buyers for certain products.
10. Make sure that the store's buyers are motivated to buy your product. Match up the physical and ethereal aspects of your product with what you know about your store's target customer. Make sure your product fits like the proverbial glove. It's not that store buyers are being rigid or obstinate (although they may be) when they resist your efforts. They know their stores and customers better than you do. And you may be missing the mark.

Seven Proven Strategies to Improve Your Current Relationships

The easiest kind of selling is through your existing distribution base. Don't neglect it. Make life easier for the channel with these ideas:

1. Customize your store materials as much as possible. Leave spaces so retailers can use your promotion ideas by just filling in the blanks.
2. Generate ideas to make your promotions more effective. For example, time your coupon expirations and "good until" dates to bring a steady stream of customers into the store.

3. Create cross-promotions that sell merchandise other than yours. When you build the retailers' profits, you are also improving yours.
4. Make sure that store managers know your programs. Don't expect them to guess. Keep them informed with a steady flow of oral and written communications.
5. Customize your advertising and promotions regionally. Don't try to develop trade promotions and dealer material for use nationwide. There are too many differences from retailer to retailer and from region to region.
6. Communicate meaningful data in your trade ads, dealer ads and trade presentations. Stay away from clichés like "great turnover" and super profits. Retailers hear the same pitch every day. They're numb to big talk and no action.
7. Plan a public relations program for newspapers and cable TV using the distributor's company as the contact.

Marketing to and Through Distribution Channels

There are many ways to win distributors' hearts, but one of the most important is to ply them with strong, gritty promotional materials. Here are some requisites:

1. Brochures, trade ads, letters, and bulletins. Make sure they're professional and speak to the store's needs.
2. Value-added items like displays and promotions for food-service organizations. Items like napkins, table tents and cups are always appreciated.
3. Multi-use promotional items that sell related merchandise as well as your own.
4. Point-of-sale materials that sell as well as show.
5. Media clips are also very impressive to distributors.

Working with Outside Reps

While using your own sales force is usually more effective than working with outside reps, independent representatives have their own sets of advantages. Reps are paid on a strict commission, which makes selling costs a variable that rises and falls with revenue. When business is good, more reps can be added. When sales are down it's easier to change reps or add new ones. In some cases, independent reps can get more sales, since they contact the same companies many times over and have already built up trust with the client.

The drawback is that you have very little control over independent reps. You have little recourse, except to revoke the line from the representative. On the other hand, if your product is not selling, the rep is not going to care anyway, so it's a moot point.

Using Middlemen, Dealers and Brokers

Whether you are a new company or an established firm, you're going to enter a love-hate relationship with middlemen, dealers and brokers. That's because unlike your own salespeople, you can't control their day-to-day operations. You can't insist on a sales quota, you can only suggest, motivate and hope.

The key to dealing with them is to make sure the potential of your product excites them. Successful brokers and middleman, more often than not, have strong egos. Take their suggestions—they'll have many—to heart. Sell the business opportunity rather than the actual product.

Keep a constant flow of promotions in the communications mix. Support the relationship with cost-effective ways that promote your product, like in store demonstrations, sampling, free offers and trade shows. Middlemen can make or break you depending on how much attention you lavish on them.

Give area exclusivity if possible. Competing for business among dealers can only lead to animosity and the tendency to look for additional brands.

Load up the distributor with as much product as he can afford. Make sure distributors advertise well. Provide ready-made ad slicks to make it easy for them.

Where to Find Middlemen and How to Keep Them Happy

Middlemen and reps have to be thoroughly researched and courted. And, once you find them, you have to stay on top of them. Here are some tips to give you a head start on the process.

1. Make sure your product quality is high and has an easily seen point of difference.

2. Create strong sales training aids and introductory advertising/promotion campaigns.
3. Be interested in the dealer's business. You can't make money unless the dealer makes money. Don't load up the dealer with more product than she can reasonably expect to sell.
4. Avoid loading a territory with too many dealers. It leads to heavy price cutting and a loss of good will.
5. Choose your dealer based on his financial ability and knowedge of how to market your product.
6. Recruit dealers at national and regional trade shows in your industry. You can also run classified ads in trade magazines and ask the assistance of trade associations.

Distribution Outlets for Creative Marketers

Here's a test question, Marketing 101 level. You've just invented a new windshield wiper blade, called Tripledge. Its so powerful and effective you offer a lifetime guarantee and charge $19.95. You try the normal distribution channels, the aftermarket automotive supply stores. Sales are fair, at best. You run a postmortem and find that your wipers are placed next to cheaper, more well-known brands and there is no incentive for the dealer to sell them.

Do you:

- Lower the price?
- Sell out to Joe's Pushcart Job Lot sales?
- Resign yourself to meager profits?

None of the above.

That was the answer the Tripledge people chose. Instead of fighting harried dealers to move its product, Tripledge marketed directly to consumers through catalogs, late-night commercials, credit card inserts and coupon ads in Sunday newspaper supplements (FSIs). Sales went through the roof. Tripledge has built up awareness so well that conventional distributors are clamoring to handle its product.

Take Advantage of Hot New Distribution Avenues

Looking for new distribution channels for your tree? Try these:

1. *Sell your product direct.*

Go directly to consumers. Selling direct is not totally new, but it can be effective. There are numerous ways, including catalogs, infomercials, party plans, even multilevel marketing programs. The infomercial approach is interesting because if you've been watching the supermarket and department stores, you'll find that last years' infomercial hit is now a hot-selling supermarket product.

2. *Factory discount outlets.*

This is the fastest growing distribution avenue. Consider selling your product through the factory store. Put the name of the outlet on your product, rather than your own brand name. Godiva Chocolates, Ben & Jerry's and Harry and David are a few of the companies that have opened up successful retail stores.

3. *Play piggy-back.*

Piggy-back companies with large route sales. They may be very excited about turning unused space in their vehicles into profit centers. This can only be done when your product does not conflict with their existing products.

4. *Direct TV.*

Wouldn't it be great if you could talk one-on-one with your customers—millions at a time?

It can happen, and did for Charmin Edwards when her product got picked up by the QVC home shopping network. Like many smaller companies she became very disenchanted with the typical department store distribution channel. She reports that, "Trying to get into department stores is very difficult because the giants of the industry monopolize the space. It's very difficult being a small new business because you don't have the money to stand up to the (big companies') advertising and promotions." She suggests a solution for another potential problem: "You have to get your share of the market without stepping on the giants" because once you have built a business the giants will knock off your product.

She likes QVC because you don't need a fortune to get started. "Its an incredible way to do business. QVC says if you have the product, we're going to buy it. They pay right on time," according to Charmin Edwards.

6. *Warehouse stores.*

These are the membership clubs that have taken the country by storm. They want quantities of product designed to sell off the floor with a minimum of consumer/store personnel interaction.

7. *Cross-promote.*

You've just developed a new game about intimacy. Go to game stores, right? Not necessarily. How about hotels, marriage counselors, lingerie shops or any other business category that might gain added sales from carrying your product?

Barbara Jonas and her husband invented An Enchanted Evening, a game to make relationships stronger. Ms. Jonas calls it "a kiss and make up" game.

Ms. Jonas initially considered three distribution channels:

- Direct marketing to end users
- A mixture of direct marketing and traditional retail outlets
- Retail channels

Instead she went into nontraditional business categories where her product would help sell additional services or products. It's called cross-marketing and really works for the Jonases.

She doesn't just sell games, she sells a total package.

8. *Multilevel marketing.*

Almost as sure as June follows May, whenever there is a rise in unemployment or a downturn in the economy, multilevel market plans take hold. Most of them don't work (as we'll discuss in a moment) but occasionally, when the product and the multilevel plan are strong, amazing things happen. LCI became one of the biggest long-distance telephone suppliers just this way. LCI used multilevel network marketing exclusively to build its $480 million residential base and, to a lesser extent, its $1.1 billion in business sales.

Instead of paying a full-time sales staff, independent sales reps sign up friends and relatives. These agents earn a small commission of 2-5 percent of the revenue generated by their phone customers and $250 for each person they recruit into their sales organization. It works for them because it relieves the churning that happens when people switch long-distance carriers. When these customers are sold face-to-face, they are more reluctant to switch their carrier to an unknown phone shill.

LCI insists that their reps pay more attention to selling phone services than recruiting new people in the network.

Beware—Hot They're Not

Here are three channels that most people think are hot, but they're really not.

The Internet. Despite the hype, the Internet is far from successful for most companies and product lines. Why? Because neither advertisers or users know quite what to do with it. Use the Internet only when your product is easy to describe and you have a lot of it. More on the Internet in Chapter 14.

Multilevel Marketing. It seems so easy. Just get ten of your friends and invite them to become distributors. Soon everyone is rich, right? Well, nobody gets rich except for the first few people. And in many cases, it's quite illegal.

Infomercials. I know, I just said they work for some people. That's true, but only for some people. They're expensive. They're faddish, and you'd better ask for a lot of money for your product. More on informercials in Chapter 14.

Strategic Advantages and Disadvantages of Some Popular Selling Channels

Discount Stores (mainstream and specialty) Over the past twenty or even thirty years, this distribution channel has assumed increasing importance. These stores abound in almost every industry. Their centralized buying facilities can make it fairly easy for a manufacturer to go nationwide with a product.

Disadvantages: The disadvantages of distributing through discount department stores are few, but significant. To begin with, this distribution channel pushes you to lower prices to the bone. It's also hard to make an appointment to get a sales call.

Specialty Stores These days, specialty superstores abound and offer many of the same advantages as department stores and discount department stores with regard to centralized buying.

Disadvantages: A limited product line and a great deal of competition.

Direct Marketing This channel is a great way to test and develop customer interest. If you've done your targeting homework, you can contact only the best prospects, make your pitch, and get relatively quick momentum behind the new product. Geographic coverage is unlimited, because you're using the mail or telephone. Best of all, because you eliminate the traditional distribution middleman, you are no longer at the mercy of retailers who are quick to pull the plug on new products that fail to gain immediate attention. Gateway computers sells millions of computers per year, all directly.

Disadvantages: Direct marketing does have its drawbacks. It can be costly to reach a large market, and startup costs are substantial. Plus, your customer never gets the chance to actually play with your product.

Distributing Through Business-to-Business Outlets

Here are a number of distribution outlets for business-to-business sales. Different as these various distribution channels are, they share at least one characteristic: All, in varying degrees, resist change. The innovation you see as a boon, the distributor may perceive as a problem. Professional buyers are trained and encouraged to be skeptical.

Industrial distributor. Primarily a sales organization, which means it will want a bite out of your revenue. Depending on the market for your particular line of products, the distributor may be slow to adopt new merchandise or may adopt it without promoting it. If the distributor already carries a competitive line, it may be quite difficult to get him to adopt yours.

Joint ventures. You partner with another firm; you make the product, and the other guy sells it.

OEM (original equipment manufacturer) programs. With OEM, you supply components for another manufacturer's system.

Private branding programs. You manufacture a product to be branded with a well-known company, usually nationally based.

National account programs. You supply goods under contract through one or a handful of distributors. The great part of this is that sales are steady. Drawbacks are that you suffer the same economic pangs as your client and you are at the mercy of your client choosing another supplier. You also lose the ability to add value to the product through distribution, and you may soon find yourself overly dependent on one or a handful of accounts.

Sell to the Big Chains

Selling to the mega companies (such as Walmart, Staples, or Price Club) is the Holy Grail to many businesses. The mass chains (those with fifty or more outlets) account for 40 percent of all retail sales. The downside is that they can tie up your manufacturing capabilities, they can be hard to communicate with and their buying processes tend to be slow. But, if this is your goal, here's a plan you can use to get in and sell:

1. Establish personal contact early on. Sell direct. These companies won't usually buy from distributors or commissioned salespeople. They want the extra dollars you spend on salespeople turned into lower prices for their customers.
2. Make sure you can turn around on a dime. Retailers may expect turnaround in three to five days or they may cancel the order.
3. Develop a clear complete program with:
   — national and co-op advertising
   — return policy
   — displays
   — product lines
   — support
   — product (yours, of course)
   — detailed info about your product and product lines, including product capabilities, prior sales, and packaging
4. Come in with your lowest price. Expect them to cut it drastically.
5. Develop alternatives if the product moves slowly (e.g., rebates, refunds).
6. Give a complete and through accounting of when and how the company will receive your product

Other Distribution Channels and Strategies

When building your distribution tree, don't overlook the obvious. Each option has its own peculiarities. But don't let that put you off. The rewards may be well worth the effort.

Resorts and Gift Shops

Sell your product through gift shops in resorts and entertainment parks like Opryland, Six Flags and Yellowstone Park. It can be tricky though. You often have to give particular venues an exclusive or create something special for them. The good news is it's a stable environment, not usually subject to the whims of department stores. There's also great potential for building rapport because you'll be dealing face to face with key people.

Direct to Supermarket "Commodities"

While it's expensive, some companies are marketing their commodity items directly to supermarkets, supplying displays, value-added items (like coffee grinders) and delivering direct. While it can be problematical to keep a driver and a truck on the road delivering in all types of weather, this is one way you can bypass brokers and independent service companies. To make this work, look for metropolitan areas with stores closely bunched together. Expect a great deal of competition.

Supermarkets as Friend and Foe Supermarkets are a breed unto themselves and can be difficult to work with. Many charge a fee for placement. These are called slotting allowances. But supermarkets have their own pressing needs, particularly because warehouse stores have taken a lot of thunder away from them. Here is what supermarkets have been looking for.

1. Proven sellers. Supermarkets don't want to take chances
2. Anything that will take business away from the warehouse stores and natural foods stores.
3. A complete program. They want to make sure you are going to sell a turnkey program.
4. Highly original ideas that have sold before in other venues.
5. Incremental profits deploying unused retail space.
6. Products with high, built-in profit margins.
7. Value-added products with obvious value-added benefits. Example: come up with a way that a supermarket can prepare a certain kind of food for immediate resale.

8. Products from minority venders. One company, owned by black people, has discovered that many chains will take its product on, without slotting allowances to build good will within communities.

Six Ways to Get Past Slotting Allowances

Slotting allowances are here to stay. Now that I've said that, here are some ways to get around them (particularly if you're a small company).

1. Instead of slotting, ask if you can manufacture product in private label form. The retailer gets more facings and you get a flanking brand. Selling products in two facings gives consumers an added frame of reference.
2. Create a product that's so strong, the retailer salivates.
3. Play dumb. Pretend you don't know what a slotting allowance is. Don't laugh, I've seen it work.
4. Go ethnic. Many chains will allow a product in without slotting if the company is owned by an African-American and has ethnic products.
5. Add value. Sell a promotion or a program rather than a product or two.
6. Give extra products instead of dollars. Your payment will be based on retail prices, but your cost for making the goods is probably well below wholesale.

CHAPTER TWELVE

Proven Strategies for Turnaround Situations and Repositionings

The trouble with life is that we have to live it forwards but understand it backwards. Marketing is much the same way. We try to research it as much as possible. But we make mistakes or encounter problems along the way. Marketing is not for the fearful. Nor is it for the person who is so overwhelmed by the breadth and complexity of the American marketing scene that he or she is afraid to blaze new trails.

Bill Gates, the head of Microsoft said it best, "In the corporate world, when someone makes a mistake, everyone runs for cover. It's fine to celebrate success but it's more important to heed the lessons of failure."

I applaud this kind of thinking, not that Bill Gates is overly concerned with my approval. America has become a nation of blamers. Everyone's lack of success is someone's else's fault. It's like that in the real world. And it's like that in many companies. If a product doesn't sell, the first solution is "get rid of the ad agency" or the marketing guru. The agency, of course, says we got faulty directions from the current marketing guru. Marketing blames R & D, but then, so does everyone.

I won't work that way. And I don't let my associates or even my clients work that way. It's just bad business.

When someone makes a mistake or tries to blame others, I say to hell with placing blame. Once we know what we did wrong, we can figure out how to make it work right. This mindset is lot more constructive and encourages people to come up with new ideas that might be successful.

Learning Lessons from Mistakes

Lessons driven by mistakes can often lead to unanticipated discoveries. These lessons can give you an edge that never occurred to anyone else, especially your competition.

Think about your R & D team. I know, it actually pains you to think about R & D, but try hard. R & D runs on trial and error. Mistakes are actually built into the scientific process. That's why they don't call it trial and success. But mistakes can often lead to success.

Long ago, IBM did a study of the successful creative person. They wanted to learn what makes a creative person...well...creative. They learned that creatives were not afraid to falter—to even fail—and to learn from their experiences how to make things right.

If success is the heart of the American dream, then failure is the engine that makes it happen. It makes us get the job done right. I make mistakes every time I write a column or article. Fortunately, I can erase them with my handy escape key. But I *react* to my mistakes rather than being consumed by them.

The trick is to find the error before it overwhelms you, and to correct the damage before you have to practice damage control.

But this doesn't always happen. Mistakes are often compounded because the executives in a company won't admit a mistake. They often hide them under 10 lb. reports. A house built with faulty underpinnings cannot stand—which is the story of how one credit card company rushed to failure with a new card, even though the reports were based on poorly thought out premises.

When I handle a project for a client, I typically come up with seventy-five to a hundred different concepts. Most of them turn out to be "mistakes." The consumer doesn't like them for one reason or another. Even my clients sometimes laugh at some of our concepts:

"It didn't work five years ago"

"It's dumb"

"Upper management won't buy into it"

But I plod on. And show the concepts to the consumer and let them point out our mistakes. After all, the consumer is the one who is going to buy our product. As I said, it's smarter to make and recognize a mistake early on rather than fix it after it's in the market.

Put Your Mistakes to Work

But suppose you do make a mistake and your mistake gets to market. Is it a disaster? Not always. You can actually make it work for you.

Consumers like it when you humble yourself by admitting a mistake. They will often buy your product at faster rates.

Recently, an associate went to an expensive restaurant. The food was good but the service was abominably slow. He mentioned his dissatisfaction to the waiter. The owner immediately came out and apologized. "I am deeply sorry for your inconvenience. It was our fault." He offered the diner a bottle of wine, dessert on the house and cut the bill in half.

Despite the sorry service, my associate recommended the restaurant to me. He liked the perks, but that was not his point. By acknowledging the mistake, the owner showed my friend he was more than a filled table.

Public Mistake? Admit It and Then Move on

When Intel came up with their flawed Pentium chip and finally admitted its mistake, a weird thing happened. The company sold more chips than ever.

When a company admits a mistake, it shows a certain amount of self-confidence—that it is willing to try new things. When a company gives a marketing person the liberty of not being afraid to fail, it opens new channels to creative thought.

Enlightened companies don't hide their mistakes or place blame. To the contrary. They go out of their way to encourage customers to complain. They bend over backwards to learn from their mistakes.

But make sure the mistake is truly public or truly damaging. More often than not, the buying public is unaware of your mistake. It may pain you a great deal but most product horror stories don't advance to the front of the consumers' minds. Even if they do find out, they really don't remember it for too long. Call this phenomenon *transient relevance.*

Campbell's Soup had a problem some years back when some of the soup cans exploded. It made for a few laughs but the problem passed quickly out of the consumers' minds. Don't make the problem worse by apologizing or by calling attention to the problem. In most cases, all you'll get is more publicity and you make the uninformed public, informed. When a mistake is made, find out how potentially damaging it is by running focus groups to determine consumer awareness. Then act accordingly.

A rule of thumb for evaluating corporate disasters is, if it runs in *Consumer Reports* or CNN, or if Mike Wallace is camping on your doorsteps with the *60 Minutes* crew, own up. If some obscure magazine runs the story, ignore it. Don't fan the fire.

Turnaround Situations

Now that we talked about public mistakes, let's talk about other problems. They include misguided positionings and products, outdated products, new competition and negatives associated with your product.

Turning Negatives Into Positives

Every product has an inherent flaw. The perfect product has never been invented. But we can turn a negative into a plus if we try hard enough.

Find two good things about your product for every negative. For instance, if you have a product like Listerine which tastes bad, your message should be that it tastes bad because it's killing germs and making your mouth fresh. Noxzema smells bad, but it cleans skin and helps relieve sunburn pain.

Of course, you should try to fix the disappointing part of your product. And once you've done that, you should tell the world about it through promotions and maybe a line extension or two.

The most important thing in righting your company or your marketing plan is to reexamine yourself constantly. As I mentioned previously, often the owners of businesses don't really know what their own businesses are about. You can create success with the dullest product providing you know what your strengths and weaknesses are.

Follow This Basic Strategy for All Turnaround Situations

1. There should be quick recognition of problems that may lie ahead or current mistakes you are making.

2. The causes of the problem should be determined, not only the symptoms.
3. Alternative corrective actions should be inventoried.
4. Work fast. Work accurately. Be ruthless.
5. Learn from your mistakes.

Now here's where I differ with almost every marketing book. Don't do what-went-wrong studies or postmortems. They're wasted and they tend to downgrade morale. Instead of looking for what went wrong, figure out how to do it right. Adapt the research strategies in the second chapter and in the new product methodology in Chapter 10 to thoroughly test the results of your corrective actions before you spend big money.

General Turnaround Strategies and Protocols

Problem: Products out-of-date, competition selling faster, more efficiently.

Symptoms:

- Market share loss
- Complaints from distributors and salespeople
- Best sellers stagnating or trending downward
- Marked superiority of competitors

The usual culprits: Managers building the line without feedback from consumers, too much internal opinion backed up by too few hard facts.

How to solve:

1. Collect facts and locate needs through customer feedback.
   - Explore new segments you might have been missing
   - Explore existing and new target markets
   - Explore product fits with these segments
2. Analyze product line from this feedback.
3. Analyze through segmentation and price/profit data.
4. Establish specific goals and timetables for product updating.
5. What do you need to change?

- Areas that have been neglected
- Areas to pursue
- Analyze new profit potential
- Develop plans for all functions
- Review plans and tasks that lie ahead

6. Implement plans.
7. Carefully monitor progress.

Problem: You have no new products or your new ones aren't bringing in business; little new business because product line is outmoded; costs too high (a symptom of new products bringing in too little cash); profit goals missed; failures dilute entire product line.

The usual culprits:

- Not enough cooperation between marketing disciplines
- Top management lacks a marketing orientation
- Management isn't committed to a new product program

How to solve:

1. Define your new product goals in detail. Recruit management's interest, cooperation and funds.
2. Mercilessly review new products through consumer feedback and the new product candidate's ability to achieve stated goals.
   - Assess deficiencies in line
   - Develop new products that buyers actually want
   - Conceptualize new products
     — for key market segments
     — assess ways to turn your customers on
     — define fit with your company's business and goals
4. Run profit-and-loss figures on winning concepts.
   - Define the profit potential
   - Optimize and analyze other criteria that can advance the concept (channel distribution, brand names, and so on)
5. Create prototypes.

Problem: Profits are low, profitability varies from product to product, your pricing structure isn't generating profits.

Symptoms:

- The trade and your sales force complain about your high prices
- Overall volume changes frequently, up or down
- Margins have been falling
- Prices are changed arbitrarily

The usual culprits:

- Competition's prices are too low
- Failure to relate pricing strategy to the marketing concept (misguided cost-plus pricing strategy)
- Ignoring competitive pricing and positioning strategy when setting prices
- Pricing by cost to reach target margins

How-to-solve:

1. Market analysis.
   - Competitive positioning review
   - Determine value of purchase to consumer
   - Work with suppliers to lower costs
2. Trade terms analysis.
   - Trade profit analysis
   - Competitive terms analysis
3. Buyer feedback on prices (qualitative or quantitative analyses)
4. Pricing Decisions.
   - P & L analyses of decisions
   - Cost reduction actions
   - Predict competitive reaction and your counter moves
5. Price Testing.
   - Further qualitative or quantitative feedback

- Concepts in context studies.

6. Develop price promotions to communicate your new pricing structure—at least to the trade.

Problem: Haphazard marketing

Symptoms:

- Sales miss quotas
- Marketing is in a state of flux
- Wild promotional and product expenditures

The usual culprits:

- Marketing isn't consumer driven, management isn't marketing driven
- No business plan or strategy

How to solve:

1. Create a thorough business plan and business mission.
2. Delve deeply into competition's strengths and weaknesses.
3. Develop more centralized marketing and brand functions.
4. Develop actionable goals.

Repositioning a Stagnant Product

Most people, when they talk about repositioning, speak mainly about advertising and promotion. While these are important, they are just carriers of the message. When you reposition a product you are, essentially, redefining your product and linking yourself to a new customer base.

Nine Repositioning Strategies That Work

Here are nine ways to revitalize or reposition a product so that it either captures a new audience or recaptures the old one. While these are all classified into problem/strategy headings it is suggested you review the entire section. One particular strategy may work for a number of problems.

Product Benefits Are Weak

Strategy: *Change the product and create alternative products.*

The goal in any product revitalization is to change your customers' perception of your product and make it more meaningful to them. You can do this by effectively changing your product or by developing a good/better/best strategy.

In changing your product, you may have to revamp it completely, leaving only the brand name. It sounds scary and a bit drastic but your tried and proven brand name can be worth even more than your factory that is making the product.

Learn your brand's strengths and weaknesses and determine the leveraging power that is still in the brand. While most brand restagings result from leveraging a brand's strengths, you can also restage a brand by deleting negatives or by flanking your product with even better performing additions to your product line.

Product Has No Clear Strengths; Consumers Find Your Brand Name Weak; Product Doesn't Perform Up to Standards

Strategy: *Change the name and the product.*

Sometimes a company may be behind the times, if not in actuality, in the consumers' perception. Perhaps times have passed the company by or it doesn't have access to the newest, brightest product technology. But all is far from lost. Any company can reinvent itself if properly motivated and if it has access to current consumer information. Here's how.

First, look deep into your product though the eyes of your customer to find, or test, unique selling propositions.

Then, hide yourself. Cast off all the negative vibrations. Create a new name and a new personna. You still have the factory and the know-how. You're simply eliminating negative baggage.

When you enter a total product/image overhaul, handle the project like you would a new product. Determine the positioning and the product at the initial stages of your revamping through customer feedback.

Your newly named product should be engineered around your new positioning strategy. Chances are you don't have to search far for that killer new product. You probably have an extensive archive of products that were too early for their time. This might be the time to make them tangible.

One-Product Company; Limited Emotional Leverage

Strategy: *Boost your brand's value through line extensions.*

Line extensions can be a terrific way to build your brand's emotional leverage providing you capitalize on the outstanding equities of your product line. Efficient line extensions are always the product of primary research where you learn your customers' wants and desires. A line extension should enhance its mother product at all stages of the marketing process. There should be a synergistic effect that you can almost feel.

Line extensions can be used to procure more space, and to utilize more of a factory's capacity. But, just as importantly, they also can be used to cement your relationship with your customer. The visual composite of your brand and your line extensions should come together on the shelf to display a complete visual unit that expresses a complete image. A true line extension is more than just a new flavor or an added variety. If a line extension strategy is adopted for a repositioning program, it should change the consumers' feelings about your entire product line.

Image Weak, Sales Down But Company Is Strong

Strategy: *Change the name or develop a new brand.*

You can alter consumers' feelings about your brand by simply coming up with a new name. A new name can help you develop an "instant image."

Clairol had a monster shampoo in the sixties and seventies with its line of Herbal Essence shampoos. When the product lost steam in the nineties they changed the name to Herbal Essences to develop a new framework and new customers for the brand in the nineties. It was more than just adding an "s" to the name that made the product work. It was an integrated positioning that played right off the health fads of the nineties.

Sales Steady But No Dramatic Improvement Seen; Need to Spike Sales

Strategy: *Add a new usage.*

Show off your product's versatility by giving it new uses. Consumers love to discover new uses for an old reliable product. Arm & Hammer and WD 40 have built huge businesses on this incredibly simple strategy.

Don't look at your product as a product, look at it as a service. Your product provides a function for consumers. Use your ingenuity to define new functions. When you provide a new service to consumers, your product is more meaningful and takes on new importance.

Create a new problem that your product can solve. The excitement of discovery works here. People love to find new uses for existing products and love to recommend them to their friends.

Product Has No Clear Focus

Strategy: *Change or highlight the descriptor.*

One of my favorite ads is one I wrote for the secretary of a client. She had a Jeep with a snow plow attachment that she had a great deal of trouble selling. I suggested that instead of running in the auto section, that she run in the business opportunity section. The ad simply said:

Business Opportunity—snow plow business for sale.

She sold the car the next day. The "business opportunity" headline was like the descriptor on the package, instantly communicating what the product was for.

Nobody talks about the poor descriptor that languishes on many packages. It's a shame too. Just changing the descriptor is enough to drive new sales. While advertising the brand name is often the key to providing imagery and an overall view of the product, most products and brands are decided upon at the place of purchase. Consumers often look at the pictures and the descriptor even before they look at the price.

The descriptor is a vital usage cue for consumers. It is the consumer's one- or two-word cue on how the product will work for him or her. Changing the descriptor changes how consumers will relate to the product.

You've Milked Your Target Audience for All It's Worth; You've Alienated Target Customers in Some Way

Strategy: *Change your selling outlets and your customer profiles.*

Seek out new niches, new regions and add new user segments that will deliver new users for your brand. A brand or product is new to anyone who hasn't seen it before.

Customers See Your Product as Too Downscale/Too Upscale; It Doesn't Relate to Their Self-Image

Strategy: *Create new reference points*

Wouldn't it be great if we could be as savvy a marketer as Microsoft, and be as personable and talented as golfer Greg Norman? If consumers can't own the qualities of the greats, maybe they can borrow their persona. A *reference group* is a group or a person with which a person identifies. Consumers aspire to be in a famous person's reference group.

STP was just another oil additive when it was introduced in the sixties. But Andy Granatelli, a former race car driver, created "racing" imagery. This imagery transferred nicely to owners of "hot cars."

Sneaker manufacturers have long known the importance of signing up black athletes for their basketball shoes. Notice I said "black" athletes. African-Americans have set the tone in sports and styles. Whites borrow this feeling and transfer it to themselves through some of the clothes they wear.

One of the most important success factors in choosing your reference point strategy is selecting your endorsers and spokespeople carefully. Make sure their emotional assets are in total sync with the ones you want your product to communicate. Emotionally dissimilar matches will actually confuse your customers.

Product Has a Commodity Status

Strategy: *Create a brand and add something unique.*

Many products are commodity products, meaning everyone sells pretty much the same thing. The ultimate commodity is probably gasoline, but throughout the twentieth century, oil refineries have been turning this liquid gold into—well—liquid gold. What's more of a commodity than water? Yet many marketers charge $2.00 a bottle for the same stuff most people can get for free. (By the way, does everyone know by now that Evian spelled backwards is naive?)

They do it by branding and separating themselves from the competition. Foxy lettuce created a brand almost overnight when it was the first to package their product in plastic bags.

"Intel Inside" became a 1990s buzzword when computer manufacturers plastered it on their computers, striving to differentiate themselves from the competition. It worked. Even people who had no idea of what was inside the computer insisted on Intel.

It's amazing what a few little stickers, plastic bags or even just a creative name can do to a commodity product when you couple it with a good branding program.

Product Has a Mediocre Image; Product Is Just Plain Old

Strategy: *Just say "new."*

People love new brands and new products. The word "new" can be used, like the delete key on your computer, for things your products or company might have done wrong in the past, providing they're not too heinous. When a mediocre restaurant puts out a sign that says "Under New Management," people will give it a second chance.

If your brand is old, people will try it again if you put a banner that says "new" on the package.

Used correctly, the word "new" can add new feeling and new sales for your product. And isn't that why you're reading this chapter?

CHAPTER THIRTEEN

Strategies to Make Your Package and Product Name Sell...Sell...Sell

Your package and name must sell...sell...sell by hooking casual shoppers and making them curious enough to want to find out more about your product.

Dynamic Packaging Sells

You have only a few brief seconds to capture the consumer's interest with your package. That's why a package is more than just a cardboard box, bottle or can. It's a free-standing, three-dimensional product story in an aisle in a store, or even right next to the cashier. Every part of your package must play a part in the sale if you're going to have an efficient selling machine.

As hard as it may be for many left-brained marketers to accept, the package is often the defining feature of whether a product is perceived as effective or good tasting.

This was shown in a vivid experiment conducted by Louis Cheskin, a packaging researcher. He sent three identical deodorants to a group of consumers. The only difference was the packaging. Consumers said that all three products were different and that one worked better than the others. He then tried the same experiment with crackers. Consumers invariably said the crackers in the most prestigious package tasted best.

Turn Your Sales Pitch Into a Package

Your package should clearly lay out both your rational sales pitch and your emotional pitch. It's got to answer all the questions and doubts the consumer has. Since you can't be there in your power suit and tie, smiling and building the relationship, your package has to fill in and sell by proxy.

Even though food never looks as good as it does on the package, showing a food shot when dealing with the product provides a fantasy of a delightful end benefit. Food usually tastes better when it's enjoyed in a fancy restaurant. Restaurateurs know that presentation of your dinner is a major contributor to a well-enjoyed meal. The package is your presentation—your menu of benefits.

The results of good packaging are speedy trial and a positive feeling about your product. A creative package reaches out to grab consumers so that the consumers reach out and grab the product, almost without realizing it. A good package conjures up clear images in the mind of the consumer of what the product is going to do.

The importance of packaging is reflected in the fact that you're reading my words. If I sent you the identical manuscript in a loose-leaf notebook, you probably wouldn't give it a second thought. Something about this book and this very page has captured your attention. Perhaps it was the way the type is laid out. Maybe it was the cover. Or maybe the publisher. It was, probably, a combination of them all. The packaging gave my words life and credibility.

People Read Packages in a Logical Order

If the first two sentences or so catch your attention, you'll read the next paragraph. If you think that paragraph has meaning for you, you'll read the next and the next. Packaging works exactly the same way.

People read packages in a set order.

- If the name and graphics on the package catches their attention, they'll pick up the package and read more.
- If the front intrigues them, they will invariably go to the back panel for more information and additional usage suggestions.
- Then they will attack the side panels for reinforcement of the selling premises and to see how the product fits into their lives.

Creating an effective package requires joint cooperation between marketing, advertising and design. Efficiency is the name of the game when it comes to something as vital as your package. You have no space to waste.

Subtlety in a Package Is Foolish

Now I'm going to get in trouble with the package designers, but the package is no place for subtlety. It should grab the consumer by the neck and shout "BUY ME." It should act like a beacon in the store. Consumers don't have time to analyze packaging. That's the marketer's job.

Good packaging cajoles, invites and persuades your customers to grab the package from the shelf and take it home. It differentiates your product from every other product. It sets your parity product apart from the me-toos. It can also transform a loser into a winner.

Packaging As Dramatic Proof

While advertising and most marketing attempts to sell by promising and delivering on a need, your packaging should dramatize the fulfillment of that need. The trade dress your product wears brings credence to the claims set forth in your ad or brochure. It continues the sales premise at the exact point your ad leaves off. Whatever the theme of your campaign, your package should convince the customers that they are really getting what your ad message promises.

Packaging Is Symbolism, Too

Although unwrapped merchandise is still sold in farmer's markets and third-world markets, in America people prefer recognizable shapes and logos. It's important to recognize that packages help confer status on both the company that makes the package and the people who buy the product.

Packaging brings uniqueness to each brand. It gives shape and tangible form to the product and the buyer's self-image. Arousing emotions through your package is of no less importance than the technical efficiency in which the package stores and protects goods. Packaging is an expression of individuality. The package is your way to create an affinity between the personalities of the product and those of the buyer.

Packaging can be too good or too luxurious, however. Fancily boxed chocolates or soap, for example, may turn off a person who may not want to include promises of romance in a gift. A person who has a down-to-earth lifestyle may resent paying for glitzy expensive packaging. Your packaging strategy depends on your target market.

Packaging is also a symbol of how a product is made. The well-designed package announces that the manufacturer thinks especially high of both her product and her customers. Consumers react very strongly to this message.

Three Strategies for Writing Labels

Obviously the front label is an important part of the package, but so are all sides of a package, including the instructions. Here are some basic strategies for writing labels and instructions:

- Specificity is better than generality. Instead of saying "this product is good for cleaning bathrooms," say "this product is great for removing soap scum from shower curtains, sinks and vanities."
- Use simple graphics instead of copy lines to drive home a point effectively.
- Although most people won't follow labels or instructions exactly, use graphics, text and step-by-step directions in your usage instructions to make your points. Clear, uncomplicated directions and simple visuals denote to the consumer that the product is a quality one.

The Surprise Package Strategy

Create drama with your package. Pay attention to the pleasures that the packaging itself can provide: a package can be suspenseful and exciting as one unwraps a product little by little to see what's inside. How many of us have opened a package in a car because we were too impatient to wait until we got home?

Some Products Demand Familiarity

Familiarity has a reassuring effect and is of utmost importance, particularly when dealing with a product that is basically unpleasant, like sanitary napkins, laxatives and hygiene items. In these products, the consumer is more likely to reach for the familiar package rather than those that don't have the expected cues. Quick—what is the color of a Dr. Scholl's package? (It's yellow.) The yellow means that the product will work. Been there. Done that. Why try a new product that may cause embarrassment or distress?

The Halo-Effect Strategy

Create packaging for new products by using the same basic graphic elements of your best-selling products. Consumers will transfer the good feelings that your first product elicits over to the new additions. Of course, if your products are not selling well, try the strategies on repositioning products in the previous chapter.

Packaging Links You with the Consumer

Your packaging is often the only way you can "meet your consumer." Use the space wisely. Talk to your consumer. Spread the word about the product and your company. Deliver a message that makes you unique. Write a personal message to the consumer or communicate a message (e.g., "we're environmentally friendly") that you know will be accepted readily or even received enthusiastically. A personal note on the package is always helpful. Create a phone number where people can contact you personally. Ask for feedback about the product and your advertising. Responses you get can be a great way to build a customer database.

The Advertising-Reinforcement Strategy

Use graphics, banners, self-adhesives, or booklets to help consumers recall an advertising theme. This can help remind the purchaser that the product will fulfill the need or want—such as fun, prestige or control over life situations—that led him to find the product in the first place.

The Lesser-of-Two-Evils Strategy

When a buyer walks up the aisles and makes three selections, the chances are he/she did not plan to make two of them. Consumers spend more shopping time negatively than positively. It takes them twice as much time to make a buy decision as it takes to decide not to buy. In fact, consumers resist picking up a package and reading it for further info. Make your package simple. Make your copy brief. Say in two or three words what used to take two lines. Use graphics to convey the message quickly and painlessly.

The Tie-in Strategy

Do multiple tie-ins of products with a complimentary nature. Don't be afraid to use dissimilar products for cross-promotions and merchandising programs. Use labels for premiums, rebates, free add-ons, and so forth.

Don't Go Overboard Over Recycling

Consumers will rarely pay for a recyclable or two-way bottle. Yet, they want to see a recycling label on the package. Give them what they want, but don't spend big money on developing a recycled package. You'll rarely earn the dollars back.

The Added-Value Strategy

The package should not only sell the products; it should also create the desire for repetitive purchases. When packaging is useful and functional in other ways than simply serving as a container to hold the product, consumers have more reasons to choose your product over the competition.

Foxy Lettuce created a revolution in the produce industry by packaging each head in a plastic bag. Both merchants and consumers were ecstatic. Now one could buy a head of lettuce knowing it was not prehandled by picky customers. Foxy quickly established a brand name in the minds of consumers. It was a solid marketing tactic—especially for the stodgy, slow-to-change produce industry.

- Create a package or bottle that consumers can use for other chores, like organizing or school projects.
- Use self-adhesive booklets for recipes that can be stored in an index card folder.
- Add value with a special opening device. Tylenol is often sold with a cap that has a long vertical extension with a hole on the top. The hole makes it easy for people with arthritis and other hand ailments to insert a pencil as a lever. Helpful packaging can make the world just a little bit nicer for people.

Keep Your Package Evolving

In the olden days of packaging, graphics were stagnant. The package graphics were set in stone. Few changes in package graphics were made because it was very difficult to make changes.

But packaging today is extremely flexible. It some cases we can change package graphics as quickly as we can change an ad.

Change your package to reflect your ad change, providing you don't confuse the customer. Use your package to make your ad succeed at the next level.

Convenience-Plus Packaging

Convenience for convenience's sake (with the usual higher price) rarely sells. When developing a convenience product, stress that the product is better or cheaper than buying the product without the convenience. Always rationalize convenience with a greater efficacy benefit.

Packaging for the Senses

The more senses you can stimulate through product packaging the better. Look is important, but so is touch. Give your product a difference that consumers can feel. This can be a special texture or a new kind of container material.

Point-of-Sale Dispensers as Packaging Hook

In an earlier chapter, we discussed the benefits of point-of-sale devices. A package is the ultimate P.O.S. unit. Tie your package into a point-of-sale theme which dispenses your product. Keep the units compact, and visually and texturally interesting. Create a revolving display that is easy to refill. By using a dispensing merchandiser you can put the package, the P.O.S. hook and the advertising hook in one impulse-sale-generating unit.

You can also use this display/package to tie in with other brands. While the big idea is to generate sales, you also get many more brand impressions than you get with only one product.

Use Packaging Instead of Price Wars

Packaging serves as an alternative to price competition. Use smaller size units to deliver smaller amounts of your product to avoid a price increase. Create multipack units when the price for one of an item is too small to make money for you. Use larger multipack units to give consumers buy-in-bulk prices.

Although *Consumer Reports* will get mad at me, use odd weights to make it difficult for consumers to compare prices.

A Small Package Often Means There's Less Inside

Don't get too efficient. Generally, customers equate a smaller box with less product inside. Whether it's true or not, that's the perception. Be very careful when you make a package more compact.

Color Strategies for Your Packages

1. Choose primary colors, and black and white. Dark colors usually fall back from view. Brights stand out on the shelf and pull the eye forward. Pastels are usually overwhelmed by other packages.
2. Pay special attention to the language of colors:
   - Red signals strength and vitality.
   - Orange looks clean and appetizing; expresses action.
   - Yellow is the loudest color. Mocking the sun, it is cheerful and sometimes sensuous.
   - Pink suggests femininity and daintiness.
   - Green is healthful, quiet, environmentally friendly.
   - Blue is cooling and subduing.
   - Black is dramatic and interrupting (but a bit overdone at this writing).
   - White denotes virtue and cleanliness.
   - Brown is strictly utilitarian. It is also environmentally friendly—rich in earth tones.

Follow the Eight-Point Packaging Checklist

Does your packaging:

- Attract attention?
- Tell the product story completely?

Eight Rules Packages Must Follow

1. The logo must stand out and be seen a reasonable distance from the shelf.
2. The logo must strengthen the brand image.
3. The package must clearly identify what's inside.
4. The package must approach and greet the buyer.
5. It must speak to the customer's needs as if on a one-to-one basis.
6. Packaging must present the merchandise effectively.
7. The package must overcome objections.
8. It must close the "deal."

- Create an affinity with the consumer?
- Look clean and sanitary?
- Facilitate carrying the item out of the store and into the home?
- Look like a good value?
- Have a name and descriptor that describes the product's benefits in a convincing way? (The name must act like a résumé, getting the consumer to delve into the product further.)
- Reflect and enhance the product's performance cues quickly, vividly and effectively? (Check out the Sony Walkman package. It accomplishes its goal to perfection.)

Naming Your Product

Where have all the great names gone—the names that have created an immediate cachet in the minds of the consumer? Names like Ivory, Arm & Hammer, Jell-O, Chanel #5, and the like? Product names are sounding increasingly alike. Originality is being replaced by ampersands and the cumbersome apostrophed 'n. Imagination is substituted by fake French words and the ubiquitous "lite" and "gold." Power words are big too—straight from a copywriter's thesaurus.

The key to a great name is simplicity of imagery with a dash of creativity...and an end benefit promise. Healthy Choice says what it is and says it quickly. Snuggles Fabric Softener is one of the truly great names of the eighties, capturing the essence of what a fabric softener should impart to a product. Snuggles' main competitor, Downy, also offers a fervent interpretation of what a fabric softener should do to clothes.

Twelve Rules and Strategies for Naming Products

Consider the following strategies and ideas when stalking the perfect name. Remember, the more memorable and precise the name you choose, the more likely that consumers will recall and respond to it at the critical point of purchase.

Offbeat Names Can Work

Offbeat names can be fun and effective when they seek an in-crowd ambiance. They create their own level of acceptance. Screaming Yellow Zonkers is still a hit after all these years. Dippity-Do and Dep are two more names that have found new generations of supporters. But wild-sounding names need to keep up with the times otherwise they may go out of date. As mentioned before, Herbal Essence was the right name for the flower times of the sixties and seventies. Clairol took the guts of the name and turned it into Herbal Essences, a more modern way to capture the feelings of these times.

Load Your Name with Benefits

Today you need the selling power of a good name, especially if you don't have a lot of excess cash to spend on advertising. A good name functions as a headline on the shelf. It reeks of self-benefit.

I was recently talking with a man who had developed a new antacid. The name was Prelief. It looked good on the package but it made no connection to the solving of gastric problems. The consumer has to make a great leap to associate the name with the benefit. Must products can benefit greatly from having a name that exudes a consumer benefit.

Shun Dull Names and Puns

The worst kind of names are those that won't take a stand or a viewpoint. Nondescript names make them instantly forgettable. Because marketers are terrified of offending anybody (you can't avoid it, guys), they develop names that affect—and influence —*nobody*.

A great name comes from a person who has immersed himself in the product. It's easy to outsmart and entertain ourselves with puns and double entendres—but consumers don't get them.

The worst names are those that connote nothing and instill no emotions. New Breed Dog Food is one name that comes to mind. Why should I buy a dog food for a new breed when I have an old mutt? Mighty Dog, Lucky Dog, Sheeba all promise a bit of fun and fantasy.

Give Your Product a Fantasy Name

Give your product a name that denotes more than what is actually in the box. Let the consumer's imagination run wild. Snuggles . . . Obsession . . . Black Diamonds . . . all promise rewards that are far out of line with what the product can logically do. Who can the resist the sin of Opium or the aspirational feeling of Black Diamonds?

You can also personify your product with a fantasy figure. Mr. Clean embodied all the characteristics one would expect of a high-strength cleaner.

Communicate an Instant Reward

One of the keys to selling to American consumers is recognizing that Americans want their rewards instantly. Americans don't want their rewards intimated or delayed—they want rewards *now*. Give your product a name that reeks of instant benefit. "Now," "at once," "express" are all good name starters that denote speed and instant gratification.

Long Names Can Work, Too

Long names can work well for the simple reason that most products are named with one or two words. Long names break through the clutter. Consumers may shorten the name when they speak about your product to others or when they write it down on their grocery list, but so what? What you're looking for is what they'll remember—and buy.

Use a Real Person's Name

Orville Redenbacher is an unusual case of people liking a name for the wrong reasons but being caught up in a mystique. Until he died a short time ago, few people thought that he was a real-life person.

Chef Paul Prudhomme has his name on a line of New Orleans Seasonings. Consumers may not be able to take a trip to his restaurant in New Orleans, but perhaps they can use his seasonings.

But don't take fame too seriously when choosing a persona for your product. Fame fades quickly and all you're left with is an empty bottle. Paul Newman's Sauces worked because he didn't take himself or his product very seriously. It was like an in-joke the whole nation was aware of. But Frank Sinatra's spaghetti sauce died quickly. It took itself too seriously.

A Note About Numbers and Letters

Although there are exceptions, names that use abbreviations and numbers appeal to men more than to women. While a man might want people to know his computer is a new Hx4 with a 2.6 Meg Nex drive, most women are more comfortable with a real name like Compaq. Names with numbers instead of words also tend to be forgotten faster.

Be Careful with Name Extensions

The big trend today is to use every brand name that your company has and milk it to the max. This can work. But you must know what your brand equities are. Hershey's, some time ago, launched Reese's Peanut Butter but it proved a mediocre brand-name strategy. Consumers thought the name Reese's meant it was too sweet for their kids' everyday consumption.

Create a Name Consumers Dislike

People don't have to like a name to buy a product. When researching names, you'll undoubtedly hear this comment from people and associates: "It sounds like so and so." If your product and name fit, it really doesn't make too much difference. In most products sold in the store, the product name isn't said out loud. It's read.

It's actually better to have a name that people hate rather than one that sounds wishy washy and takes no stand. Bully was a wildly unpopular name in focus groups, but it was remembered and that's what sold tons of Bully Toilet Cleaner.

Have Fun

Choose a name that's whimsical for a not-so-serious product. Toilet Duck is one of the best names of the decade. Cleaning the toilet is arguably the worst job in the house. But consumers look at the product and say "That's cute." Don't be afraid to have fun with your product.

The same company that developed Prelief also developed a product to alleviate gas. They called it Beano. Is gas serious? Probably, but the product created a bit of levity in a category chock full of serious names.

The Foreign-Sounding Strategy

I don't know why it is, but the Japanese like American-sounding products while Americans like European-sounding products. Viva Le Dijon and Häagen-Dazs are both foreign-sounding names that are made in the good 'ol USA. You can create instant prestige by going foreign.

Ten Basic Strategies of a Good Product Name

It should be memorable.

It should contribute value to the product.

It must elicit interest and trial.

It should communicate your strongest benefit. It should be flexible enough to allow for line extensions.

It should be easy to READ.

It should differentiate your brand from any other product on the shelf (unless you're trying to be a me-too product).

In that case, use a name that sounds like the market leader's.

It should reflect the consumer's most wanted performance cues.

It should create performance expectations (it's up to your product to deliver on these expectations).

It should actively prospect in the aisle.

CHAPTER FOURTEEN

Strategies for Marketing Through the New Media

I've been in the marketing business a long time now (a couple of decades or so), and never have I seen so much hype over new media. The people who are most excited point out the similarities between the birth of the Internet and television in its infancy.

But there are many more differences than similarities. In fact, the only real similarity is that both media are delivered through picture tubes. And the differences impact greatly when marketing strategy comes into play.

Back in the fifties, we had limited choices. We were further limited by the comparatively few channels we were offered. Advertisers could reach the general population quickly and economically; there was not a great deal of segmentation at that time. Also, at that time, radio provided the training wheels to the then-new medium. People were used to setting aside time to be entertained, so marketers simply adapted their radio strategies to television. Television was a destination; it was place to go to be entertained. If we had to endure commercials, so be it. After all, advertisers were footing the bill.

Now we have choices. Boy, do we have choices. We can log onto over half a million "stations" on the Internet. While we can look at the ads and browse an Internet site, it takes just a simple mouse click to make it all go away. But the big difference is that television and radio commercials were relatively painless. They were helpful, in fact, because they provided time to use the bathroom or to get a quick snack. And we had no real alternatives.

Nobody talked about interacting back then—and surprise—people don't talk about interacting now, except for the people who sell space on the Internet—which seems to be everyone these days. Interactive TV has proven to be a failure, except for the home-shopping networks and infomercials which we'll get to later. People don't want to interact with advertisers. They want to veg out.

The Internet and the World Wide Web

I'm starting off the new media section with Internet and the World Wide Web for a simple reason. Everyone is talking about them. It's hard to pick up a magazine without seeing an article on the potential of the web. And that's the problem. The web appears to have potential. But you can't make money on potential. You need hard data. And the data just doesn't warrant most sellers having a presence on the web. But, on the other hand, everyone is jumping on the bandwagon because nobody wants to be left out of the new "hot" thing.

Almost every major company now has a website but it's like the dog who runs after a car. Once he catches it, what does he do with it? Even companies that make their money by selling computers aren't exactly sure how to make the web work for them. In a recent discussion I had with Hewlett-Packard, a key player in the computer industry, it admitted the company had no idea how a website should be run and exactly what its web strategy should be.

Most of the web propaganda falls into the "you can" category. "You can" order pizza... "you can" order seafood... "you can" search for 12,001 websites that start with the letter "A." So what? "I can" doesn't translate into "I will" or even "I want to."

Typical of webspeak is a site for Nabisco. In meeting after meeting, brand managers wanted their own space on the proposed Nabisco website. Nabisco developed a "Neighborhood" themed website. It featured recipes, brand information and even financial data about Nabisco. How's it working? Said a Nabisco spokesperson, "We're not betting the farm on Internet commerce. We realize that it says something to be on the leading edge. But we've got a realistic long-term approach. We're all sure something is coming, but we're not sure what."

Uncertainty about how to do online marketing stems from the nature of the web itself. It's more a means than an end. A big part of the web is in the links, which allows surfers to jump from one site to another. Thus, there are few true destinations, just the experience of logging onto or surfing the web itself.

In order to attract and hold your visitors, you have to keep your site fresh. While this is no different than traditional media, hard-sell media approaches are ruled out because surfers can send you to marketing oblivion with a click.

Although most websites can be classified as advertising on an accounting spread sheet, websites are built to inform, not to actually sell. If you were an advertising agency and told your client, "Well, we're not actually trying to sell...," you'd be looking for a new client rather quickly.

And then there's the problem of publicizing your website. Many companies use traditional media to publicize their websites, but are not sure of what to deliver once a surfer gets there. Did you really want to have a dialogue with Arm & Hammer baking soda or Bully toilet bowl cleaner?

Nevertheless, the numbers can be fun if you're into that sort of thing.

ConAgra's Healthy Choice website gets some 500,000 hits per week. That sounds impressive, but it can't be traced to actual sales. A ConAgra spokesman takes the same "down the road" as Nabisco, seeing the opportunity for e-mail ordering and the like. It's a lot easier to go down to the local supermarket. The ConAgra strategy is to use the web as a connection to customers. They get suggestions, questions and even new product ideas. But even this is not without its drawbacks. ConAgra gets time-consuming e-mail about things that people would never call up about. Queries run the gamut, from "Does an old friend still work there?" to "Can you help me with a class project and also send me your marketing plans and advertising budgets?"

But if you insist on a website strategy, there are things you can do, provided you have a strong focus.

Should You Be on the Web?

Yes, sales are now estimated to be over a billion dollars. Companies that benefit the most from the Web are those that sell hard goods that are easily shipped and described simply. Other such companies include:

1. *Companies who sell to people who have an interest in computers, like computer supply houses and software marketers.* Their natural audience consists of people familiar with computers and those who have semitechnical know-how. These people actively search for computer websites for great bargains and the next hot computer gizmo.

2. *Companies that have hard to find products.* Sites that offer collectors a new acquisition seem to do well. There are many sites that offer products like outdated Beta VCRs and hard to find auto parts. These sites have two things in common—surfers are emotionally involved with their subject matter, and the company's customer base is highly targetable. Finding the website is almost as much fun as getting the merchandise.

Ah, but there's a rub, too. If you start a business or launch an online site, competitors will follow as quickly as ants to a Smuckers jelly picnic. When CD Now, a record company, launched its website, there were no other record companies to compete with. Now it has competition from all sorts of record companies, including such well-heeled spenders as Tower Records and Sony.

3. *Companies that sell by bulk in a price-intensive environment.* In this case, looking through the Internet is just another way of locating suppliers. Merchandising in this mode is most effective when you have a limited product line and face-to-face communication is not necessary.

4. *Companies that provide added value to the "look what I found on the Internet" game.* For example, companies that provide sites to play games sell space to the game manufacturers.

5. *Companies that offer a website as an adjunct to their direct-mail operation.* But the website should only be used for a supporting function. It does not replace a catalog, telemarketing strategies or a live 800 number.

Six Key Concepts Affecting Your Web Focus

1. *The four key words of a successful website are educate, invigorate, advertise and sell.* If you bore customers or sell too hard, you're only a mouse click away from oblivion.
2. *Content is king.* People aren't looking to be sold. People pay to be online. They want to be entertained, or at least informed. Provide content that your competitors aren't providing. Give visitors information of value. Update your content and your page monthly if possible.
3. *Know what your customers will and won't buy through the Internet.* It's ludicrous to think a visitor would buy a box of Cheer when he or she can run down to the local supermarket. Websites generate more leads than actual sales. Follow up leads through e-mail. While people may

check out a particular website once or twice a week at most, they always check their e-mail.

4. *Customers rarely buy anything from their initial visit.* Keep them coming back for more by continuously adding value to your site. The Internet is a different kind of media. People have to come to you.
5. *Create a strong, powerful, easy-to-remember, easy-to-type website address (DNS).* Just one incorrectly typed hyphen means your prospect won't be able to find your site.
6. *Focus, focus, focus.* Become an expert in your field and stick with your area of expertise. Offer only a few related product lines and save your diversification for new websites connected by links. You'll also get a great many more "hits" from the search engines.

19 Proven Strategies for Websites

1. *Generating leads is the most realistic and immediate source of benefits.* Create a custom database and deliver coupons to your customers via e-mail. The coupon should be large enough and clear enough to leave no doubt in the purchaser's mind that it is an actual coupon. Call attention to the coupons on your opening page and cross-reference the coupons with links throughout the site. If your product is a service or a complicated product, advertise a free telephone consultation.

Reinforce cross-promotions by adding links to the companies that you are participating with. Try to work out reciprocal web relationships with your participants. For instance, they advertise on your website and you advertise on theirs.

Amazon books (http://www.Amazon.com), based in Seattle, has a strong website that is heavily advertised on other websites. But Amazon considers its actual sales much less important than the mailing list data they obtain.

Develop a strong follow-up process to convert your leads into sales. Use e-mail as the central tool to provide most of this information.

2. *Sell through hominess.* Virtual Vineyards (http://www.virtualvin.com), a wine-selling firm, has created a strong website by creating an image of informality. The site exudes trust and credibility. Because it caters to wine fanatics and offers a lot of tips and buying information, people take the time to see what new products the company is offering.

3. *Stay in touch with your customers by motivating them to give out their mailing address.* Use free information packets, newsletters, free samples, and so on. Follow these leads with a hard copy of your catalog. These can be print or online catalogs. Print materials work better than electronic catalogs. People still value paper over electronic blips. Try to do both.

Online trust is built the same way as with traditional businesses. Provide valuable information. Respond immediately to every inquiry. Follow through on all of your promises.

4. *Register with the search engines under as many key words and categories as you can.* When people are searching for a specific product or service, they use search engines to find what they want. There are dozens of search engines as of this writing. The top ten search engines get 90 percent of the hits. Yahoo, Excite, Alta Vista and Lycos are some of the bigger ones.

5. *Keep communications flowing by updating your web product line with practical enhancements surfers can download.* Reference your company website in all your print promotion and advertising, and with everyone who sells your product.

6. *Find other websites that can link with your company.* Offer these sites strong content to put on their site. Editorials that educate your customers about expensive product lines can be a great help to purchasers.

7. *Use autoresponders (software that automatically sends out e-mail to people who inquire about your product or service).*

8. *Design a column or feature article for your site that you can change every month or so.* Use a banner or a flag that says "new" to call attention to your new, value-added features.

9. *Save money by bartering goods for free ad space on your site.* You'll have to keep strong statistics about your hits to do this. One website sold its space to a broadcast company in exchange for radio ad time.

10. *Create headlines for each webpage.* Make them links to consumer enlightenment material. Make this content lively—go easy on the hype. You want surfers to read further. Hype turns surfers off. If they used search engines, they probably worked hard to find your site (14 of 15 hits are usually duds). Reward surfers for finding your site.

11. *Ask for feedback from your visitors.* Amazon sells books but encourages visitors' feedback. Its customers can even publish reviews of

books. Amazon also sends out e-mails on all new books related to a customer's interest that they use as a continual base of contact and a way to keep visitors returning again and again.

12. *Create new profit streams by selling ads on your website.* CD Now carries ads for record companies and charges 4 cents an impression (an *impression* is defined as someone's clicking on a page carrying the ad).

13. *Use existing online services (America Online for example) for your site rather than the World Wide Web.* They get more traffic and users are less concerned about security problems with credit-card transactions. Another advantage of online services is that, while you've got to be semi-literate to navigate the Internet, online services are designed for the technologically impaired. They are so easy to navigate that users usually just have to push a button to get where they want to go.

14. *Don't forget to close the sale.* You're not developing a Web site to impress—you're creating it to sell. Make sure your closing argument is strong. If possible give your customers a choice of products, for instance, Product X or Y. You'll get more sales when you offer an alternative choice than if you ask your customer to order Item X or nothing.

15. *Banner ads (rectangles that often cover the width of a webpage) are the most effective advertising tool on the web.* Bright blues, greens and yellows are the most effective colors to attract attention.

Include animation. Animation has been shown to improve response rates by up to 29 percent. Web banners are usually shown for 15 seconds at a clip but you can get them for 60 seconds or more.

Questions in a banner are also effective since a person is only a mouse click from getting the answer to questions.

16. *Always include text alternatives to the graphics on your pages so people with slow modems can find your messages quickly.*

17. *Since people will rarely buy on a first contact, keep using your list to send second, third and fourth inquiries.* If people eventually want to be taken off your list, don't fight it.

18. *Test your sales approaches online.* Test headlines, direct-mail hooks and selling strategies. Market research on the Internet is cheaper than a full-blown ad test. Online you can find out what people are buying and, through surveys and e-mail, you can ask them what they need. You can

adapt your overall sales approach to their likes and dislikes. Your customers, typically active participants, will actually help you build your business.

19. *Use your website as a starting, or reference, point for any marketing campaign.* The movie studios do this constantly. Use a line in your advertising such as "for more information visit soandso.com." Websites never sleep and never get tired of giving out information.

Six Creative Web Strategies

Conduct a treasure hunt on the Internet, hiding prizes in related sites. This generates traffic and strong market data. Ask surfers to give their names and addresses as the entrance "fee."

Give away prizes for the best ideas or feedback about your website.

For some reason, people seem to like filling out surveys on the Internet. Use a survey to determine how consumers are reacting to your product line or a specific product category in general.

Develop a traditional media promotion that requires people to go online and register first. This will publicize your site, deliver information and help you collect names.

Whether you ask for an e-mail address or not, stay in touch with your customers through your site by offering monthly tips, special reports and catalogs.

Sponsor a Sweepstakes. It's an excellent way to draw prospects. Publicize the sweepstakes in your media advertising and in the major search engines. Match the sweepstakes offer to the goals you are trying to achieve and the audience you are drawing.

There's Big Money in Infomercials

Talking about the new media always brings up the subject of infomercials. An infomercial is a program-length commercial, usually thirty minutes or so in length. They are usually run at very late hours or during light viewing hours. People talk about them as if they were a new thing. They surely aren't. In the early days of TV, the hard sell spiel ruled as the new medium looked for anything to provide revenues. In a classic episode of *The Honeymooners*, circa 1955, Jackie Gleason did a spoof where he tried to sell a kitchen implement with the show's sidekick (Art Carney) on TV. It was funny then and it's funny now. The sets are more sophisticated now and there are better production techniques, but there are surprising similarities between today's infomercials and yesterday's video pitches.

Infomercials are a great medium to learn the emotions that can drive a product. As a rule, infomercials are highly researched. The consumer feedback is the sales generated through 800 numbers. These sales are monitored every day. Infomercial makers are always testing new pitches and ideas.

If you're looking for a new product, knock-off the products featured in the most successful infomercials. You can tell who's successful when you see a particular infomercial so often that you're almost ready to buy the product.

Notice how sales are driven by emotion and backed up by a rationale. Enthusiasm is contagious—and infomercial producers milk this excitement. Notice how excited the studio audience is. People actually give standing ovations to the Wondermop.

Infomercial products are so popular that they are now filtering down to the "legitimate" distribution channels. There are now at least five companies making a "Wondermop" look-alike for retail chains.

The Basic Infomercial Strategy

Following the basic principles we've discussed in our research strategies, infomercial producers keep what works and throw out or improve what doesn't. Copy the most successful ones. Producers are always testing new pitches and ideas.

The basic components of todays infomercial are:

- A dramatic product demonstration shot before a live studio audience
- Many testimonials
- Hard sell two-minute commercials spaced approximately seven minutes apart

This format was not set by accident or whim, but as a result of extensive consumer research.

The research that goes into an infomercial is, perhaps, the most accurate research in almost any medium. If the 800 number lines aren't ringing off the hook there's something wrong with either the commercial or the product.

Use This Formula for Creating a Successful Infomercial

- Relate your product and message to a familiar consumer problem
- Sell the audience members on how your product can enrich their lives by solving the problem
- Keep your audience excited through the pitch showing what the product has done for others
- Wear your audience down with your enthusiasm

Reinforce the emotion of the pitch. Use hard-sell inserts placed into the body of the commercial three or four times, approximately seven minutes apart, at the infomercial's most uplifting moments.

Eleven Criteria for Infomercial Success

1. *The product should be unique.* You should be unable to buy the product in stores. Infomercials rely on hope. With most infomercials you are selling only benefits—the more emotional the better.

Richard Simmons' fat-reducing products feature heartfelt testimonials about getting slim and rebuilding your life.

More than in any other media, the product should offer a unique way of solving a problem. The problem can be emotional, useful, instructional or recreational in nature. You can't be too slim, too rich or too hungry. Products that promise to solve these problems are infomercial staples.

Since consumers can't touch the product, the message must be so strong that consumers will pick up the phone instantly and then wait eagerly for the product to be delivered.

2. *The product must be demonstratable.* Dramatic demonstrations of the product and its benefits capture and hold viewer interest. Before and after photos may seem hackneyed, but they do work.

3. *Infomercials are more efficient in terms of effect and cost when run during passive viewing hours such as before and after late movies or talk shows.* During these periods, consumers are more likely to go to the phone.

4. *Your product can be purely informative.* American Express ran an infomercial showing how to pick a travel agent. After calling the 800 number viewers received a brochure about American Express Travel Services, an invitation to an American Express film, and of course, extensive callbacks. It resulted in the lowest cost per sale in American Express' history.

Merck runs infomercials on allergies that carry the hidden message of asking for the Merck name at the doctor's office. Allstate and Ford both run infomercials that are cleverly disguised as real shows.

5. *Frequent mentions and displays of the mandatory 800 number is essential to success.*

6. *Use verbal exclamations in your infomercials.* Words like "finally," "at last," "new," "breakthrough" and "amazing" still carry value after all these years.

7. *Provide information overkill.* If consumers are going to buy a product they haven't seen, give them as much important information as you can squeeze in.

8. *Repeat the name of the product as often as possible.* You want a consumer to say "I want to buy the Tread Faster 2000" rather than "I want that product I saw on TV."

9. *Show as many close-ups as possible.* Show the product in static form and in use.

10. *Use emotional appeals.* Sound effects and happy people enhance emotional appeal. Appealing to emotions can be as effective as rational explanations. Adventure, fun, enjoyment and the desire to become a better person in one form or another can drive sales for a long time. Paid studio audiences add to the emotional appeal.

11. *Use an on-screen actor instead of voiceovers.* George Kennedy was a super choice for Breath Assure breath fresheners. Your character will be identified with your product after a while.

Infomercial Costs

You can produce an infomercial using freelance camera people and your friends as actors for under $35,000. But if you do it professionally, the cost rises to $100,000 or more. In fact, the average professionally produced infomercial is over $200,000.

Using a telemarketing company to handle orders can run $2.50 to up to $30 per qualified lead or order. Media can add another $50,000 on up, depending on your target market. The most profitable times to run infomercials are late night, mornings, Saturday and Sunday afternoons.

Or, you can slash upfront costs by hiring an infomercial direct-marketing service that does everything. But you'll give up control.

Does Your Product Stack Up As a "Practical Product"?

Does it solve an obvious immediate need?

Is it unavailable in local stores?

Does it save time, money or effort?

Do most people have a need for it?

Does it make the user more appealing—more attractive physically or sexually?

Will the users and their friends see a visible appearance change?

Does your product make the user feel more confident?

Are the product benefits something that almost everyone has a desire for?

Is there some unique aspect that makes it exciting?

Is your product timely?

If you can answer all the questions with an honest yes, than you should be exploring the infomercial market.

Home-Shopping Shows

Cable TV has nurtured the concept of home shopping to giant behemoth status. There are many reasons to pursue the Home-Shopping shows as trade channels. One is that many entrepreneurs have become disenchanted with typical department store distribution channels. They're expensive. It can be difficult to find the money to stand up to a larger company's advertising and promotions. With the shopping networks you can stimulate sales without worrying about stepping on the toes of the giants.

Sales can be incredible. At one time selling $10,000 worth of product in an hour was considered good. Now, some stations do it in a minute.

Another reason is that appearing on a shopping channel can lead to sales from the very retailers that spurned you only a few months prior. An hour or so on a TV show can be wonderful exposure, and you're not paying for a penny of it.

What Sells on the Home-Shopping Networks

Women's and family-oriented products do best. Jewelry accounts for about 50 percent of sales. Products that lend themselves to demonstration also sell well. Fitness machines, computers, and engine additives also do well.

On the flip side, discounted products—closeouts and overruns—can also sell fast.

Approximately three times as many women watch the channels as men. The average household income is about $35,000.

Exclusive products are also strong. In fact, home-shopping networks crave exclusivity. More and more home-shopping networks are looking to introduce products that are not available anywhere else.

QVC, which claims to be the largest home-shopping network is always looking for new products, and says, "If you have the product, we're going to buy it." The network claims to reach 50 million homes.

While QVC is actively looking for new products to sell, like other home-shopping networks, it has a number of things it looks for before accepting a new vendor. The product must be easy to demonstrate, it must be shippable and the vendor must provide QVC with an adequate quantity of merchandise (it varies with every product) in time for it to hit the airwaves. Since most programming is thematic, product selections are based on how they will segment between programs. For instance, a cooking show might attract both men and women, but an apparel hour might only attract women of a certain age and sex. The retail price of the item should exceed $15.

The key to selling on these networks is the intensive product demonstration. The demo is programed for a particular segment and is run many times over a selected time frame, usually a month or two. Because viewing a home-shopping channel is often the product of mindless channel surfing, it is imperative that your demonstration stops people in their tracks.

How to Get on TV

To start the process, request a vender relations kit from the network. You'll receive a form to fill out about your product and material addressing the most frequently asked questions.

Then you'll be asked to send in a quality control batch and, if you're lucky and the product is good, they'll run a low-volume market test in off-hours. Your product will have about 30 seconds to 4 minutes to prove itself (or not prove itself).

The Consignment Factor

On some stations, if the product doesn't move, not only do you not get paid, you get all of your product back. The network is actually buying on consignment. If you choose the network-shopping route make it an adjunct to your other marketing channels. If the product sells well, it can be your marketing focus for years.

CHAPTER FIFTEEN

Strategies for Fund-Raising

Whether you're developing endowment programs for giant institutions like the Girl Scouts or collecting funds for a local church, as a fund-raiser, you are usually very committed to a cause. You wonder aloud why other people are not as emotionally vested as you.

Welcome to the wonderful and headachy world of fund-raising for nonprofit organizations. Fund-raising is marketing at it grandest. It's probably the most frustrating kind of marketing too because there are so many variables beyond your control.

There are basically two types of fund-raisers—those that are marketing oriented and those that are out begging for money.

The fund-raiser who is not marketing oriented is sometimes stunned that the prospect doesn't share the same commitment and enthusiasm that he does. He is blissfully unaware that a particular prospect may be bombarded by over a hundred appeals per month that are blasted in every form of communications—including the home telephone.

As mentioned in other parts of this book, the savvy marketer uses every tool at his disposal to create new funds by learning and using new consumer hooks and constantly evolving his or her approach.

Plan First, Ask Later

Strategic planning of your fund-raising campaign is critical to success. With strong planning and delegation you can manage many ongoing fund-raising projects simultaneously. Seat-of-the-pants projects usually implode as the campaign or a particular program gets closer and closer to fruition.

Fund-raising is probably the most challenging kind of marketing because in many cases, the prospect is not receiving anything tangible. That's only one difference between not-for profit marketing and traditional marketing (we'll call commercial marketing, traditional marketing for the remainder of the chapter for the sake of brevity).

Key Strategic Differences Between Fund-raising and Traditional Marketing

Here are the key differences between nonprofit and traditional marketing:

- In most cases, you're not selling anything tangible. If you are selling something tangible, like candy bars, a huge chunk of the profits go to the company that manufactures your goods.
- You're usually on a skeleton budget. Fund-raisers never have enough money to do what they really want to do. It comes with the turf. Accept it.
- In most cases you are dealing with non-professionals both inside and outside the organization. It makes for a hard sell. In many cases you're dealing with a cadre of volunteers, who, despite their zeal and well-meaning enthusiasm, don't have a clue as to marketing and selling.
- There is often an element of distrust when dealing with potential prospects. People aren't always sure what you're going to do with all that money. This is a learned reaction. The media have made many potential givers skeptical about giving to new organizations. Separating the sincere from the slime can be very problematical for potential donors.
- You are usually dealing exclusively with a person's disposable income. People in their early life stages simply don't have the money to give. Elderly people are usually living on fixed incomes and are sometimes afraid to give money for something without a return.
- It's critical to build a relationship. The first gift, as small as it usually is, should simply be a stepping stone to more continuous—and larger—giving.

Key Similarities Between Fund-raising and Traditional Marketing

There are also some striking similarities between fund-raising and traditional marketing.

- Most people give with their heart rather than for a rational reason. Your pitch must be a combination of emotional and rational appeals. If you are targeting businesses, you must mix the emotional with a rational business building pitch. Businesses want to make money while helping you.
- Your prospect wants some kind of product benefit, even if it's merely a psychological reward. Just as consumers want to know that a company will stand by their product, donors want to know they are appreciated. And they sometimes want physical benefits too, in the form of trinkets or premiums.
- You are in competition with many, many organizations that are plowing the same fields as you are.
- Successful research is at the very core of your success.
- It's critical to build a relationship. I know I mentioned this in the previous list, but in fund-raising you have to develop and keep relationships—in different ways. Businesses know that the best customer is one who has bought from them repeatedly. Fund-raisers know their best donors are those that have given often.

How to Kill Your Program Before It Starts

While there are many fund-raising strategies that work, there are many practices and mind-sets that can make even the most well-intentioned fund-raising program severely dysfunctional.

Here are the top ten ways to maim a fund-raising effort. I've also included some advice for working around them.

1. *Not researching your prospects fully.* Segmentation strategies (chapter 2) are even more important in fund-raising than in traditional marketing. In order to get a donation, your prospects must be READY, WILLING and ABLE to give. You might want to hang these important words on your bulletin board, for these are the three main components of a strong prospect—and a hefty gift.

2. *Creating an attitude of "this cause is so important, we don't need to learn salesmanship or marketing."* As a marketer, you are a salesperson (there's that dirty word again). Your primary missions are to sell both to your organization and the outside world. You must imbue them with knowledge, salesmanship and enthusiasm.

3. *Relying too much on volunteers but not inspiring them.* It's the "we have a truckload of volunteers, I don't need to sell and do the down and dirty work" syndrome. You need to train these volunteers and constantly help them make their sales pitches more effective.

4. *Oversimplification of your goals.* I've been in many fund-raising meetings where the conversation was something like this. "If we can get ten donations of $10,000, we'll make $100,000." If it were that simple, you wouldn't need the money. Fund-raising is hard work. You've got to keep current givers happy and continually attract new givers.

5. *Not planning for every event and not having a core strategy.* All events should build on each other to continuously bring in funds.

6. *Not testing and retesting mailing and phone lists.* You should be continually trying to reach new people. Experimentation should be ongoing and failures looked upon as learning experiences.

7. *Inadequate funding or inefficient use of funds.* It costs money to make money. Even basic telephone solicitations and direct-mail programs can consume funds to a high degree.

8. *Inordinate use of time.* Use your time to go after donors who have the money to give. Spending hours and hours going after only one $100 donor may not be as financially profitable as spending two hours going after many smaller donors or spending weeks coddling a high-potential prospect.

9. *Not being professional or sincere.* Potential donors look for reasons NOT to give. If your materials are weak or miss the mark, prospects will be very, very wary of giving. Be professional and have a plan for everything you do.

10. *Not showing your prospects where the money is going.* Prospects want to know that their gifts are being used wisely. Create as many "before and after" success stories as you can in your verbal pitch and written materials.

What to Ask for Can be Just as Important as How You Ask for It

If you ask for too much money, your prospects will think you're being greedy and that they are being taken advantage of. On the other hand, if you ask for too little, the prospects may think your cause is not all that serious and that you really don't need their donation. They'll save their money for a cause that appears more needy. I recently worked on a fund-raising project for a local organization. The organization had developed a video tape that showed the facility looking so clean and well-funded that the prospects did not want to give because they didn't think the shelter needed their help.

Identifying and Learning about Your Target Consumer Base

The key to asking for the right amount is to know about your donor's income, lifestyle and assets. You can get a great feel of your target market by going through government census data. It's available on the Internet.

Here are some of the things you must know—at the very least.

- What are the population trends in your market area?
- What are the income trends?
- What do the various occupations in your area pay?
- What is the ethnic makeup of your market area?

Here are some other specifics point you should know about your prospects to create a donor profile.

- age
- marital status
- gender
- education
- presence and age of children

A telephone survey can help you get this data. This material can also be gleaned through a campaign of telephone "thank yous." Try this approach when you receive a donation:

"I just received your gift and I wanted to call and thank you personally. It's going to help our cause dramatically."

In the course of the call ask the donor how his or her family got involved and why they feel strongly about the cause. You'll be surprised at how much information they will give you if you ask.

Written mail surveys may also be used to get answers to specific questions. Keep your survey short and expect a response level of about 20 percent to 50 percent. The rate will increase if you offer a small incentive, say a dollar bill or an invitation to a special event.

Another way to get rough demographics is through a bit of detective work on the actual check and envelope from your donors. If the check sports a high check number, chances are the donor is older and has used the account for several years. A shaky signature might show the donor is an elderly person. The return address lines and who signs the checks may show you who in the family is actually sending you the money.

You can also get information to build you data bases at the local library. Look for such resources as Infotrac, Nexus and Lexus.

Rating Your Chances and Your Prospects

If you're planning on going after gifts personally, focus your efforts on quality prospects. Here is a donor rating sheet to make sure you're spending your money and time wisely. Each question should be rated on a 1-5 basis with 5 being strongest. Information can come from your mailing lists, donor lists, lists from organizations similar to yours, from your preliminary conversations with the prospects or cold calls.

Donor Qualifications Rating Sheet

Potential. Does the prospect seem to have strong sources for giving? ______

Propensity. Does the prospect frequently give large sums to charitable organizations? ____

Affinity and knowledge. Does the person have shared values with your organizations and its principals? _____

Does the prospect have a personal or business relationship with member of the board of directors or other ranking people? _______

Is the person a current giver?______ (add five points for yes.)

Does the person do volunteer work for your organization ?_____ (add five points for yes.)

Scoring.

25 or more: Strong potential.

15 - 25: Worth spending some time and effort in prospect cultivation.

Under 15: Spend your time elsewhere.

The Giving Life of Donors

It's important to learn the giving cycles in a typical donor's life so that you can make strong use of your time and funds. It can help you focus your fund-raising appeals more advantageously and put your census data into more of an actionable context.

People give to charities in different ways throughout their lives. The primary aspects of a person's giving propensity is the source or a person's income, his or her lifestyle priorities and how much disposable income he or she has.

Young Adulthood

Let's create a mythical couple. When our couple is 23 to about 34 year old, their disposable income is usually limited to one or two salary checks. These people are primarily small givers because disposable income is earmarked for (paradoxically) necessary living expenses and luxuries. Our couple are "Me Generation" thinkers. Charity is not a big expense because they are very self-involved. They are using their money to solving the great mysteries of adulthood and saving toward raising a family.

They live check to check and the higher salaries they will slowly earn is all accounted for in their minds. Larger sums, if acquired, are used to pay back bills, family emergencies, home improvement projects and vacations.

Our people have few accumulative assets or investments. They do, however, respond to offers of free trinkets (address labels, note cards, etc.) but will not usually become high-level donors.

Advanced Adulthood

Later in life, at about ages 35 - 45, accumulated assets are growing. Our people are comparatively well off. Their assets can be home equities, inheritances, job bonuses, stock growth, and richer paychecks. At this stage

Illustration 15.1
Giving Life of Donors

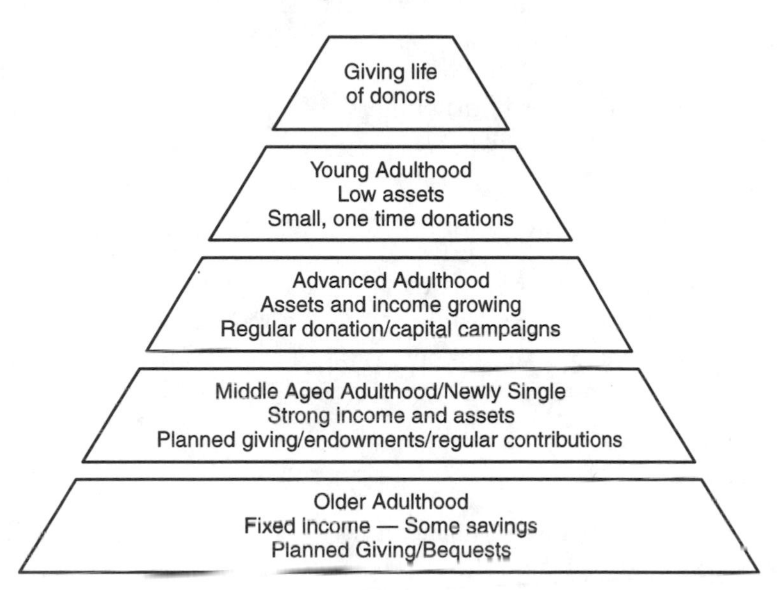

in life, they are more likely to give to capital campaigns—perhaps a reasonably large sum will go toward building a new church wing.

At this level, they have come to some decisions about which charities to support and the causes that interest them. This is a prime age group to help you "grow" a donation. Keep in mind, the same people who sent, at an earlier age, for the note cards or address labels may now be counted on for increased and more regular donations.

Middle-aged Adulthood and a New Demographic—The Newly Single

As our mythical couple ages into their late forties, they start thinking of retirement and stowing away funds. Pay checks, now at their peaks, are leveling out. The children may be in college. But there's a new dynamic working here. The baby boomers are exerting demographic force. Because of the divorce rate that is approaching 50 percent, they are as apt to be single as married. This downsizing of the household gives them more discretionary income. Add this to the fact that they have appreciated assets, these people are often ready, willing and able to make gifts from these assets.

Older Adulthood

As these people continue to age, cash flow becomes more scarce but our couple may have strong investments, insurance funds, social security and retirement incomes. They are a bit nervous about the future but may be in the position to offer endowments, planned giving programs or may even give money in their wills.

Annual Giving—The Backbone of Your Fund-raising Program

Annual giving can be defined as the giving of gifts in annual time frames. It is how most charities meet their annual expenses and necessary operating capital requirements. Annual giving provides the base for all other kinds of giving—capital campaigns, planned giving, special events, etc.

Key Numbers

Once the donor has been recruited, you have the responsibility to keep the donor's contribution coming in. Your goals will be to get your donors contributing on a regular basis and to up their donations as much as possible. You must also constantly recruit new members. Here's a breakdown on what you can expect of your new and pre-existing donors.

20 percent of your current donors will lapse next year.

80 percent of your donors will generate 20 percent of your charity's revenue

20 percent of your donors will equal 80 percent of your charity's revenue.

While the split will never be this neat, it will stay pretty close. It's easy to see that you have to keep getting new members and keep your existing donors satisfied.

The Planning or "Case Statement."

The case statement is a document that you can leave with potential donors. It's also a blueprint for your organization that can guide you to success. It has a great deal in common with mission strategies that we spoke about in Chapter 4.

Because of the huge amount of both bogus and genuine fund -raising organizations, potential donors are more skeptical than ever. They will go over your organization with a magnifying glass looking for reasons not to give. The case statement is a vital tool in earning credibility. It can be as short as three or four pages or as long as thirty or so. It should be pithy and professional, guiding your prospects through the ins and outs of your organization. Above all, it is a selling document, answering objections (as much as possible) in advance, without waiting for them to rear their ugly heads at inopportune moments. You will use it to persuade individuals and businesses of the worthiness of your effort.

The case statement should consist of:

- your mission statement
- your history and track record
- goals, strategies and objectives
- facilities and resources
- background of your key people

The case statement may be going to various types of donors so consider adapting your case statements for direct mail, corporate and local giving, sponsorships and grants.

You can also excerpt portions of the case statement for such necessities as.

- volunteer training
- staff and board training
- special events
- public relations
- The rationale for support

Here Are the Questions You Must Answer

Why is your foundation or organization so compelling that it must ask for gifts? What makes you special? What makes you unique? Why should someone give you money and leave out other groups?

- Your mission statement strategy—your reason for asking for money. It helps you to make decisions and take actions that are consistent with solving your task. It also helps you communicate the charity's role to the public.

- Your marketing plan. How will you go about raising funds? How much money do you really need and why do you need it?
- Your management. Who are the key people running your organization? What are their qualifications?
- Societal needs. How is your charity or foundation going to make life a little better for someone?
- Common Values. How does your organization relate to potential donors? What are the prime similarities that hold your people together?
- Sense of achievable goals. People want to know where their money is going to do the most good. What are your works in progress. What have you already achieved? People want to know that their donation is achieving something. If you are raising money for a new church or synagogue, what do the blueprints and proposed renderings look like? Who are the affected people and what are your parameters for working with them?
- Future goals. What is your future and what are the building blocks or milestones you need to achieve?

An Abbreviated Example of a Case Statement

The following mythical case summary is extremely brief, but it shows how the key components work together:

The Case for the Sanderson Speech Therapy Center

The mission of the Sanderson Speech Therapy Center is to provide a learning environment in which speech handicapped adults acquire the ability to speak so that they can interact with others to achieve more for themselves, their families and for the community.

For the last fifteen years, the Sanderson Speech Therapy Center has provided the support and training to empower speech impaired adults to get jobs, live normal lives and to achieve successfully in both business and social environments. Some of our graduates have even gone as far as to found successful companies and many have risen to become elected officials.

The Sanderson Speech Therapy Center has assembled an expert staff trained to develop specific communication skills tailored to our clients' needs. We have also developed state-of-the-art computerized therapeutic equipment which we have shared with schools and institutes throughout the country.

Our Center, with your help, will keep providing speech impaired people the training and support that is available no where else in the country. No individual is excluded and while many pay modest fees, we need ongoing help to meet our operating expenses and to develop new, breakthrough speech apparatus.

Our Board of Directors includes Dr. Simon Thorenson who has written the defining books on the subject and who is known world wide for his innovations in speech therapy. His biography and qualifications are included in this report.

A Five-action Strategy for Achieving Larger Scale Donations Through Personal Contact.

Successful fund-raising requires a combination of relationship building skills, strong selling materials and the ferreting out of opportunities through a list of strong donor prospects.

The strongest prospects are those that have given to similar organizations. Most donations (the larger ones) are the product of a five-action program. They usually require face to face, personal cultivation and solicitation. Larger donations are the product of a progressive hand-holding relationship.

Action One—The Prelims

Make your own pledge commitment first. This doesn't necessarily mean a monetary investment but it can be in terms of time spent, people contacted and research generated. In fact, all volunteers or paid fund-raisers must pledge time or effort. They should be constantly monitored to make sure they are attaining their goals. If a commitment is not given, than you can be sure that they volunteer is not going to generate donations. One strong volunteer who commits to a goal will achieve more than five "casual volunteers" who would like to help out but don't really have the time.

Action Two—Learn Everything About Your Organization You Can

Familiarize yourself, your salespeople and your prospects with all the details of your organization. Create rich before and after case histories. These details and case histories bring interest to the organization and vividly show its worth. This information can be manifested in printed material, slide, tape or computer presentations, or a volunteer's notes.

Action Three—Give Your Prospects a Vivid Show and Tell

Schedule a meeting with each of your prospects. Give the prospect at least two possible meeting times. Try to avoid lunch or dinner dates. It tends to obscure the immediacy of your need and prospect might think that your organization is too extravagant. No matter how you plan your meetings, be ready to deal with reluctance. Go over your sales points, calmly and businesslike.

Action Four—The Decisive Follow-up

Entertaining is over. Now is the time for the gift or pledge commitment. Build rapport with the prospect. Recap your story. Ask for a SPECIFIC gift. Invite and assuage objections. The bad news here is that you might get too many objections. These fall under the range of:

"I need some time to think it over."

"Everyone is hitting me up for money."

"Do you have a pledge card you can leave with me?"

Action Five—The More Decisive Follow-up

Don't leave things dangling. Follow up with each prospect at a predetermined time to allay their fears, keep the relationship going and (hopefully) collect a check.

Another Sales Strategy

Volunteers and hired personnel are much more comfortable in making pitches via telephone or personally if they know what to say. Add a cup of motivation and you will have a sales achiever. Here's a more formal and detailed 10-step approach put together together by William Doyle, a noted fund-raiser and fund-raising trainer.

1. *Prepare for the meeting. Familiarize yourself with the case statement and materials.* Make sure you are sincerely committed. Insincerity can kill a presentation in a nanosecond. Also bone up on special donor programs like lifetime memberships, special privileges for reaching donor levels and recognition dinners, etc.

2. *Know as much as you can about your prospects.* Just like in traditional marketing, information about your customer is vital. Try to develop concrete information about a prospect's giving history, complaints about your particular organization and any previous association with the organizations' participants or directors.

3. *When you set up appointments, DO NOT discuss the gift over the phone.* The goal of the phone call is to set up a face to face meeting. It is greatly more effective in getting large donations than just a phone call.

4. *The visit. Go easy on the small talk unless you're really good at it.* Your prospects will know why you're there and appreciate your keeping the visit as short as possible.

5. *Share your reason for being there.* Tell about your recent programs and successes, the organization's role in the community, why they should get involved and how the gift can benefit both the prospect and the prospect's business (if it's a business call).

6. *Ask for the gift.* There are basically two situations you may encounter. In the first case, the prospect may be a previous donor. In this case, say something like this.

"For this case we hope you will consider a gift in the $_____ range."

If this is a new prospect you might say:

"Ms. Johnson, many companies similar to yours are being asked to consider a gift in the range of $_____. We would, of course, be happy to have your support at whatever level you are comfortable with."

7. *Shut up. Handle objections. Listen.* How you handle objections is important to current and future sales. Rephrase the objection to make sure you understand it. Don't argue, ever.

For instance:

Prospect: "We gave last year, but I don't think we can afford it this year."

You: "Yes, you were very generous and I can understand that the business climate makes it hard to give again. But can you afford to give a gift at the $____ level. We've appreciated all the things you've helped us do in the past and we want to continue to support the community."

8. *If they still won't nibble, set up a time for a callback. Be persistent with your calls.*

9. *Write a thank you note.* Send a short personal note thanking the prospect for the gift or the time.

10. *Stay in touch.* Keep sending written notes and updating the prospect on the charity's works and successes.

The Phonathon Strategy

The phonathon is a tried and true method for raising funds. A well-orchestrated program saves you time and money. It's productive, easily trackable and can be run by a group of volunteers. A well-planned program can help upgrade donors and finely target your efforts. A disadvantage is that every fund-raiser seems to using the telephone as a major marketing tool and respondents are getting very resentful.

Phonathons are also consistently good in getting donors to increase the size of their gifts. Another plus is the ability to learn what it is about your charity that causes donor to support it.

To make your phonathon work at it's optimum, you should try to integrate it with all of your fund-raising tasks, including direct mail, and special event planning.

All effective phone programs start with a planning meeting and going over goals and objectives. Goals should be realistic and attainable. Goals can be as finite as determining the money needed to buy a new ambulance or they can be more general, for instance collecting enough money to fund operating expenses.

In the first planning meeting you should determine your calling strategy, the amount of call hours that will be needed to reach your financial goals and dates. A key decision you will have to make is whether to use volunteers, hired help or a combination of the two. Volunteer help is, of course, free but often volunteers can't commit the time and wherewithal you may need to plan and achieve your goals. When you pay for help, you get more control and can demand more from the people who man the phones. On the other hand, paid solicitors can cost a great deal and they may not have the emotional commitment you need.

Train Your People Well

Whether you are going with volunteers or hires, training and managing them correctly is critical to success. A script should be developed and care taken to insure that the callers know the ins and out of the organization. They must know how to respond to questions and objections. Make sure that callers believe in and are enthusiastic about the cause. Incentives can be developed in the form of bonuses, salary increases for achieving certain levels and premiums like tee shirts or jackets.

An important part of the instruction is the use of role-playing and fake calls from previously successful telephone fund-raisers.

Hints for Calling Success

Whether you are doing the calling or managing the call center, here are some helpful hints on getting more from your call strategy.

- Keep a happy tone.
- Be enthusiastic. It really is contagious.
- Be prepared. Have all the information at your fingertips.
- Use your own style—within reasonable bounds of course.
- Ask a person for a specific amount whenever possible.
- Have morning and afternoon advisory sessions where callers can share the day's experiences, and tell how they got around various objections.

- Handwrite thank you notes to givers and maybes. You can save energy and time by having another person mail the pledge form, stuff envelopes, etc.
- Keep refreshments available.
- Don't forget the follow-ups. Send notes and pledge reminders to tardy givers on a regular, predetermined basis. Research shows much better results when a reminder system is in place.

A Successful Telephone Script and Responses

"Hello . . . may I speak with Jeremy David. This is Nancy Baker. I'm with a group of volunteers calling on behalf of the Seaside Animal Shelter. We greatly appreciated your support last year. This year's funds will be used purchase a new kennel. We've saved so many dogs last year that we need the kennel to house more pets and save them from being destroyed. We'd like to ask you to help out again this year with a gift of ?? (Up the amount from the previous year.) Can you help us with ??"

If the prospect says yes, thank the donor. "We'll mail you a pledge card and return envelope. Is this the correct address? You can also charge it to any major credit card."

If the prospect is undecided, say, "I will send you a pledge card and return envelope to use if you decide to make a pledge."

If the prospect says no, say, "We will miss your support but we understand your situation completely. Thank you again for your support."

Direct Mail

You call it direct mail. The people who get it call it junk mail. However you phrase it, direct mail is the targeting and mailing of fund-raising letters and material to people who are most likely to respond with contributions. After the phonathon, it's probably the most frequent kind of fund-raising program.

It can be expensive and tricky. That's why many large fund-raising organizations go to outside advertising agencies for their expertise.

Here are the main components of a direct mail fund-raising program.

The mailing list. You can purchase it, rent it or create it yourself. The best mailing list is one you have built over time consisting of prior donors and regular donors. The next best list is of people who have donated to groups like yours or who have an affinity to causes like yours. You can also test lists of those who might share the same belief systems that you do. Sources of lists are other fund-raising organizations or mailing list brokers. A good broker can help you plan your entire direct mail attack. Here's my favorite mailing. It's not slick, but it works!

Direct-mail Fund-raising Campaign

It starts with a teaser envelope . . .

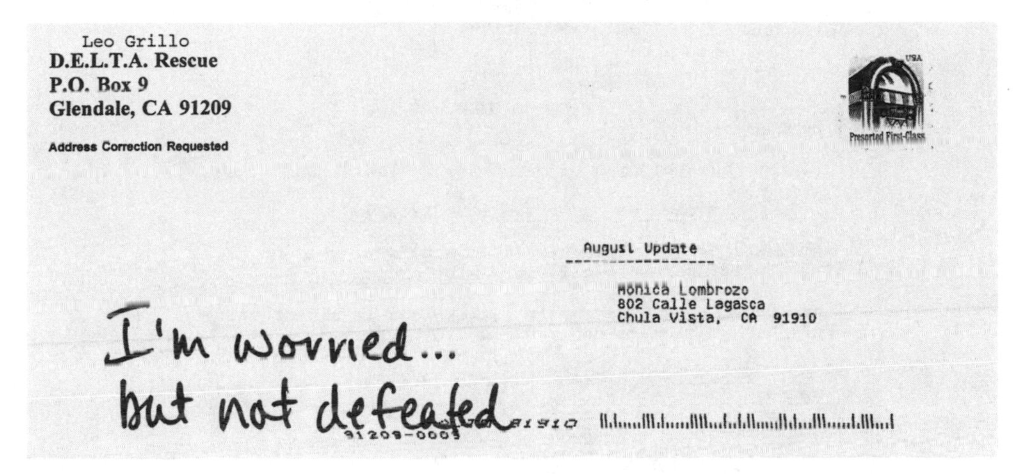

The return card

Attention: Leo Grillo

Thank You

D.E.L.T.A. Rescue
P.O. Box 9
Glendale, CA 91209

for animal rescue . . .

A super sales letter with all the right notes, including "faux" handwriting

Help!

we are out of catteries,
our dog yards are allocated,
and our hospital is overflowing —

June, 1997

Dear Partner,

I have two colonies of cats, now in isolation . . .

. . . that need to be housed immediately.

And with over 1,000 cats and dogs to oversee, our two hospital buildings are overflowing with patients!

At our 94-acre Supershelter, flat land is almost used up. We can put just a few more dog yards on it . . .

. . . but we can't build another hospital, or the catteries that we need desperately. And in a few months, we will be out of room for newly abandoned dogs.

Our situation looks bleak.

Over the past few months, I have been agonizing over what to do. Then I remembered something that I planned on 11 years ago, should this situation ever arise . . .

. . . to buy the Lewis property next door!

It's the last piece of private land in our valley. On it's flat 21-acres, there is a 3,000 square foot house that can be turned immediately into enough shelter for six colonies of cats!

But there is only one problem . . . Mr. Lewis wouldn't sell this prime land at any price . . .

. . . until now!

You see, the retired Mr. Lewis just bought another, smaller home for himself and his wife. Now he is selling his land.

But before it goes on the general market and is lost to us forever, he offered it to us at a very fair price . . . and I said we would take it!

over →

Paragraphs should be short, sentences to the point

By the time you get this letter, we will be in escrow on this land . . . without the money to buy it! We will have to raise the cash price of over $300,000 within a month!

So what does this mean to the animals?

Getting this 21-acres and the huge house on it means:

- *Our two stranded colonies of cats will have a home, along with four new colonies not yet rescued.*
- *Over 300 more dogs can be housed by developing the flat land area of this parcel.*
- *We can build a new, third hospital building to care for the sick, injured and geriatric animals that we have.*

Will you give $150 to help us buy 500 square feet of the Lewis ranch?

By breaking the 21 acres into small, affordable pieces, **Deed Shares**, your special gift . . . added to the others . . . will make our dream come true! Deed Shares *begin* at 500 square feet.

If everyone gives $150 extra this month, for this emergency purchase, we can do it! We can expand our shelter, convert the Lewis house into six giant catteries, build yards for 300 more dogs, and eventually build another hospital for injured and sick animals.

And to thank you for this special gift, we will send you a personalized **Certificate of Appreciation** to display . . . and we will inscribe your name . . . or your pet's name . . . in our **Golden Book Memorial** which will be on permanent display at our shelter.

Please fill out the enclosed reply coupon with your regular support gift, and then fill out the Deed Share, tear them both off and mail them today!

For the animals,

Leo

Leo Grillo, founder

PS: Our animals need your help every month. So first, please send your regular gift to support our 1,000 abandoned animals. Then, second, please give at least one **Deed Share** to honor a loved one and to save countless animals for years to come.

Questions and answers cover points not addressed in the letter

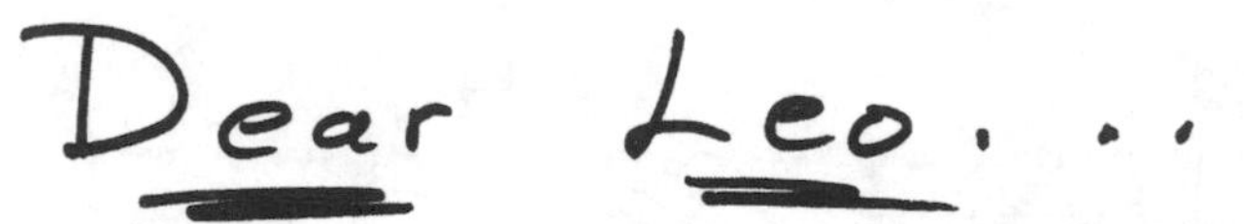

Why do you solicit each month? Why not have a membership to D.E.L.T.A. Rescue that could be billed once a year?
RE, Annville, PA

I rescue animals constantly . . . and I need to feed them, medicate them and care for them . . . constantly. Our bills come in monthly and that's why we need your support monthly.

Memberships do not raise spendable money . . . they break-even with mailing costs so that the host organization can then ask their "members" for donations during the year. When you find out that all the money raised in "membership drives" was to pay the cost of the drive, and no money went to the animals, you can't get upset! *Memberships are for the people, donations are for the animals.*

Memberships also allow some organizations to report the cost of fund raising for memberships as "membership costs." This allows them to list "fund raising" as a lower amount on their IRS reports. One large humane organization -- without any animals at all -- reported a fund raising cost of 3% recently! With cost of membership drives it is really way over 60%!
****

I love what you do for these beautiful animals, but how do you get detailed past life information before they reach D.E.L.T.A. Rescue?
SK, Hamburg, MI

It's sometimes very easy to piece together from having done this for 18 years. Clues, evidence, condition of the animal. Sometimes campers tell me what they know and I put it together. For some angels, animal communicators pick up images from them and can see what they've been through before I rescued them. This month, with poor Shiner, it was pretty easy to figure out.
****

My 8-year-old cat licks the hair off her back legs and tummy. Three vets have given her steroids with little improvement. Another tried holistic remedy and nothing has helped. Do you have any ideas?
KH, Denver

I've been through it for years and I finally found a cure for my problem - maybe it will help your cat: Many times my cats have caught mice that ran the gauntlet through our cattery! When I see that they are still alive, I rescue the mice from the cats. Sometimes the mice need medication, fluids, etc. (Really!)

When they are well, I release them in a new area and they are back to nature as was intended for them. When I have to keep

over

the mice for a few days or more, I put them in a reptile cage with a screen on top. This looks like a glass fish tank. I line the bottom of the cage with white paper towels and give the mice things to chew on and nest in.

One such treatment didn't work and the mouse died after two weeks. When I went to clean his cage, I noticed tiny dirt particles on the white paper. Under a microscope, they were live mites! And they were everywhere the mouse had been.

At this time, my cats had the same symptoms as your cat. Nothing worked until I figured out that the problem was mites! I dusted my cats with flea powder and the problem went away.

Now I spray them lightly, rubbing their tummy and legs (they sit on mites in mouse areas), and then I spray the ground and floor under the cats. Since then a number of vets have offered this diagnosis with great results. Try it and let me know.
****

I have a 9-year-old shepherd mix that has partial paralysis of her back leg/hip. Specialists say there is nothing to do for her. Can you recommend literature or experts so I can further my knowledge?

RT, San Diego

If you are on computer and online, there are vet boards and chat rooms run by vets. Mainly, make her comfortable. Ask your vet about SOD, Cosequin, etc. If she eventually needs it, K-9 Cart company can build a rear-wheels scooter for her. Call me (805-269-0410) for their number if you need it.
****

We're so close!

So far we've raised half of the money for the Lewis 21-acre ranch property, next to our Supershelter, which will contain seven new catteries for seven colonies of rescued cats . . . plus 15 more acres of dog yards!

But we're still a long way off. If you haven't donated yet, please consider filling out the **Deed Share** that I mailed to you last month and send it in with your gift today. Remember, when you send your **Deed Share**, please fill in the name of the person you would like to be remembered by this gift. Mine is made out to "All the Grillo Animals" of which there are dozens.

If you've already sent a Deed Share, why not send another to memorialize another pet! The soul that you honor will be named in the ***Golden Book Memorial*** which will be on display at the shelter for years to come. Please help this dream come true for the animals. Send an extra gift for this new shelter land today.

Thanks, Bob

Another strong letter

Shiner was dumped
for not fighting.
then he was attacked
anyway...

July, 1997

Dear Partner,

I heard about a guy from Mexico who sometimes shows up at one of our feeding areas and turns his fighting pit bull on the dogs there.

This guy brags that he regularly wins money . . .

. . . $100 . . .

. . . by fighting his pit bull in the alleys near Paxton St. and Glenoaks Blvd. in Los Angeles!

His tortured dog is reportedly a mess . . . covered in painfully infected wounds herself. But she kills the other dogs because that's what she is forced to do.

Animal Regulation in Los Angeles has been contacted about this many times, but has yet to do anything to stop it.

These streets are dangerous, and gang-ridden. Only undercover humane officers could catch the suspects in action.

If I ever see this guy turning his dog loose in our feeding area, I will arrest him myself . . . a citizen's arrest. I've done that before. Meanwhile, poor Shiner may be the first proof we have that this guy is really out there.

When I first saw Shiner, he wasn't moving. He was holding his swollen, infected eyelid on the ground to ease the intense pain.

Quickly, I set up a trap and baited it with meat and dog food.

Shiner headed toward it at first, but with his high fever and aching head, he wasn't hungry and wouldn't go into the trap. For the next two hours, I followed Shiner through the field, coaxing him to a spot where I could move in and rescue him with a

over →

come-along.

Twice, when I got within ten feet of him, he whimpered . . .

. . . worried that I was going to hurt him some more. I could see that his left eye was huge and swollen shut . . . teeth had punctured his lids above and below.

There was a colored discharge coming from the wound and I thought his eye had been bitten through.

His body was full of holes too. Shiner had been suffering for days before I found him . . . at a feeding station you help support.

My heart ached for him, and all that he'd been through. I just had to get him some help. But he was too afraid to let me.

Finally, through a lot of maneuvering, I got lucky. Shiner ran into a Park's Department service yard and I closed the gates behind him.

As I moved in on him, he froze . . . and whimpered . . . hoping I wasn't going to hurt him some more.

Slowly I put my rope around him, and one foot at a time, I pulled Shiner forward, into my waiting truck. When he was safely inside, I talked to him, calming him down . . . I was elated when he half-wagged his tail at me!

And close up, now, I could see that under that swollen mess, his eye was okay . . .

. . . I knew he needed lots of treatment at our hospital, but that he would recover from all his wounds . . . thanks to the help of people like you!

Shiner is one of the lucky ones, because you were there for him. Please continue your good work . . . send your best gift to rescue, care for . . . and love these little angels, today.

For the animals,

Leo

Leo Grillo, founder

PS: Shiner has had a rough life . . . he's a lover, not a fighter. When he was abandoned in the wilderness, another pit bull was sent to attack him. He nearly lost his eye, and his life. But thanks to people like you, Shiner is safe now. Please keep up the miracles. Send your finest love-gift now.

D.E.L.T.A. Rescue • PO Box 9 • Glendale, CA 91209

Another compelling letter, complete with specific success story

They come from far away to help us, we cannot forsake them.

February, 1997

Dear Partner,

Seashell's mother was abandoned months ago at a primitive campground by the ocean . . .

. . . where she learned to hide in the brush, staying away from people because they were mean to her . . .

. . . throwing rocks and bottles at her when she came out, looking for some scraps to eat. She must have felt really abandoned by a world she was sent to help.

She did her best, giving to the world with all her heart, and this was her reward . . . being dumped, left to die alone in a cold, wet place.

Meanwhile, Seashell was born, in that wet brush.

This little guy lived off his mother's milk until that ran out. Then she taught him to catch bugs. But that wasn't enough nourishment for his body to grow on.

Soon she brought him scraps of food that she found in the camp's garbage dumpster.

It was not nutritious, but it filled the painful hole in his belly. Still, Seashell was not growing the way a kitten should.

When I found his mom, I suspected that there might be a family of kittens somewhere . . .

. . . so I carefully followed her to her den.

I heard Seashell meowing from inside the thick bush before I saw him. I set a trap baited with really fine cat food and it was just a few minutes before this hungry angel dove into the trap and devoured the food.

It was almost too easy . . . as if I was meant to be

over→

there at that exact moment in Seashell's life.

When I put a towel over the trap to calm Seashell down, Mom ran out from under the bushes and disappeared around the bend. When she didn't come back hours later, I knew I had to get Seashell to our shelter for treatment of parasites.

Seashell hid in the corner of his cage during the long trip to our shelter, hissing at me when I peaked in at him. He was afraid . . .

. . . and he missed his mom.

Mom never returned to the site . . . either she was afraid of being caught herself, or something happened to her.

But I will keep looking for her . . .

. . . she may even have more kittens somewhere who need our help.

For now, her little Seashell is safe and growing like a weed with all the good food he's getting.

When I took his picture for you, I noticed that Seashell is quite tame now . . .

. . . all the love he's received from our staff has reassured him.

Someday he will be a gloriously large fluffy cat, happily spreading his joy to all who come near. All because you cared enough to be part of this mission.

But I have to find his mom now . . . and tell her that people like you really care that she lives and completes her mission. This is our mission.

For the animals,

Leo

Leo Grillo, founder

PS: Giving your love to these animal angels is signified on this plane by the amount of the gift that you send in for their support. Please be generous today and enclose your best gift in the envelope provided.

D.E.L.T.A. Rescue • PO Box 9 • Glendale, CA 91209

A strong return card asks for a specific amount

❑ ***Yes, Leo!*** I will continue to help you rescue abandoned pets like our little Seashell. Here's my monthly gift of ...

❑ $20 ❑ $15 ❑ $25 ❑ $30 ❑ $50 ❑ $______

❑ to rescue abandoned pets, like Seashell, in the wilderness.
❑ to spay/neuter and medically treat these suffering animals.
❑ to care for them daily at our beautiful "no-kill" mountain-top sanctuary.
❑ to expand our shelter to help even more helpless abandoned animals.

This gift is in memory of my dear ______________________

Please make your check payable to: D.E.L.T.A. Rescue, PO Box 9, Glendale, CA 91209

❑ Master Card ❑ Visa ❑ Am Express ❑ Discover Expires: ____________

□□□□ □□□□ □□□□ □□□□ ______________________
Signature

Name ______________
Address ______________
City, State ______________
Zip ______________

How D.E.L.T.A. created tangible deed shares

DEED SHARE
ONE HUNDRED FIFTY DOLLARS
$150
GIFT ENCLOSED FOR
500 SQUARE FEET OF LAND
GIVEN IN THE NAME OF
Please print name to be inscribed

DEED SHARE
THREE HUNDRED DOLLARS
$300
GIFT ENCLOSED FOR
1,000 SQUARE FEET OF LAND
GIVEN IN THE NAME OF
Please print name to be inscribed

DEED SHARE
SIX HUNDRED DOLLARS
$600
GIFT ENCLOSED FOR
2,000 SQUARE FEET OF LAND
GIVEN IN THE NAME OF
Please print name to be inscribed

DEED SHARE
ONE THOUSAND TWO HUNDRED DOLLARS
$1,200
GIFT ENCLOSED FOR
4,000 SQUARE FEET OF LAND
GIVEN IN THE NAME OF
Please print name to be inscribed

DEED SHARE
SIX THOUSAND SIX HUNDRED DOLLARS
$6,600
GIFT ENCLOSED FOR
1/2 ACRE OF LAND
GIVEN IN THE NAME OF
Please print name to be inscribed

DEED SHARE
OTHER
HERE IS MY GIFT OF $__________ FOR
__________ SQUARE FEET OF LAND
__________ ACRES OF LAND
GIVEN IN THE NAME OF
Please print name to be inscribed

Your Package

This includes the entire direct mail program and should consist of:

- a "personal" letter
- a promotional brochure, or perhaps a newsletter
- a response mechanism, typically a small reply card
- the return envelope
- optionally, a small gift or incentive. Address labels, calendars, note cards and key rings have been popular for many years. A caveat however. There's a backlash against premium items. People are getting annoyed and perceive that it takes money away from the fund-raising organization.
- a database created from donors. Since people who have given in the past are going to be the heart of your process, you should create and continually update your database.

Prospecting for Donors and Mailing to Previous Donors

When you are prospecting for donors, you are going after people who may not know of your cause and are leery of contributing. That's why your mailing lists should always be tested for response levels.

When you target previous donors, you will get the best response. You can mail to these people up to a dozen times a year without getting them too upset and causing a backlash.

Response Rates

A correctly done direct-mail package mailed to previous donors should elicit a response rate of about 13 percent. A virgin mailing can achieve as low as 1 percent.

What Goes into a Successful Mailing?

A strong mailing consists of these components, working from the outside in:

- The outside envelope. This should always have a teaser about what's inside. Using a line like "Save this Child" with a photo of a young boy or girl with big eyes will get prospects to open the envelope. But there are people who will say they won't open the envelope if a child looks too needy. That's why it's important to continually test your mailing to learn what works best.

- The appeal letter. This is the most important part of a mailing. The letter should be sincere and moving—targeting your prospect's heart. Here are some tips to make it even stronger.
- Underline key points with a blue or red marker (a printer can show you how to do this so that it looks like it was hand-done).
- Use portions of the margin to "personally handwrite comments." These "callouts" are usually the first things read.
- Vary the size and length of sentences, line sizes and margins. They all increase readership. Reexamine the letter writing strategies in Chapter 4.
- Reiterate the strong points you are making in your promotional literature.
- Be as credible sounding as you can. Talk about how long your organization has been around, etc.

The Return Card

- Don't forget to allow for credit-card donations.
- Give the respondents the choice of specific amounts, i.e., $15.00, $25.00, $100.00.

The Premiums

As mentioned, address labels are strong these days. Using premiums for mailings usually get mainly small, one-shot donations. They work best for larger organizations that can get a large volume of smaller donors and for organizations that are building up their mailing lists to rent or sell.

The Return Envelope

Use bulk mailing imprints from the post office but tell your prospects they can save money if they use their own postage.

Other Kinds of Giving

There are many kinds of giving, far too many to list in one chapter, but here are some categories worth mentioning.

Cause Marketing

This is when a business uses advertising dollars for a particular fund-raising project. It makes them look good in the eyes of consumers and their stockholder. A typical program is a "Save a Rain Forest by buying Ben & Jerry's Rain Forest Crunch Ice Cream." In this promotion, a fraction of the purchase price goes to a specific cause. The Make-A-Wish Foundation uses a great many programs like these.

Create and pitch your own program to companies by adapting some of the cross-promotion ideas in Chapter 14. Another way cause marketing works is when a company sponsors a special event or cause, i.e., The Special Olympics.

Planned Giving

This is the act of making a financial commitment of fairly large sums of money at predetermined intervals. The prospect is usually somewhat advanced in age, well-to do and very committed to your cause. Endowments through wills are also very popular, particularly with older people.

Special Events Fund-Raising

The sky's the limit in special event fund raising. In this kind of fund-raising, you come up with occasions and events to rally people to your cause or supply some kind of service to raise money. Some examples are auctions, car washes, even rent-a bachelor promotions.

Pledge Drives with Premiums

It seems the only time I find a program I like on Public TV is when they are having a pledge drive. But it works. Their strategy is to target unique segments with programming for many tastes. The also make use of very expensive premiums—tote bags, videos, shirts and jackets. Such products are beyond the reach of many fund-raising organizations, but they can be effective for fund-raisers with a high-profile causes. You can also hit on manufacturers to get the goods free with a promise to promote the organization.

Create Opportunities to Give

Many people want to give to charity but are not always sure how. Some respond to telephone solicitations, some to mailings, some to personal visits.

Some want something of value like address labels, note cards, coupons, and even frequent flier miles. Some people will only give if their is a matching fund from businesses or other organizations.

Some want to have fun. They like to couple their contributions with dinners, auctions and theater tickets. Here are some more ideas for your fund-raising appeals.

- Give Frequent Flyer Miles. Miles can run 500 for ten dollars or less. Check the airlines for specifics.
- Put a member in jail. Here's how it works. A member (hopefully one with a sense of humor) is put in a humorous jail. The back room at your town hall can work well. The person gets "released" when he gets enough pledge money from friends for "bail." People have a good time with this one.
- Cross promote with local businesses for matching funds for a popular and well-regarded charity.
- Hold a "thon." Walkathons, swimathons, bowlathons—they all can be effective and the ideas are limited only by your imagination. People pledge money for a certain amount of miles, walked or swam, strikes bowled, etc.
- When fund-raising for capital improvements, sell bricks or even small parcels of the land that needs to be bought. Check out D.E.L.T.A.'s land sale in the illustration on page 286.
- Silent auctions always draw well. Ask businesses to donate such items as diners, hotel stays, classes, sports and theater tickets.
- Sell flowers right before Mothers Day (sometimes the best ideas are the more obvious ones).
- Sell box lunches and picnic baskets at fairs.

- Don't forget to create "Playbill's" and sell ads for free band concerts, dance recitals and the like.
- Have members of your organization bring back interesting items and tee shirts from places they've been to sell at an auctions.
- Annual dinners are a great way to create enthusiasm and cash.
- Hold a fashion show. Tie it in with a retailer's goods.
- Card decks are useful for well-known organizations or for selling premiums. They're not as effective as a well-developed direct-mail program but they allow you to target your list. Your choice of the card deck to use, like your direct-mail list, will play a critical part in your success.
- Create a joint promotion with an already-on-board business or manufacturer. They already know your cause and believe in it. Strategize ways that you can both earn money.
- Internet providers usually donate some free advertising and promotion. Try the major online providers.
- Try to get goods you need, instead of cash. For instance, office suppliers may balk at a hefty contribution, but may be able to supply some slow selling desks or bookcases. Create a pitch that makes it worthwhile for the giving organization, for instance getting rid of outdated inventory and taking a tax write-off. Timing is important for this kind of giving. Companies want to get rid of inventory when the economy downturns.
- Memorabilia, especially sports, is strong at fund-raising auctions. Link auctions with the ubiquitous charity golf tournament, basketball game, etc.

CHAPTER SIXTEEN

Strategies for Cashing in on Business Alliances

Not long ago, I went into a local supermarket to hunt up the latest batch of cross-promotions for my marketing column. No problem. Since cross-promotions are the hottest marketing strategy of this decade, I found many. But then, deciding I wanted a somewhat nutritive snack, I bought some lettuce, apples and bananas. What did I find? More cross-promotions. They were plastered right on the fruit. It seems that everyone is getting into the act. Advertising on apples? It's the wave of things to come.

Cross-Promotions

Cross-promotion, or *partnering*, as the phenomenon is called, has become a way to extend the value of marketing dollars. A cross-promotion is defined as two or more companies getting together to create sales by expanding the playing field.

By dipping into each other's markets, both companies (or three or four, if your cross-promotion plans get really ambitious) can result in higher visibility and efficiency than you might be able to achieve by going it alone. There are many reasons to cross-promote.

It can be said that Bill Gates, the head of Microsoft, is the world's greatest cross-promoter. His success has more to do with partnering than his computer programs. Gates' first foray in cross-promoting was with IBM. His group developed MS-DOS, the main operating system for IBM personal computers. The MS are the key letters. They stand for Microsoft.

This was to be a match that IBM would be sorry for. Gates never sold the operating system to IBM. Instead, he licensed it to them and every IBM computer sold meant dollars in Gates' pockets. Thus, Gates road his partner's coattails to success. IBM then tried to create its own proprietary operating system, but DOS was too firmly entrenched.

Gates' next stroke of cross-promoting genius was developing Windows, the software program used in the majority of the world's computers. The fact that it was far from ideal and looked suspiciously like the Macintosh computer screen was of little concern because Gates partnered with computer manufacturers to have Windows preinstalled. Windows became the standard mostly because of the innovative cross-promoting ideas of Bill Gates.

Cross-promoting works. By choosing the right partners, you can get your message and products into more kinds of stores. Your memorability increases because your promotions are more unique. Credibility is increased because when you partner with a respected company, its image can be transferred to your product. Microsoft achieved strong credibility because it partnered with the largest computer manufacturer in the world. Every dollar IBM spent on advertising promoted Gates' company as well.

Cross-promotions help you extend your reach. You can reach more potential buyers by partnering with companies who reach a similar demographic as you or you can partner with a company that is targeting people you are missing. Frequency of impressions increases because your promotion appears in front of both customer bases.

Follow These Requisites for Choosing a Partner

While you might be saying "cross-promotions are for me". it's wise to be very careful about the company you are considering partnering with. I'm sure that in hindsight, IBM would have reconsidered its alliance with Microsoft.

Some of the requisites you should be looking at when choosing a potential partner include:

1. *Shared vision.* Partners must respect each other's businesses.
2. *Commitment.* Partners must have equal commitment to the promotion.

3. *Brand Integrity*. When you join forces with another company you are linking reputations. Choose a company or a person that can enhance your product's value in the consumer's mind. If you have an upscale chocolate syrup, for example, don't partner with a low-budget-brand ice cream.
4. *Added value*. Your prospective partner should offer something extra, such as marketing resources you lack or access to markets you can't reach.
5. *Role delineation*. The rules and roles of both companies must be defined beforehand. Be very specific about what each of you will contribute. Consider time frames, employee involvement, product delivery times and available store space.
6. *Complementary and natural fits*. Choose a partner who seeks a similar audience as yours. Look for similar market segmentation and buying demographics. However, if your partner's product is related to yours, you can also gain a market advantage by cross-marketing to a market segment that you don't currently reach.
7. *Point-of-sale match*. Both parties should have similar merchandising objectives in terms of in-store promotions. Know the strategies before you deal.
8. *Synergy*. The cross-promotion should result in economical gains for both parties or at least offer the perception of added value to your partner. The product of the match should be more than the sum of both partners.

Building Sales Through Business Alliances

Courting a partner is a little like dating. The prospect may be a bit shy and wary of what you're offering. Start slow and progress further as you get deeper into the relationship. Hey, it's a lot like dating!

1. *When approaching your partner prospect, don't make a sales pitch*. Couch the offer as a chance to be part of an outstanding promotion. Build up the perceived value. Sell the partner the dream. That's the best way to get agreement.
2. *Target a specific market*. Choose a niche and go after a company that is currently serving that niche well.

3. *Allow adequate planning time, especially for complex pairings.* Plan at least six months in advance. Poorly planned promotions cost time and money.
4. *Create merchandising and advertising that satisfy the needs of both companies.* The stated benefit of the ads must draw on the product strengths of both parties.
5. *The promotional investment must involve both parties.* Both should share in the costs and in the creative development.
6. *Keep it simple.* Don't confuse the consumer.
7. *Take a long-term, as well as a short-term, approach.* A good partnership should ripen as it matures.
8. *Watch your distribution channels.* The promotion should create a sales advantage in the channels that both of you inhabit.
9. *Test often, test well.* If possible, choose a low-risk, limited budget promotion to test the waters. Research the possible benefits from your partnership in advance of the deal. Make sure the partnership is meaningful to consumers.
10. *After the promotion, check the results.* Decide whether you need a stronger partner or other ways to continue and improve the relationship.

Eighteen Hot Ideas for Cross-Promotions

These are some cross-promotion ideas you might consider. While we can't select every industry, use them to jumpstart your cross-promotion thinking.

1. *Create a cross-promotion scheme that adds value for your trade customers.* For example, if you've published a romantic novel, create a cross-promotion for a company like Victoria's Secret. Perhaps it could be used it as a premium for its catalog sales in return for inserting a flyer for its nightgowns in the book.

2. *If you're a retailer, cross-promote with other stores in your area.* Choose stores that cater to the same people demographically as you do. If you're a retailer who sells sportswear, place your clothes in a local sporting goods store. In turn, you would carry displays and coupons for its merchandise.

3. *Sports is always a good hook to hang your cross-promotions on.* Coca-Cola teamed up with Nascar (an auto racing association) for reciprocal promotion of their products. Coke furnishes ads for the walls of Nascar race tracks; Nascar gets free publicity in Coca-Cola promotions.

On a smaller scale, The National Fitness Center teamed up with a local tennis club to offer a fitness program for tennis players with a low-cost introductory membership. These introductory offers led to annual memberships from the tennis players who visited the Fitness Center. The tennis club was happy to offer this "perk" to its members.

Bausch & Lomb Sports Optic created a "Fan of the Game" that appeared over the large screen TVs in sports stadiums. To help pay for the cross-promotion, it partnered with MCI to finance and coproduce the extravaganza in exchange for advertising.

4. *Build channel loyalty by cross-promoting with new merchants.* Send cards to your customers introducing them to a new retail store. Offer discounts or special deals at these and other retail stores where your product is placed.

In the same vein, develop a cross-promotion with many stores that feature your product. Furnish cards that can be punched where purchases are made. When the cards are filled customers get a small prize or discount of some kind. Or you can develop stickers to be placed on a card. This ties in with the frequent buyer promotions mentioned earlier.

5. *If you offer credit cards, offer a free holiday basket of goods for shoppers who visit a particular store and use the card.* American Express offers two-for-one dinners with restaurants for their card members in selected areas.

6. *Cross-promote with other manufacturers who serve a similar niche as your products.* Banana distributors have long created promotions with cereal companies who also made deals with milk producers who made deals with strawberry growers who made deals with...well, you get the picture.

7. *When offering a cross-promotion though retailers, particularly for a discount or free sample, make sure you say "compliments of the store."* It implies that the partner has secured the savings.

8. *To make a cross-promotion more effective, give each of your partner's employees a discount or token of some kind.* Your partner will appreciate it as much as the employees. Small gifts keep everyone on board and remind the employees of the promotion.

9. *Take a tip from the airlines, especially if your product is a parity product.* In order to differentiate themselves from the competition, airlines are cross-promoting with everyone, and being very creative. United Airlines serves Starbucks Coffee and promotes it heavily. Most airlines continually cross-promote with rental car companies and hotels.

10. *Tie in supermarket cross-promotions to the holidays.* For instance, if you make hot dogs, create a promotion (or help supermarkets create a promotion) with bun manufacturers, beer brewers and the like for Memorial Day, Independence Day, and Labor Day cookouts.

11. *Piggy-back on an exciting new technology.* To reach tourists more effectively, The Tahiti Tourist Board created a cross-promotion with Kodak. It jointly produced a Tahiti Photo CD. It's a CD-ROM that shows pictures on a computer. The promotion showed off the new Kodak technology and also displayed beautiful Tahitian tourist spots. Everyone benefited.

12. *Introduce a new technology.* Roland Musical Corporation created a musical video that was attached to an *X-files* (the popular Fox sci-fi show) videotape. Both Fox and Roland created an integrated marketing thrust and a sweepstakes to publicize the video. The results were a dramatic increase in visitors to the Roland website and more than 15,000 contest entries.

13. *Computer industry cross-promotions.* America Online enters partnerships with many companies to build new revenue streams. It now has more than 10 million members and scores of business partners. It's even partnered with banks to offer its own credit cards.

14. *Save money when you partner with media.* Arden Cosmetics cross-promoted with CBS to reach their joint customer base of women.

15. *When you get creative with your cross-promotions, even the most mundane of products can be brought to new heights.* Bennetton and Motorola rolled out a designer line of pagers. The goal was to make the pager part of a total fashion statement. Motorola provided the pagers and Bennetton provided the name and design expertise. To further the promotion, the "United Colors of Benneton" logo was stamped on the pagers.

16. *Partner to offer discounts.* American Express has also partnered with Mobil to offer small businesses an 8 percent discount on gas when paid with an American Express card.

17. *Partner to court new customers or offer new services.* GTE, Sprint Cellular and the Automobile Club of America created a cross-promotion to sell Auto Club Cellular. They programed cell phones to automatically call AAA if a driver suffered a mishap. Consumers loved the safety net.

18. *Partner with service groups to create good will and sales.* Campbell's Soup Company has been partnering with schools for years. People save their labels to buy audio-visual hardware for schools.

Sports Marketing

Scenario 1: You're watching the Superbowl and the star quarterback is taking a hit of Gatorade. At the end of the game, the winning coach is drenched with Gatorade. Is the keg of Gatorade there by mistake? Does everyone on the team love Gatorade? Probably not.

Scenario 2: You're watching the NCAA basketball game on TV. Everybody is wearing the same brand of sneakers. A coincidence? Hardly.

Scenario 3: You went to the Brendan Byrne arena to watch a New Jersey Nets basketball game. But wait. The name is now the Continental Airlines Arena. Are they using the building as an airplane hanger?

Sports marketing is big. Real big. Sports marketing started back in 1935 when Gillette sponsored the broadcasting of sports events. Gillette is still a heavy spender because applied creatively, sports marketing works.

Six Benefits of Sports Marketing

1. *It can increase public awareness of your company dramatically.* That's why arena names are "rented" for fees ranging up to, and above, 1 million dollars annually.
2. *Sports can be used to link a particular lifestyle to a manufacturer's product.* For instance, Jose Cuervo has gotten extraordinary lifestyle mileage by sponsoring beach volleyball. Beach volleyball is now an Olympic sport! Its followers are young and hip. It rubs off on the Cuervo brand.
3. *Sports marketing can help you differentiate a product or service from the competition.*
4. *It can help you access new marketing opportunities.* Giveaways and free trials to spectators can help you build a targeted marketing base and

introduce a new product. Corporate sponsors and local business people have long used Minor League baseball to build interest and excitement in their businesses.

5. *There's a strong entertainment aspect—a shmooze factor—in buying sports sponsorships.* Heavy sponsors are granted use of sky boxes and hospitality booths to entertain clients. Clairol spends heavily on the U.S. Open in Flushing NY. Its current and potential trade customers line up for invitations to the event.
6. *You have a captive, highly emotional audience both at the game and on TV.* The signs surrounding a playing field get picked up by TV cameras. It is estimated that a quick exposure on TV has the effect of a 30-second TV commercial for about the 1/4 of the total cost.

Strategies for Making Sports Marketing Work Better

Sponsoring a sporting event can be extremely useful if done right. But you can take a bath, too.

Manco, a supplier of duct tape, was a sponsor of an auto race. It seemed a natural fit, since race car drivers use a lot of duct tape on their vehicles (God knows why). It was fun, but hardly worth the money. In fact, it was almost a public relations nightmare. Some of Manco's customers called to question the sports buy and asked why the prices were so high.

Tips for event sponsoring:

1. *Sponsorships should be supported by other activities such as promotion, point-of-sale and advertising.* Source Digital Systems, a seller of video-editing systems gathered 128 prospects near the Baltimore Orioles new ballpark, Camden Yards. It demonstrated its product video-editing capability with videos showing how a baseball coach could use the product to train his charges. Two months after the event, the company closed $420,000 worth of sales. Not bad for a $15,000 investment.

2. *Sponsor a variety of smaller enterprises, rather than just one mega-event.* Just choosing one or two events has been shown to have limited impact.

Frozfruit sponsors road races and smaller events to distribute coupons and give out product samples. It spends about $100,000 a year, targeting mostly smaller events which give the company greater exposure and where the sponsoring fees are lower than in "glamour events."

3. *Sponsor events that match your demographics.* A monster-truck pull will give you limited exposure to an upscale audience. A boxing match between two Hispanic fighters may give you a strong Hispanic audience of males. A title fight may bring in whites and females of a higher-income echelon.

4. *Use a sports event to soften a harsh company image.* John Hancock Insurance has invested heavily in the Boston Marathon. It finds that the program has improved its image, making it easier for its salespeople to get appointments. Now a fixture at the Marathon, it finds that sales improve greatly after each race.

5. *Reach new and greater market segments.* More than 108 million dollars were spent by eight major companies for the 1994 World Cup Soccer Tournament. For many marketers, there were two strong goals. The first goal was to reach the growing Hispanic market in the U.S. The other was to reach the 16 million kids playing youth soccer. The sponsors achieved world-wide awareness for their products.

6. *Make the locals love you.* By sponsoring an event or series of events, you can prove your loyalty to a special location where you have business.

Successful Strategies Used by Top Sports Marketers

Anheuser-Busch is one of the heaviest spenders in professional sports. Its strategy is to have the average fan identify with the brand through the company's winning sports image. Besides owning the St Louis Cardinals, the company maintains an advertising presence in other ballparks. Anheuser-Busch also cross promotes with other major spenders to stretch its sports dollars. For instance, it cross-promoted with *USA today* to distribute the ballots for the Major League Baseball All Star game. Much of the advertising and promotion plays off its sponsorships.

Nike's success is a mixture of product innovation and aggressive advertising. Like Anheuser-Busch, the company wants sports fans to identify with its products, but goes about it differently. It bonds with the personality of its sports stars, and use star athletes to demonstrate the products to attract teenage males. The company makes deals with coaches to equip an entire team with top-of-the-line shoes, effectively locking competing brands out.

Nine Rules for Choosing an Athlete/Personality

You don't just pick a star and hope for the best. You have to make sure that the athlete is going to be working for you. It's easy to get burned. Here are some requisites.

1. *The star must be legitimate.* He has to be authentic. The consumer must believe that this endorser is a truly superior player.
2. *The star must have credibility.* This is particularly important when introducing a player to distributors. Both consumers and distributors look critically at athletes. If the bond doesn't work, the program is a useless—and even negative—expense.
3. *Use your athletes for their advice.* The input that a pro gives should be taken seriously. He is the expert in his field and should give strong input on performance, comfort and durability.
4. *The level of achievement must be grandiose.* The athlete you choose should be in at least the top 10 percent of the athletes in her sport. A mediocre athlete will be perceived of as a mediocre athlete by your customers no matter how much hype you give her.
5. *Personal characteristics should be impeccable.* This person must convey a message, should speak reasonably well and offer a good appearance.
6. *Charisma.* It's hard to explain this one. Certain people, like Michael Jordon have it. Many more don't. The athlete should be a person that people aspire to be like.
7. *The personality should communicate the message you've created.* Nike sponsors such "bad boys" as Charles Barkley and Dennis Rodman. They work because the message is be yourself, be independent, or as Nike says, "Just do it."
8. *Don't use an athlete as a crutch.* Far too many companies choose athletes because "they're available." Using Michael Jordon for Sara Lee may have impressed a lot of distributors but it did nothing for the brand.
9. *Be careful.* Check out everything you can. Relationships between athletes and consumers are fragile. Mike Tyson and Magic Johnson were considered great endorsers before each had difficulties in their private lives. Before you latch onto a star, make sure the endorser can carry the weight.

McDonalds uses sports to communicate a value proposition, and spends tons of money on using sports as a vehicle to communicate an "All-American" message. Among the sports McDonalds sponsors are the NBA, NHL, World Cup Soccer and the Olympics. McDonalds waits for a potential endorser to prove herself in the marketplace. They count on the athlete's good will and public ethics to promote the company.

As a hedge against the "famous right now, forgotten in an hour" nature of athletic fortunes, Hanes uses a variety of athletes. If one bombs there is always another to take his place. Hanes' ads feature the likes of Michael Jordon, Joe Montana and Steve Largent.

Slim•Fast used sports to change the perception of its product and to obtain acceptance with males. Tommy Lasorda showed that he could lose weight by using the product and still be a man.

Put Your Product in the Movies

When *E.T.* was released to rave reviews and gigantic grosses, one company wasn't overly thrilled. That was Mars, the candy company. The company was approached by the producers to have M & Ms featured in the movie as E.T.'s favorite food. Executives voted down the move, much to the delight of Hershey's, whose Reeses Pieces quickly became E.T.'s favorite food.

Product placement is the time-honored and effective way of getting nonpaid exposure to promote products. In the early sixties, *The Hustler*, a movie starring Paul Newman, showed the gritty underworld of pool halls. Despite the fact that pool halls were shown in a grungy, low light, the pool table industry boomed.

Plugs are reaching epidemic proportions. I counted more than twenty-five product placements in the movie *Honey I Shrunk the Kids*. The movie, as they used to say in the trades, "went boffo" and the manufacturers who had products in the movie rode it to success. A master stroke of product placement occurred at the end of the movie. The miniaturized kids were found in a bowl of Cheerios.

Rayban sunglasses entered product placement nirvana when its sunglasses got a key role in the blockbuster movie, *Men in Black*.

Product placement in films or TV is an effective strategy for gaining exposure and promoting products. When shown in the film's main storyline, the products achieve higher credibility than products in ads. This placement also increases product loyalty because consumers know that the products they use are so good, they're in the movies.

Highly visible product placements like the Mercedes used in the *Dallas* TV series or the Pontiac Trans Am in *Smokey and the Bandit* are especially sought.

When a product is placed in the movies, its life can go on and on seemingly forever. While an ad flight runs and is forgotten, movies go into international distribution, video distribution and even TV distribution. And don't forget that major studios can spend fifteen million dollars or so in promoting the movie your product is in.

There are many opportunities. Each studio plays by its own set of rules. The best places to go, if you want your product to become a movie star, are specific product placement agencies. You can find them by contacting E.R.M.A., the Entertainment Resources Marketing Association. These agencies receive scripts and act as go-betweens for their clients and the film studios. You can also go straight to the studio. There is an least one executive dedicated to product placement in most of the major studios.

Mega Marketers like Anheuser-Busch, Ford and AT & T have product placement departments. AT & T had five hundred placements in 1993 while Ford had 350.

Even moviegoers don't seem to mind a product placement (even though they will object vehemently to viewing an actual commercial in a theater). People don't mind them as long as they are not "hit in the face with the product." To them, the placement of an actual product adds realism to the movie.

Some companies react very negatively to product placements. They feel a negative image can downgrade a brand or product. *The Hustler* proved that this is not necessarily true. Even a poor placement is better than no placement at all.

Effective Strategies for Product Placement

While product placements may look like free rides (most movie studios won't charge for the privilege) there are many ways to build on the effectiveness of the placement.

1. *Tie in your product placement with heavy-duty promotion.* The Reeses Pieces name was never actually shown or heard during *E.T.* It was Hershey's promotion of the placement that made it work.

2. *Play up the association of the product with the film by using banners in ads and promotional materials.* Place an interrupter on your package, such as "As seen in the Movie *Dynamo*."
3. *Cross-promote with the studios to create excitement in the movie and in your marketing mix.* Licensing opportunities also abound. But be careful. You may be committing to a bomb.
4. *Track your demographics closely.* Movies deliver a well-defined, measurable audience. A new film is a new product introduction. Even before a movie is made, producers know what kind of audience the movie should receive. The movie's demographics should tie in closely with your product's demographics.
5. *Know in advance the context in which a product will be used.* Ford, for example, makes it clear that they want no involvement in a scene with failed breaks, a dead battery or in any situation where an accident is caused by an auto defect.
6. *Opt for a no-cost product placement.* While most placements are done in strict barter arrangements, some film studios will charge a fee for a small placement that has no real bearing on a story.

Licensing

You can rent well-known brand names and use their equity to build your business. Worldwide licensing hit $110 billion dollars last year.

You can use licensing to get a quick sales bump, or you can use it to build a brand. The success comes when you can relate an image to the product. For instance, Popsicle boasts 100 percent brand-name recognition among adults and children.

Supermarkets see licensing as a mixed blessing. As a rule, they accept licensed products only if the image is in great demand. What works in apparel and toys, isn't always a success in food. When licensing works, it can make the product stand out from the pack. As brands continue to fight for attention, consumers will choose the product they know best.

Choosing your licensing properties is more critical than ever. You can't just slap a name on it and hope it will sell. The image should be thoroughly researched both on and off the product.

Franco American uses Waldo, Gargoyles and a host of other products to get children yelling "I want that Waldo Macaroni." What does licensing cost? Expect to pay 5-12 percent to the licensor over the life of the agreement. You also must factor in the costs of product design, merchandising and promotion. When you consider licensing, negotiate the longest possible contract, which gives you time to establish your product in the marketplace.

Try to place your products with similarly licensed goods in store displays and plan cross-promotions with other licensors that have the same products as you do.

CHAPTER SEVENTEEN

Private Label Strategies Pay Off for Retailers and Suppliers Alike

You can instill added value in your product through a strategic private label program. A private label means the same thing as a store brand.

Private labeling works for retailers who want to build their own brands and reap strong rewards. It's also for manufacturers who want to brand their goods with the name of the retailer. This chapter is for both manufacturers and retailers

Big Profits in Private Labels

The Europeans knew about private label prestige long before we did. In Great Britain, private label is king. Some private label products hold a 40 to 50 percent share of market. The major brands are featured as an afterthought. Here in the U.S., we're still in the infancy of private label brand development.

Using private labels allows the supplier to save money on advertising and consumer promotions. The store promotes, the supplier supplies. Both do what they do best. Developing a private label program for retailers usually means you won't gain the status of having your own brand, but the profit potential can be enormous.

Private label used to mean "cheap." But not anymore. For a long time, the business was dominated by brokers who were used to getting the product out fast and furiously. But that's not where the money is.

Private labeling was (and still is to some extent) dominated by a commodity goods outlook for even the most prestigious of products. But that's not where the real money is.

The private label marketing approach used to be to sell the most products for the least dollars, but that's not where the real money is.

The real profits lie in creating "house brands" that perform better in some way, or have a strong point of difference with national "name" brands. You can do it with imagery, creativity, and strategic deals (yes, price deals too) that ultimately lead to a strong consumer feeling.

Private labeling has reached a critical mass of power where it isn't always a necessity to develop a low price platform. In fact, charge too little for your goods and the consumer is going to think your product doesn't work and will buy your product as a low-thought compromise. In a discretionary purchase, that usually means it won't be bought again. When the price goes up, sales will come down.

Private Labeling Is a Win/Win Strategy

Everyone wins when a strong private label program is implemented.

Retailers

- Can undersell the competition
- Can create strong consumer loyalty by convincing the customers that their venue is the only place they can get a particular product
- Can control their product sources to a degree that they can't with branded products from various manufacturers
- Can add prestige to their stores with superior products
- Can take great advantage of price elasticity
- Create added value for their consumers and can create more reasons for repeat purchases

Manufacturers

- Can get more for their products at the wholesale, and sometimes the retail level
- Can supply several tiers of products structured by price allowing retail store clients to have a more flexible pricing policy

- Can be more flexible in dealing with their retail store clients because manufacturers are offering a program, rather than a product
- Have a leg up on competition because retailers feel that they're getting something extra and perceive manufacturers as cost-efficient suppliers
- Create an ongoing relationship with their retailer's customers and are no longer just selling soap

Additional Benefits of Private Label Strategies

Using private label strategies is a great way to eliminate the problem of paying high-slotting allowances because you're delivering products for your manufacturing costs (plus a little for yourself, of course) instead of paying high fees. You're producing at your actual cost, taking advantage of volume scaling but charging your standard wholesale prices.

National Brands Can Benefit with Private Labeling

Even if you're a national brand you can still build profits if your ego doesn't get in the way. By delivering private label products along with your own goods, you keep more of your facings. This actually is a great marketing tool, helping to preempt shelf space and keep smaller brands out—maybe even your competition.

Private Label Marketing vs. Retail Marketing

Private label marketing is different than standard retail marketing. It has to be, because unfortunately many consumers suffer the preconceived and unfounded notion that the basic house brand may be somehow inferior to highly advertised brands. Consumers had found that only by choosing a "second tier" product could they stock the cupboards fully, instead of leaving a pile of groceries at the checkout stand.

This negative mindset is changing rapidly. Private label products have improved greatly in quality. Now, the best of them even outperform the known brands.

The *Swing Shopper* Explores Store Brands with Gusto

A new kind of customer is the *swing shopper*. The swing shopper treats the private label product as another brand option. The swing shopper is most likely to believe that the quality and reliability of store brands are improving greatly. This is a major attitude change of a decade ago, when consumers had been burned by inferior store brands and took great pains to avoid buying them.

As consumers try these "new brands," they are getting more comfortable with choosing them over branded goods. Survey after survey has shown that once you get a consumer to try a private label product, if the product is seen as being on a par with a branded product, the consumer will purchase it again. For instance, 50 percent of ketchup is purchased with private label names.

The Supplier-Retailer Relationship

The word partner, although overused, is tremendously important whether you're a store looking at a supplier, or a supplier trying to court a store. In branded marketing, it's standard procedure for the manufacturer to provide marketing and merchandiser help in the form of advertising, promotion and slotting allowances.

Store-brand marketing requires an even greater partnership or else much private label merchandise will gather dust on the retailer's shelves. No one will know it's there.

In order to make things work, both retailers and suppliers have to get in bed together. Wholesalers and suppliers should get involved and even create store-brand promotional programs. Invest in your retailers, create tie in promotions, TV advertising, displays, and even direct-mail aids. Drive customers to the store, just like the national manufacturers do.

What Stores Want from Suppliers

The major success formula lies in developing whole programs, not just selling products. Loblaw's of Canada has gotten rich selling stores a complete creative package which includes labels, P.O.S. and advertising slicks. Adapt the strategies in this chapter (and in this book) and develop entire programs around your offerings. Cott beverages, based in CT, has had enormous success—to the tune of more than 400 million cases or so a year—with their own private label programs. Cott, like Loblaw's, offers a total marketing package to retailers, including product development, package design and retail merchandising strategies. They are suppliers of Master Choice at A & P, World Classics at Dominicks and Sam's Choice at Wal-Mart.

The Better-Package Private-Label Strategy

As I've seen it, manufacturers of store-brand products don't mind spending money on what's inside the package, but they hate to spend money on what goes on outside the package. It's a shame too, because how you spend money on the outside impacts tremendously on how the consumer perceives what's inside.

Let's talk about a product most of us know and love beyond any sense of reality—Godiva Chocolate. Liquor may be quicker but Godiva is more than dandy. I know we all know and love Godiva because after I complete a project for clients I send a box of Godiva Chocolates to them and they are enthralled. Are these chocolates any better than the myriad of products I can buy at any good department store?

Well...no. The truth is there are only a handful of manufacturers around the world that make the raw materials that chocolate companies need for finished chocolate product. But Godiva products are wrapped in expensive looking gold foil. Would I really earn points by sending them A & P chocolate bars?

So are Godiva chocolates special? Do they taste different? The answer is yes...and, yes.

Why...if they are made of the same basic material that our private label chocolates are packaged in? Because the gold foil and elegant boxes give them the magic name—Godiva. If it's packaged better, consumers perceive it also tastes better. And the upscale wrapping allows the retailers to charge 100 percent more than competing products.

You can play the same packaging tricks with your private label goods. Store brands have come past the age of plain vanilla labels. They've passed the age of "value pricing" to a more flexible pricing strategy. Stores can command higher prices if the "look and feel" of the item sways consumer perceptions, even if it is a parity product.

At Pathmark (a supermarket chain in the northeast) confection packaged in glitzy foil (without the Pathmark name) can command a higher price than a similar product packaged in typical private label clothes.

A private label product can gather the strength of a branded item when it offers the supermarket a point of difference that's clear to consumers. That's what the Orville Kent family did. They were selling a deli salad product line to stores and they made okay margins. But they came up with the inspired idea of making their product better than what the stores, and consumers, were used to. They worked closely with store to make a more elegant presentation and created a revolution at the deli counter. Orville Kent is now one of the biggest deli providers and has successfully branched out into other areas where its store brands can be looked upon as just a little better than its competitors. It can't keep up with the demand. Make your store brands a better product, not a bare-bones parity product. Instill your brands with emotion, fun and prestige. That's the way to build and keep store brand loyalty. Stake out your territory and guard it with the ardor of a newfound lover.

A Better Product Can Make an Entire Store Shine

Just like a footprint, every product and service is unique.

Smith's is a major retailer in the southwest. Time and time again I have heard consumers say that its apple pies are better than most of the major branded items. Consumers feel like they're discovering something and are genuinely excited about bring home a superior product. It builds up Smith's store equity as well as the equity of the other private label products it sells.

D'agostino's in New York and other savvy retailers around the company offer private label products that are better than similar branded products and price them at the high end of the pricing spectrum. To make this work you have to have a DEMONSTRABLY better product or imbue your product with luxury cues.

The "As-Good-as-the-Next-One" Strategy

A cornerstone of a popular private label strategy is to make your store brand on a par with the national brands in terms of active ingredients, inactive ingredients and packaging. To make this work effectively, the trade dress must be similar in terms of graphics and production values to the leading national brand. As folksinger Woody Guthrie said, "Plagiarism is endemic to all cultures." I never knew Woody was a marketing guru.

Constant testing is the rule of the day. Your product has to have the same quality appeal of the branded products, even if it costs you more (and sometimes it does) to make it.

This means working with suppliers to keep a constant vigil on what your competitors do. When the national brand zigs, you must zig. When it zags, so must you. Don't try to outdo. Mimic instead. Lean on your suppliers and make sure you make your change when the branded products do. Benadryl changed the alcohol level in its formula so suppliers of the rivate label knockoffs made the same changes (to great success, instantly).

When you do it right, private label sales of certain items can sometimes even exceed the national brands. For instance, Drug Guilds' knockoffs of Cort-Aid sells more than the name brands. The Cort-Aid clones achieve five times as much shelf space as the branded product.

The Association Strategy

Join forces with other similar stores to create a regional store brand. Valu Merchandisers was formed by Associated Wholesale Grocers. Its mission was, and is, to provide their 800 member stores with health and beauty care and general merchandise items, including a 350-product store-brand line. It uses the same name—Best Choice—that it uses in its food line. This integrated brand thrust transformed its previously helter-skelter mix of private label logos into a lean, mean selling machine. The goods are priced at a level where consumers will try the product and both retailers and suppliers will sport strong margins.

A unique part of the strategy is the triad partnership that was formed between Valu Merchandisers, its retailer customers and their various product manufacturers. Prices and costs are coordinated to supply a steady stream of mid-priced goods that consumers perceive as high-end performers. Everyone makes money—and that's what a strong private label program should do.

Promote Your Brand

Here are some hints for the retailer who is selling private-label products.

In order to make a program work fast, your promotion should be equivalent to the national brand's in packaging, quality, and promotion. But because the money is amortized over hundreds of items, the ultimate "true" cost can be very efficient. You may not have enough money to go "mano a mano" against a particular national brand, but you can make up for this with a comprehensive program for all products. You can engulf the competitor through the weight of sheer numbers.

Drug Guild, a $400 million retailer, runs at least four promotions a year, specifically for its private label merchandise. All are customized by region. It has one of the strongest private label programs in the country.

Eleven Low-Cost Promotion Strategies

Some store brands suffer image problems. They're like the famous character actors in the movies. They're always in demand but they never get the starring roles or the glamour. And they never, ever get the girl. These perks always go to the heavily publicized brand names—the stars that everyone knows about, mainly because of the interest stirred up by the flacks at the publicity mills.

Your private label products can become big stars if you get the word out.

But you don't need a huge budget to get your message across, just a bit of creativity and follow-through. Here are some ideas. They're all effective in making your consumers choose your store brands over the competing BIG NAMES. Most of these tactics can be executed in less time than you spend making up your weekly ads, and with considerably less expense. They're all guaranteed to bring good will.

1. *Display your private label at the store's entrance.* It can be incredibly simple. Try a small table at a store entrance and show the savings your customer can receive by switching to your private label products. This allows customers to compare your private products with the brand names BEFORE they make their purchase decision at the shelf. Furr's Supermarket in the southwest has a table where it does just that. One side of the table shows the brand-name product and the cost savings between the two. The other side shows the comparable Furr's product. Simple. Effective.

2. *Use your local paper to build interest.* Your local newspaper can be your best friend even before you pay your ad bill. Keep a steady stream of recipes and features about your house brands flowing to your local food editor. Local newspapers are starving for fillers on food days and are forced to use national brands' copy and artwork. Don't forget the little *Pennysaver*-type publications, too. They often carry an influence and reach that goes way beyond their small size.

3. *Sponsor a contest featuring your private label.* This neat trick will build good will as well as your brands. Why not sponsor a contest with your customers donating recipes that they have concocted with your private label's brands and then submit them to the newspapers? You can even work with your local high school's home economics classes to come up with ideas.

4. *Sponsor a Label-rama.* Campbell's has had a long-standing promotion in which consumers exchange a certain amount of labels for audiovisual equipment and computers. Allow consumers to save their store-brand labels in exchange for a contribution on your part to a school or other charitable organization. You'll be surprised to see how local media will pick up

on it. This is a variance on the "receipt saver" promotions but you can make it work for your store-brand goods. It doesn't take much time, it makes money for you and leads to immense good will.

5. *Giveaways can work wonders.* A & P has a special holiday offering where it gives out calendars, recipes and coupons—all in one easy to carry booklet. This can be economical too, because you can get preprinted formats which leave room for your specialized copy and coupons.

6. *Build a mailing list.* This is easier than it sounds. Giving away a small prize will more than pay for itself in terms of the lists you can compile from entries. Use the list to precisely target your customers in their home. Have regular mailings touting the savings consumers get from their house brands.

7. *Sponsor demonstrations of your product.* An example would be a cookware demonstration on your local-access home cable TV shows. The stations will be glad to get the material and the free goods. The selling message is that your customer doesn't have to pay expensive prices to enjoy a high-performing product.

8. *Offer samples.* This is a staple of name-brand items—offering product samples in the stores—and it can work wonders for you, too. Back it up with coupons. It vividly shows how well your private label products can stack up against the big name competitors. You can even ask consumers to compare your product with the branded items.

9. *Produce a coloring book. Feature your own store brands.* They keep the kids happy and they pay off double when the kids show their art to the bill-paying mommy or daddy. The big chain restaurants have been doing this for years and it helps to keep their family images strong.

10. *Offer premiums.* Cookware, dishes and encyclopedia premiums are not new but, to my knowledge, they've never been used strictly as a vehicle for store brands. They work the same as our Label-rama. Consumers redeem store brands for premiums.

11. *Create a character for your store brands.* Who says they should only be created by the brand names? Shoprite uses its Scrunchy bear as a mnemonic for its Teddy Graham knockoffs and sells Scrunchy Bear Teddy Bears at Christmas. Any time you inject life into your store brands, you're injecting sales and personality.

Take a Cue from the Ultimate Private Label Programs

In downtown Chicago there stands an homage to the once humble sneaker. It's called Niketown. And it attracts more visitors—purchasing customers—than the region's famous Museum of Science and Industry. Right next door is a Sony Showroom with hundreds of Sony products and hands-on displays. Both are ultimate environments for store brands.

Since successful profit development is as much about image and salesmanship as it is about actual products, upgrade your store brand's selling environment. Food actually tastes better in a well-appointed restaurant. And we all know how good warm beer and hot dogs with the texture of solidified gruel can taste within the confines of a ballpark.

Many supermarkets are actually becoming mini-malls. Supermarkets now feature flowers, huge food courts, video sections and banks. Visually, merchandise your packaged store brands with the same fervor that you're putting into branded goods departments and kiosks.

I'm not saying you should devote your whole store to private labels, especially since you're selling against name brands that bring the customer into the store. But take a cue from the Wal-Marts and Nikes of the world and try and develop mini "boutiques" for certain categories.

All it takes is some end display units that you probably have tucked away in storage, some creative signage and well-performing products.

It's going to take some effort to create your own Niketown, but building your store's image through strong private label merchandising programs developed from the ground up is a strong, strategic start.

Cross-Promotions and Private Labels

What do you get when you cross a store brand with a national brand?

A helluva promotion opportunity. It's sort of like cross-dressing, only a great deal more acceptable in mixed company.

While the managers of name brands are livid with the private label explosion, they're not going to turn down a fast buck when you show them how your private label products are going to help their products turn a large—and quick profit.

Cross-promotions and cross-brandings are currently hot with national brand manufacturers. (See Chapter 15 for more cross-promotional ideas.) Healthy Choice and Kellogg's teamed up for a new line of cereals. Ocean

Spray has teamed with just about everyone for new beverages and candies. And you can team up with the branded people to create extremely effective promotions.

After all, just because you're selling a private label product doesn't mean you can't steal the tactics of the branded manufacturers. That's what made them big to begin with, isn't it?

Cashing in on Cross-Promotions

Essentially, a cross-promotion works as follows. You pair your private label product with a branded product. When you do this, you're actually borrowing the prestige and equity of the branded product. This also means incremental sales for your branded products and savings for your shoppers. Valu Merchandisers (mentioned earlier this chapter), uses cross-promotions extensively to create marketing excitement and a synergy between its private label and branded products.

Traditionally, cross promotions have been initiated with manufacturers of branded items, but it doesn't have to work that way. For what seems like eons, cereal manufacturers have been teaming up with retail store produce departments to ally cereals with fruit.

Ideas are virtually limitless. Contact the distributors or manufacturers of branded items to come up with store-brand promotions. It's cheaper to tap the resources of the company that promotes the branded product than to use your own promotion agency who is usually too busy creating your own weekly ads.

Your ads, in fact, can serve a great purpose. Tell your branded suppliers that you'll give the extra space, or even banners in your circulars, in exchange for a cross-brand promotion. They'll probably be delighted because the money has already been allocated from their trade dollars.

Seasonal promotions are probably the greatest opportunity because they're always timely for consumers. How about a promotion teaming your store-brand ice cream with Dole Bananas or Hershey's syrup? It's a win-win situation for everyone. Or, since we're talking about ice cream, team your frozen desserts with a branded product like crushed Oreo Cookies. The promotion line can be... "it's extra crunchy because you mixed it up fresh." Since we're still talking summer, offer your ice cream with discounts on Coke or Pepsi products for a cooling ice cream soda. Liquor retailers have long been using cross-promotions with flavorings for their products.

Bacardi and Coke has been a staple promotion in liquor outlets, so manufacturers are well aware of how effectively they can work.

School openings are a great tie-in or cross-promotion opportunity. Since kids are going to be needing paper, rulers and other utilities, tie it in with a school snack or new clothes. Offer a discount on your store-brand products and cookies with each package of paper bought. For variety type stores, this will give you sales in two sections of the store. Be sure to reference your cross-promotions with signage at both ends of the promotion in your store.

Film and video department stores or departments are another potential growth area because they're closely related to each other in the consumer's mind. Try a discount on your store-brand film with three video rentals...providing they bring the film back to you for the processing. If you have one of the one-hour developing machines, you'll keep the expensive machines swamped with work.

Use your private label milk as a tie-in with cookies. It's usually done in reverse, but companies like Nabisco will probably give you some hefty allowances for your expensive inserts.

The deli department is a natural for cross-promotions. Offer a discount on your store brand cheese with each purchase name brand (such as Boars Head bologna, for instance).

What you may be noticing about these promotions is that you're building your brand while selling the name brand at the same time.

Pitch manufacturers the whole promotion, not just the deal or the slotting allowances you want. You can even do a mock up of the promotion so that the branded manufacturers can actually see how it will work. Make sure to stress the benefit—the extra sales they're going to get from your store-brand promotion—and watch the sales role in.

The Potential Is Endless

Walgreens uses store brands to build strong price/value images. Its packaging is not showy but the product packaging looks unmistakingly like low-cost knockoffs of expensive products (which they are). Customers like that.

CVS adds prestige to its product lines with high-end knockoffs of famous label cosmetics. It borrows interest from the name-brand products and offers slightly lower prices. That way customers don't feel like they're losing too much when they buy the low-cost choice.

Wal-Mart has a double-tiered offensive game going with its private labels. It offers Equate, a parity HBA product line and Sam's American Choice, which purports to be better than the private labels. The superior quality of Sam's American Choice is a great start in building an exclusive and high-profile brand equity. Are Wal-Mart's peanut butter cups better than the venerable Hershey's owned-product? Could be.

A Strategy for Building Private-Label Brand Identity

For long-term success, retailers and suppliers must think of their brands, not as labels, but as an integral part of the store that enhances the store's image in the shopper's mind. Here is a strategy that can help you introduce a new brand or change an existing one.

1. Determine the store's image among current shoppers. What does it communicate?
2. Determine the motivating power of the store. Is it its convenience, selection, price, quality or service?
3. Key in on your customer's demographics and psychographics. This might take some hard-nosed research.
4. Assess your current store's brand image. Does it reflect your store's philosophy?
5. Define what you want from your store-brand program. Should it be part of an overall umbrella strategy or positioned specifically against national brands? If the umbrella image is chosen, the brand should work equally well across categories.
6. Determine how many lines and subbrands you want. Should you use a one-brand strategy or develop a good/better/best strategy?
7. Decide how integrated you want the brand to become with the store. Should it be incorporated in image advertising and signage? How big a role do you want your store brands to play in your store's overall success?

Once these are assessed, your brand-development program can begin. It should work in all media, including such taken-for-granted media as shopping carts, uniforms, and price-off stickers and hangtags.

Look at all strategic options. While me-too approaches are still very popular, they do little to build a store's image. When sourcing or creating products, run consumer research on how the product should be made. Ongoing consumer research will ensure that the product's quality and graphics meet the original objectives and are on target.

Store brands should be promoted heavily, especially at first. Use trial programs and taste tests within the store to generate enthusiasm and excitement for the new brand.

Low-Cost Tips on Marketing Your Brand

Your displays and your store's image should enhance and be enhanced by the marketing environment you create. It should be totally integrated into your store's environment. All the parts should work synergistically with each other or they probably won't work at all. Add some glamour and sex appeal to the once-and-never-again humble private label.

Here are some category-specific ideas to create a strong selling environment for your store brands. Adapt these to fit your marketing situation.

A Breakfast Nook Gather all your breakfast-type foods, rolls, private label juices, private label cereals and oatmeals, breakfast bars and shakes under one banner. You can include coupons for your private label milk, eggs and breakfast meats. You might even have a subsection for breakfast-on-the-run. Add low-priced brewed coffee to the mix and you not only have a strong selling unit but you can create strong early morning traffic.

The (Your Store Name Goes Here) Refreshment Stand Slotting fees are nothing to sneeze at, but keep some valuable floor space for yourself especially for this coming summer. Have a second facing of your store-brand sodas in addition to your shelf facings of store-brand sodas. You have thirsty customers coming into your store. Hit them up big time. You can feature your sodas, shakes, bottled water, juice drinks and powdered mixes. Use strong signage and aisle end displays.

The Beauty Bar The displays from the large cosmetics companies are fabulous and, more importantly, they sell. Appropriate some space for your own women's cosmetics and over-the-counter drugs. Wal-Mart has done a strong job with its Equate brand of drugs. Pay special attention to graphics and banners. Give them a high-fashion look. In the cosmetics sector, women are much more lured by fashion than by prices. But the markup on these items leaves you plenty of room to create a strong selling unit.

Remember, your customers are coming in for brand names. You have to sell them on your store brands. You have about six seconds to get them to pick up your brands impulsively. But if your product is a strong performer in terms of taste and quality (which should be a given) these ideas and your own additional thoughts will make these six seconds very profitable to you. It's a great new way to separate yourself from the warehouse discounters.

Nine Strategies for Spreading Your Private Label Messages

1. Ingredients set the product apart. Use "read and compare" stickers and banner; focus on origin and presentation of ingredients. Use these on product packaging too.
2. Make your private label communications fit well with the "smart shopper" trend: "Your search for premium products without premium price tags has ended."
3. Show how your private label efforts represent leadership in understanding and responding to consumer needs.
4. Develop media information and sampling kits. Create variations on the traditional press kit, featuring product samples along with product information, all packaged to underscore the premium image. Include fact sheets on ingredients and comparisons.
5. Use the "affordable indulgence" positioning, emphasizing quality ingredients and the low-price point combo.
6. Capitalize on nineties trends toward "responsible consumerism" where quality rather than brand loyalty motivates purchases, and focus on ingredient-driven product development.
7. Use lifestyle PR placements. Hit "what's hot" columns in consumer magazines. Reinforce the gourmet image of the product line. Use the "responsible consumerism" position to highlight comparable-or-better quality product characteristics.
8. Radio personality sampling programs are wonderful. Deliver product to the stations in a memorable way. Provide scripts for DJs. Target drive-time and peak programming periods.

9. Create a brand attitude survey. Results have hard news value, providing a solid hook for news stories. Sample consumer attitudes regarding brands and purchase decisions. This underscores the logic of premium private label products as a response to consumer trends, and demonstrates that the retailer is staying in touch with consumer behavior and needs.

CHAPTER EIGHTEEN

Exciting Marketing Strategies for Retail Businesses

Retail marketing is, perhaps, the most exciting, dynamic business of all because it puts you in direct contact with your buyer. More than just sales, retail allows you to exercise your individual personality and creativity and to closely interrelate with your customer. It is more an art than a science.

There's no right or wrong way to market your product when it comes to retail. But there are many ways that you can bring your personality, as well as your individual sense of fun and excitement, to the marketplace. And, in return, the marketplace will reward you well.

If you can remember this, your retail business is guaranteed to achieve outstanding growth and profits.

In the past, the trend was to convey a somewhat pompous image in the marketplace. The image that companies worked to achieve was typically one that said, "Look at how big and successful I am." It got so bad there for a while, that you couldn't tell who was who. The dress for success formulas had everyone in business suits and spewing out scripted sales pitches. And, no matter where you went you could count on everyone dressed in some sort of uniform. Well, that worked then. But, hey, the market is changing.

We're learning that people buy people. They buy fun and excitement. They want real. Buyers want to do business with people who understand them.

Today's woman will not buy a cereal that is marketed as the "breakfast of Champions" nearly as readily as she will buy one that promises to give her the stamina to get through a grueling day at the office and an evening wrestling with hyperactive kids while playing catch-up with household chores. She buys foods that are nutritionally balanced and easy to prepare. All things being equal, men much prefer shopping for a sporty Jaguar or a four-wheel Blazer that will take them out into the wide-open spaces to shopping for a four-door coup that will take them back and forth to work. And kids, well, we all know that they will spend their money and time on a computer game or the latest fad—no matter how expensive—because "it's fun" and because "all the kids are doing it."

Selling to People

The key to successfully selling to people is to understand them, pure and simple. Find out what they want and give it to them. It's really not that difficult.

Here's how:

1. Be yourself. Stop and think about what's important in your life. Recognize that your interests are very much the same as the interests of your potential customers.
2. Be yourself. (This is one idea I can't emphasize enough.) Be natural. Be real. Nothing will stop potential customers from buying faster than mixed messages. If you're dressed in a three-piece suit selling mechanical tools, they are going to find it difficult to believe that you understand the challenges they face working under the hood of their cars.
3. Remember that people like to do business with those who are very much like themselves. They respond best when they can see that you understand them...that you speak their language...that you and they have things in common.
4. Take the time to become intimate with your potential market. No, I'm serious. You can't know your customer too well. You do need to know what they eat for breakfast and what they do with their free time and what turns them on.
5. Put some energy into finding ways to make it fun for people to do business with you. It's a well-known fact (but all too frequently forgotten) that people spend more money when they're having fun.

Establish an Evolving Retail Marketing Strategy

Marketing does not happen by accident. The well-planned retail marketing strategy clearly defines who you and your business are, what you have to offer your market, who you are competing with, who your customers are, and how you go about satisfying the needs of your customers.

It's good to have a marketing plan (we all learned this in Business 101), but no one ever told us that this is supposed to be an ever-growing and evolving document. It's just as important to be responsive to the needs of your customers. It doesn't hurt to deviate from that plan when it will stimulate or fill a need of your customer.

While a formal marketing plan helps crystallize your retail marketing strategy and provides a road map for your sales activities, the real trick to the success of this document is to make sure that it is never finished. Keep revising and adding to it.

If you do, your retail marketing plan will become a tool that will help you to identify what makes you and your products different. It will clarify who is your ideal market and why the market should want to do business with you. It will become your best guide for being THE company that people will think of first when it comes time to spending their hard-earned money.

How One Company Made a Name for Itself

Gateway 2000, a world-class computer manufacturer with roots in Sioux City, Iowa and strong values based on common sense, respect, caring and fun, understood that. When it entered the marketplace, Gateway might have chosen to be like those companies who were already out there selling computers. Its employees might have dressed in business suits and built offices that followed the model already established by companies like IBM: the same business attire, same distribution channels, same formal business procedures and sales tactics. After all, IBM had clearly identified its market as corporations and governmental agencies and had found a successful formula for marketing in those arenas.

No doubt, Gateway's founders explored all those options. But they didn't stop there. They recognized that they were up against some pretty tough competition. And, they were unwilling to follow the crowd. Using some common sense, they developed a comprehensive marketing plan that clearly identified their unique personality and place in the marketplace.

Rather than copying their successful competitors, they chose to capitalize on their own best qualities. Gateway 2000 chose a Holstein cow and humorous advertisements to tell the world that it stood for the down-home Midwestern sense of values, integrity and fun. It chose direct mail for its retail channel and are beginning to open "country stores" to market its computers. Every element of the plan was developed to emphasize Gateway's uniqueness.

Gateway sells custom computers with a vengeance and proudly ships them in black-and-white-spotted cartons. Why? Not because its more technically astute than the competition.

Gateway understood people wanted to enjoy all the games and fun that computers offer, but didn't want to be "wowed" by technical jargon. It saw people that wanted affordable and dependable computers for work, and a supplier that was willing to give them a product and technical support that they could rely on. They saw people who wanted to be treated with respect in spite of the fact that they didn't have the technical savvy and the megabucks of larger corporations.

IBM carved out its niche. But Gateway did too. Each has grown and prospered, and each will continue to. Their secret? They each know who they are, who they want to do business with and how to give their customers what they want and need.

So can you.

Develop a Retail Marketing Strategy By Asking Questions

Your retail marketing strategies should begin with a lot of questions. The more the merrier. The better the quality of your questions—the more likely you are to find out which strategy works best for you.

- Who am I? What are my greatest strengths? What are my weaknesses? What do I like? What really upsets me?
- What am I really selling? Is it a widget? What does that widget do? Or is it convenience? Pride of ownership? Prestige?
- Who exactly would want this widget? Why? What do they expect to happen in their lives when they own this widget?
- Who else sells these widgets or ones like them? Are they successful? Why? Why not? What can I learn from them?
- How can I get this widget into the hands of those who want and need it?

- Why would anyone buy widgets from me rather than from someone else? What can I do better/different?
- What will the people I want to sell be willing to spend for this widget? Why?
- Once I sell this widget to someone, is that all there is? Can I sell them a second or third widget? Are there other things that I can sell my customer along with this one widget?

  Well, you get the drift.

Gathering Information About Your Market

Of course, questions don't do much good unless you can start to find some answers and see patterns. They don't do much good unless you can tie all those pieces together either.

The idea is to start looking for clues. Getting information is a lot like an Easter egg hunt. You look everywhere, but you have to go where the eggs and the chickens are—and the excitement grows with every clue you find.

You can get some information by studying statistics and documentation that has been gathered and published about your market. There's lots of resources available and you don't have to spend a small fortune finding them.

Some of the better places to look are:

1. *The government.* Here's where we get back some of that hard-earned money we pay for taxes! The government is a veritable goldmine when it comes to statistics, research and documents.

Begin with the U.S. Bureau of Census (a division of the Department of Commerce). Here's where you can begin to identify the basic stuff that makes up your market. From the latest census, you'll find essential information on the demographics of your chosen market area. You'll find out what percentage are men and women, how many of each in any age bracket you might choose, how many are employed and in which industries, how much they make, how many in their households, and much more.

Check out the Small Business Administration. They have several Business Information Centers in Atlanta, Houston, Los Angeles, St. Louis and Seattle as well as offices in all major cities throughout the U.S. Among their other services, you'll find the Small Business Institute Program and

Small Business Development Centers. Be sure to ask about all the publications that are available, many at little or no cost to you.

2. *Gather information from your Chamber of Commerce and any professional organizations in your area.* They're in business to provide information and because they're on top of the specific area you'll be working in, they'll be a little bit more current.

Although costs and time limitations may not allow you to join all of them, you'll find that the time spent networking with the members is well spent indeed. Attend each one as a guest at least once. Most will allow you to attend as a guest two or three times. Then, if you wish, choose one or two that you feel are the most productive and that you feel are the best fit for you.

Do be careful to keep your priorities straight. You're there to research and learn. Socializing is definitely an added benefit but it is secondary.

3. *Check out your local colleges and universities.* Their business libraries are generally quite good. More than that, you may find a particularly knowledgeable and enthusiastic professor or student who would be happy to do a little extra research to help you get started on the right track and to give you some expert feedback.

4. *Rediscover your public library.* When was the last time you stopped in for a visit? They've become powerful resources for information. Now, some are better than others. Typically, you'll find that some will be repositories for government publications, others specialize in business, yet others in music, and so on. Find the one that has the most comprehensive business collection and plan to spend some time there on a regular basis. You'll check out the books, of course, and the reference section. But don't forget the trade publications, popular magazines and the local newspapers as well.

In fact, keep in mind that magazines and newspapers generally are much more current than books. Published monthly, weekly or daily, they have a shorter lead time and strive for up-to-the-minute information.

Looking for more insight? Take a break from the statistics, and check into the publications that talk about psychology and motivation. Look for publications that are targeted to salespeople and advertising media. They're dealing with many of the same issues that you are. Each one will offer another nugget. Each one will hold another clue that will help you answer those questions that you need to be successful.

Learning from People

You'll learn a lot from what you'll find in print. But you can learn a lot more from people.

Do you have customers now? When was the last time you asked them what they think? You can learn a lot from people if you ask. They'll tell you why they're buying today or what they would like to buy from you if you offered it. They'll tell you what they like most about your particular widget, and what it does for them to own it. They'll tell you what you're doing right. And, of course, they'll tell you what you could be doing a lot better. Well, they will, if you ask and if you show a real interest in what they have to tell you.

Sometimes you'll get the best information by simply taking a minute to talk with them in the course of doing business with them. Other times, you might want to conduct a formal survey—one that doesn't require that they sign their name. Or, you might try prominently displaying a suggestion box. Try several methods; each may give you a different perspective.

And how about those people you'd like to have for customers, but they're not yet? Do you know what they want? If you ask them, they'd probably tell you what the most important things they look for in a shopping experience are. And you can tailor your retail marketing to fill that need.

Study the Competition

Remember those others? The ones that you're competing with? Your competition can be your best allies! I highly recommend that you make it a point to get to know them well.

Observe them. Watch what they do and how they do it. When do they do major promotions? How do they treat their customers? Look for their best qualities, which you can learn from, as well as their faults, which you can improve on.

But don't be afraid to talk to them, too. Lots of times, they will be very happy to share their experiences openly with you. If you ask, they may even share trade secrets. Better yet, you may find ways that you can work together to enhance your service to your customers.

Ok, ok. You are competing. But on the other hand, your market and theirs won't, or shouldn't be, exactly the same. They're different people. They have different personalities than you do and their customers will not necessarily be the same as yours. Besides, competition makes us all stronger and promotes a healthy business climate. That's why wherever there's a McDonald's you'll also find a Wendy's and a Burger King nearby. This is also why clothing stores like being in major malls—right next to other clothing stores.

Other Ways to Learn from the Competition

- Watch your competitors' sales and promotions. Be placed on their mailing lists and watch the local papers for their advertisements and announcements of sales.
- When you're at the library go back and review the past year's marketing efforts in your area. Scan the local papers; you'll begin to see established patterns. You may want to capitalize on local promotional efforts designed to stimulate business in the area and may wish to deviate somewhat to strengthen your own individual image. But whatever you do, you want to do it with an eye to what your potential customers might expect.
- Become a customer. You and your family or friends might call or visit businesses. Observe how you are treated, how they handle your inquiries, how they dress and behave, and display their merchandise.

While we're on the subject, remember what I said earlier about cross-promotions? Once you know who your ideal customers are, you can go to other merchants, who already serve them.

Maybe they sell hotel space to visiting businesspeople and you offer secretarial services or a haberdashery. Not only might you find a way to team up with them, but you can find out more about what those business-folk are asking for and what they need—things that you can offer.

If you're handling high-end gift items, you might want to team with a florist and bridal shop and offer a package deal to prospective brides.

Sporting goods stores work well with sneaker outlets, ski stores and bicycle shops.

Pricing Your Products and Services

While you're gathering this information, you're learning more about yourself and your customers. As things evolve you're going to discover that you are not like everyone else. You and your business have a very unique personality, and you relate better with some kinds of people than you do with others. You will begin to get a clearer idea who you get along best with and who your ideal customer might be.

Knowing this, pricing is relatively easy. You know what it costs you to present your products to market, your normal costs of doing business and what kind of a profit you need to make. At the same time, you're learning what is important to the customers you hope to deal with.

Some of your customers will pay any price if your widget does the job and gives them a sense of prestige while others, much more frugal, will drive miles out of their way to get a bargain. How do your potential customers think? You should have an idea of this from your surveys. If not, go back and ask.

You have very real costs of doing business: rent, telephone, sales staff, advertising, cost of making or buying your product, and so on. You expect to make a profit. Well, if you don't then you shouldn't be in business! Somewhere between that point and the amount that a customer is willing to spend is a happy medium.

You don't necessarily need to cut prices to keep customers. If you do, it might change the character of the customers that you will be dealing with. Do you want to do that? Then go for it. Lots of businesses have been very, very successful basing their income on high sales volumes and low per-item profit.

But you can just as easily price your products at the high end and go for custom and value-added. You may sell a lot less in volume but, because your profit margin is higher and you're offering extra benefits, you will do just as well, assuming that you've targeted the right market niche. It just depends on your customer and your expectations.

Let's say that your potential customers are busy executives. You know they start their typical business day at 7 A.M. and they frequently work 'til 5 P.M. at which time they rush straight to a dinner meeting with clients at 7 P.M. Arc you going to set your hours from 9 A.M. to 5 P.M.? Well, I hope not. Now, what do you suppose they are going to appreciate when they get to your shop? Will they be shopping casually for bargains? I doubt it. But you can bet that they will appreciate any service that makes them feel special, even pampered. They're probably going to be thinking about purchases that will help them appear more energetic and "with it."

On the other hand, the employee who is catching a fast lunch in the middle of a two-hour deadline isn't going to be looking for a place for an elegant, leisurely lunch. "Get me in and out FAST," he's thinking. There are two ways you can handle the situation. You can give him bare bones, on-the-fly lunch at a moderate price. He won't even notice what color flowers you have on the tables. But you can also deliver that same lunch, nicely boxed, to his desk and he'll most likely consider any additional charge a real bargain.

Price is more than just dollars. Price also includes convenience and benefits and "What's in it for me?" What you're striving for is to make an offer your customer simply can't refuse.

Marshall Fields established a reputation that made his stores a legend. He did it by basing his marketing on the simple premise that "the customer is always right" and that customer satisfaction was guaranteed for the life of the purchase. Customers flock to Neiman Marcus, another of the really great retailers of all times, where price is really not the factor; people love shopping there because they know they'll be treated like Royalty.

Attracting Customers

Marketing and sales should be fun! I hope you're not one of those businesspeople who haven't learned that yet. You know, the kind of businessperson who is always stressed about how to keep the doors open and how to get people to come buy.

The reality is that customers are like fish. They're a hungry lot. But they don't go looking for worm-laced hooks to nibble on. Customers are the same way. They make do with what they're familiar with. They normally don't go out of their way looking for something different and new people to do business with. They like the comfort of convenience and the tried and true. But, give them something different—make it enticing and make them want it ....

Remember people buy because they *want* long before they buy because they *need*.

Tailor Your Marketing for Fun

So, you know the kinds of things you enjoy and what turns on your potential customers? You must get them excited enough or curious enough to come check out what you have to offer. How do you do it?

Well, you certainly don't want to corral them into a meeting and give them a whole lot of statistics and try to convince them that they need you. Heck, they've gotten along well enough before you came into the picture.

You have a party! You get your business all spiffed up and you invite some local celebrities and you have music and you devise activities that will show off the very fine merchandise you offer. Have dancing and music and balloons or a picnic or a "Getting to Know You" Party. And you send out invitations to all your potential customers.

Now, of course, you don't have to go to quite this extent—and if you do you may only do it once a year. But you can make every day an exciting day to do business with you.

Look for Opportunities to Put Fun Into Your Marketing

Here's how:

1. Identify times in the year that you can do something special. Christmas, Valentine's Day, Easter, Mother's Day, Independence Day, Father's Day. Everyone does that. But how about the first day of Spring, or your Birthday, or your Company's Birthday, or Elvis Presley's Birthday or Frank Lloyd Wright's Birthday? What about the first day of the hunting or fishing season?
2. Maybe you're Italian or Irish and have special national holidays that most people don't know about. Why not make them gala marketing events?
3. And don't overlook the possibility of extending any of these holidays or events into a week-long extravaganza.
4. Devise a different kind of sale. Consider a sale that would give a percent discount to everyone who has the name of "Henry" one day and to everyone named "Matilda" the next. Or offer a discount to all customers who are dressed in purple, or everyone over 6 feet tall. Or perhaps consider giving a special discount to each buyer on his or her birthday. You could start a whole series of these minipromotions and bargain shoppers will start watching for ones that particularly suit them. You'll gain quite a reputation for being the business where people can get special recognition for being different.
5. Consider holding a "Give Something Back" sale or devise a promotion that generates a percentage of sales to be given to a specific charity.

People respond well to opportunities to help others in need, especially when they can do with very little inconvenience.

6. Sometimes you'll want to coordinate your sales at times when other retailers are holding theirs, but maybe there will be times when you'll choose to hold your prices when they're holding sales and schedule yours at off-times sales. Always look for the way to generate interest and create excitement.

No matter which kind of promotional event you choose to develop, consider these opportunities for you to go the extra mile. In addition to discounts, you might offer a special presentation, entertaining programs, opportunities to meet local celebrities, activities for young and old alike, or inexpensive giveaways.

Pay Attention to Details

Whatever the event, you'll want to be very thorough. You'll want your windows and doors to announce the event in some memorable way. Decorations throughout the store should reflect the theme—colors, posters and other decorations should clearly emphasize it. Background music and drawings for prizes should tie in with your theme, and, of course, so should the refreshments.

Use live props regularly, both in connection with your special events and "just for because." You may call on a celebrity to make spot appearances, or have an employee (or someone else) dress in a costume from a local theatre group, hire a robot or a live mannequin or a magician, an artist who specializes in caricatures, or that star athlete we mentioned earlier in this book. You would be surprised at how much excitement these will generate. And, they go far in keeping children occupied while their parents are shopping.

Be sure to have refreshments. People love the pause that refreshes, especially when they're killing time, waiting in line to be checked out or sitting in your office waiting to meet with you.

Some businesses have discovered the power of this simple idea. Look at the bookstores like Barnes & Noble. It's expanded its services and increased its business significantly by offering a coffee bar and a sit-down area where people can peruse purchases in a leisurely environment before buying.

Creative Retail Marketing Strategies

Take Advantage of Spare Corners and Down Time

Barnes & Noble has also started offering space where writers, artists and local organizations (all potential customers) can hold meetings and do book signings and special presentations for potential clients.

You could do something similar. After all, you do have floor space that isn't used during parts of the day—either when business is typically slow or before and after business hours, don't you? What would happen if you made that space available to people that you would like to have as customers? Do you suppose that they might think seriously about buying from you?

Get Out and Circulate

Consider taking your product or service outside of your business establishment?

Most communities have special events scheduled throughout the year, such as family fests, carnivals, art fairs, community picnics, county fairs, and flea markets. These are all events where people gather. They're there because it's fun, they're looking for bargains, yes, but they're looking for ideas. They're looking to meet new people. They're prime for you to get in front of them.

Of course, you're not going to do any in-your-face sales. But you make contacts, and they find out where you are and what you have to offer. Better yet, they see you as a person who enjoys the same kinds of things they do.

A bookworm buried beneath a stack of books rarely has many opportunities to win friends and influence people. A businessperson who is nose-to-the-grindstone rarely does either. Get your nose out of your business regularly. Get out and have fun doing the kinds of things that you, and the people that you've chosen as your target market,. like to do.

It's said that more business is conducted on the golf course than in all the boardrooms across the country. Learn that and you're in for some really exciting business opportunities. Tennis, swimming, golf and other team sports are wonderful business-building tools. So are hunting and fishing.

Community and volunteer activities are also wonderful for building recognition as a mover and shaker. This is a long-term effort on your part. But if you play your cards right, you will be seen as one who can be depended on to come through in a pinch, one who cares, one who is a professional.

Better yet, look for those events, fund-raisers and auctions that ask for donations and doorprizes for worthy causes. These usually generate a great deal of interest and excitement, and significantly enhance your visibility.

Become a leader. Don't just tag along. Sponsor a scout group or a contest (home video contests work well for camera shops and video rentals; pie baking for grocers; bike races for sporting goods). Or simply organize a coloring contest for your customers' children. Children are great motivators. Parents love showing off their children's accomplishments and doing business with businesses that pay attention to them.

Children, by the way, are the greatest motivators and the very best salespeople of all bar none. If you get their interest, you're going to get the parents involved.

Give Customers Recognition Where Recognition Is Due

One more strategy. Remember, people like to receive recognition and support. You are in a unique position to give that. Think in terms of ways that you can do something extra for your customers. What about a simple bulletin board posted by the front door that customers can use for their personal announcements. baby-sitting, rentals, furniture for sale, music lessons, all the peripheral concerns that a typical customer may be dealing with? Many of the larger grocers have been doing it with much success. People know they can go there to get information, and pick up a few items at the same time.

Publicizing Your Business

Of course, you're the greatest and best business around and you offer outstanding merchandise at the very best prices. But, even with all this information and activity that you've been generating your work still isn't done. You don't just run off willy-nilly in all directions and expect people to know and understand what you're all about. You can't wait for word-of-mouth to build your business. And you certainly can't expect that just because you have a storefront on the busiest intersection of your city people know you're there and how wonderful your merchandise is.

Planning and execution of your marketing strategies is critical to your success.

Gaining Publicity for a Major Event

You're probably going to spend a lot of time planning for a major event, as well you should. You want everything to go just right. I'd suggest that you begin planning each event a good six months in advance to make sure that you don't overlook anything.

But there's another reason that this time is important. It's so you can coordinate all your advertising and promotional materials—so that your invitations will go out in a timely manner and so everyone will have adequate time to schedule and plan to attend.

Your announcements need to build excitement. And you really shouldn't rely on just one. You know what your desk looks like at the end of the day and how difficult it is to keep up with the paper work. Well, your customers have the same problem. But you're a smart marketer and you want to be sure that they won't miss the opportunities you're offering them.

So, you're going to announce your events, using every media opportunity to keep your business event in front of the public you want to get pleasantly involved with you. And you're going to do more than just one announcement. Because, you see, people are busy and preoccupied. Unless they're specifically looking for your information, it typically takes 6-7 exposures for them to notice.

Guidelines for Spreading the Word

1. *Choose the media.* The media's purpose in life is to convey news and to tell people about what's going on. Media wants to promote you. But you have to have something to work with.

Here's the deal. You have a Halloween Sale scheduled. You want it to be written up in the paper. So, what? That's what the editors and program directors are going to say. About 95 percent of the businesses they cover will be having a Halloween Sale. Sales are going on all the time. What makes you different? Why should people care about this one? Is Mick Jagger going to be there? Are you going to give away $1,000 for the most unique costume? Maybe instead of a pumpkin giveaway, you're going to have everyone bring a pumpkin and a piece of candy to donate to a children's orphanage?

Or maybe you've just run a promotion and as a result of the turnout you're sending a customer on a week-long trip or your star employee has earned a special award for service above and beyond the call of duty.

Do you see? They want news! They want different! They want excitement! And, they want information about people.

2. *Check out advertising space.* It's relatively expensive in most cases. But you can shop for bargain rates here just like anywhere else. And don't forget to check with your local community station. There are community producers (people learning the business and volunteers) who would love to shoot your exciting and novel event for airing on public TV.

3. *Try radio.* Yes, even in these high tech times, people listen to radio a lot. Spot announcements during prime times and during programs that appeal to your target market make a significant impact. But do be sure to repeat your announcements several times.

4. *Local newspapers and newsletters are wonderful!* Their primary role in life is to inform the public. You support them by buying advertisements and get your name in front of the public. But don't forget the opportunities that they offer to have a full-length feature done on your business—often complete with pictures. Of course, you won't get all your information into the paper. Space limitations can be difficult even in the best of times. But, hey, the exposure is free. And, if you keep the editor informed of all your major activities in a timely fashion (a month or two in advance), you stand a good chance of getting some solid coverage—especially if you invite the editor to the event and if it is truly unique and newsworthy.

5. *Use trade and general interest publications.* This would depend on your particular market. The real key here is to know your potential customers so well that you know how they spend their time and what they read. Then you go where they are.

Pay Attention to Your Customers

While it's quite common for the everyday demands of retail marketing to eat away at your time and energy, remember that your job is to pay close attention to your customers. It's particularly important that you observe and react quickly to changing times and the needs of your client base. Remember, it's a whole lot easier to make repeat sales to already established customers than it is to get new ones.

All too often, in the heat of trying to increase market share, retailers forget that. They get so wrapped up in building numbers that they forget those who have been loyal repeat customers. Never, ever take them for granted. People will not normally deviate from their normal shopping patterns unless they feel that they're no longer getting the fine service that they have always gotten and deserve. More often than not, in cases like this they will simply go elsewhere rather than raise a fuss.

Adapt Your Plan to Your Market

Unfortunately, when you have an established location you get into a routine and forget that the world outside isn't necessarily the same as it was six months or a year ago. That's why you want to keep revising that marketing plan and re-evaluating the information you have gathered along the way. Time was—maybe even when you first opened your business—that the primary shopper was part of a family unit consisting of 3-5 individuals. Today, the percentages are swaying more toward single heads of households. Single parents have very different needs and interests from those that are shopping for traditional families. Why should you care?

Well, more parents are bringing their children along when they're out shopping. While this could be a mixed bag, and highly stressful situation for the parents, you, recognizing their situation, can take the necessary steps to make shopping at your establishment that much more enjoyable. A children's play corner has proven successful for some and isn't all that expensive. Or, would it make sense to provide small wagons in which parents could pull their tykes around with them?

The same goes for catering to your elderly customers. What could you do to make doing business with you an easier, more enjoyable event? Walgreen's is one of many, many retail establishments that have set up small waiting areas including a couple of chairs, magazines and even a TV, for the convenience of its customers.

Also reconsider the packaging of your merchandise to take into account your customers' need for smaller per-use portions. This may have a significant impact on purchases.

Think convenience—and think fun!

It really doesn't take a major investment, but it does take you being out there with your customers attending to and staying ahead of their needs. It also requires that you stay on top of your sales staff.

Occasionally, throughout the year, you'll want to touch base with frequent shoppers and shoppers that you haven't seen for a while. Where possible, you want to maintain a database of customers. These databases can be compiled from data on purchases made by check or credit card or from drawings and business cards that you've collected along the way. In fact, some have found that having a fish bowl at the register so that business people can drop their cards in for a special drawing works wonders.

Direct mailing (remember we talked about that earlier) can be a great way to maintain communication with your customers, or it can a disaster. The secret is to make your mailings very personalized. Use the capabilities of your computers to develop mail-merged letters and address each customer individually. And, wherever possible, make sure the message is carefully targeted to the specific interests of your customer. The alternative is to do a blind mailing, which is most often a waste of money.

Getting Your Sales Staff to Go Along

Don't let all this valuable information and enthusiasm stop with you. Let your sales staff in on the fun!

1. Hold a staff meeting each week, with an educational segment that might cover such important topics as how to answer the phone, handle an irate customer, or take care of special requests. Tall about all the wonderful things you've learned about people and about what your expectations are. Help staff understand the difference between being assertive and helpful and being pushy! Better yet, have your staff members share their experiences while shopping at another retail establishment. Let them tell you how they felt about the service, the dress codes, the look and feel of the establishment and so on.
2. Look for ways to build pride of ownership among your employees. This one strategy will work wonders in the way your business will be

perceived by customers. Why is this important? You're not still trying to be everywhere at once are you? You can't do it! You need to delegate and rely on your people to reflect your high standards.

3. Reward your staff for outstanding service. Perhaps an "Employee of the Week" announcement on the employee bulletin board. Treat them to a lunch or give them an extra couple hours off with pay. It's the small things that count. You'll be amazed at how enthusiasm builds when it's recognized.
4. Consider being a little (not a lot) looser with your break times. Of course, you don't want this get out of hand. Psychologists have proved that frequent short breaks and brisk walks during the day increase productivity and accuracy significantly.

Window Dressing

It doesn't matter whether you specialize in a few products, have an extensive inventory, or whether you are appealing to an upscale clientele or bargain hunters. It's essential that you pay close attention to the look and feel of your establishment.

The way you care for your business is a direct reflection on your pride in your business and what you think of your customers.

Now we all know that it's easy to let details slide. And it's particularly difficult to stay up with the cosmetics when you're handling high volumes of people, your profit margin is low and you are open 24 hours a day.

But, I can tell you this. When I have a choice I always choose to shop in a place where the floors and windows glisten and I don't have to bulldoze my way through cluttered isles to find what I'm looking for. I spend much more money in places when I feel good about being there.

Eight Strategies for Making a Good Impression

I'm not saying you need to hire an interior decorator to dress your windows and carpet your floors. It's the little things that make the difference. Here are a few examples—a list of my pet peeves, yes, but things that affect your buyers, nonetheless:

1. When it comes to overall appearance you can't apply too much spit and polish. Your parking area is a fine example. Police it regularly and make sure that it stays free of trash.
2. If you have a storefront with lots of windows and glass doors, make sure that they're cleaned regularly. I know, there's something about glass that attracts fingerprints and grime like a magnet. But, first impressions are critical.
3. Stand back and look at your front counter and check-out areas from a customer's point of view! We all know that this is where you rely on impulse buying to increase sales. And this is perhaps your most valuable spot. How does it look to you?
4. Pay special attention to lighting. A dark, or poorly lit establishment is a definite turn-off. More lighting is a wonderful, cost-effective way to highlight and promote special items. Perhaps you could alternate mini-spotlights around the store, thus subtly reminding your customers that you carry items that are frequently overlooked.
5. Make sure that your sales staff understands that your customer is the priority! Unfortunately, all too often employees get caught up in paperwork or stocking shelves or whatever assignment you've given...and they forget.
6. Want to increase the personal element? Have your salespeople wear name tags. Wherever possible, have them call customers by name. This is really quite easy, especially when customers pay by check or credit card. This one strategy works wonders in generating a warm, fuzzy feeling that will stay with them and keep your store in mind long after they've left.
7. Evaluate the normal traffic patterns within your business in relation to your customers' buying patterns. With a little ingenuity you can make browsing a really enjoyable experience. Creating natural zones and strategically positioning your key products can go far in increasing sales and making shopping fun! Keep the guesswork out of where your shopper might find what they're looking for.

Each and every business is different. And point-of-sale will vary, as will how you handle those items that you need to keep a close eye on. But if you listen to your customers, you'll find out what is best for you and for them. For example, when shoppers constantly ask you for a particular item, it might be a clue that you need to reposition it for more visibility.

8. You may want to talk with your suppliers. Tell them what your plans are well in advance, and work with them to devise special banners, signs and displays. They are there to help you maximize sales and are outstanding resources for these kinds of sales aides.

In short, we all want to do business with people who care about us. It's your job to make it easy—and fun! And you can have fun doing just that in retail!

CHAPTER NINETEEN

Strategies for Contests and Sweepstakes

You're soaking in a nice leisurely bath when you hear a knock. Grabbing a towel, you hesitantly open the front door. Ohmygosh, standing before you are Dick Clark and Ed McMahon with a fleet-sized camera crew fully equipped with microphones and lights. Dick and Ed are holding a giant sized check for $1,000,000 and your towel falls at your feet as you look with stunned amazement.

That's the dream for millions of people as they send in their envelopes for American Family Publishers, Publishers Clearing House and scores of other marketers. The dream for marketers is, perhaps, not so grandiose—increasing their business through the use of sweepstakes, contests and other interactive tools.

Win! Big! Free! Your dream comes true! Those are the buzzwords for successful games, contest promotions and sweepstakes. We'll call this whole category prize promotions.

According to the *New York Times*, a sweepstakes mailing for a magazine subscriptions company is five times more likely to generate a subscription than a mailing without a game. Not only is the front end (the direct-mail piece) loaded, so is the back end (later orders and database collection). Follow-up direct-mail letters to people who have purchased through a prior contest promotion can achieve a response of 10 per cent or higher.

Contests come in all kind of forms. There are giveaways, trivia quizzes, scratch-off, slogan and essays contests, raffles—and on the web—scavenger hunts. In exchange for the fun and enjoyment they seem to bring to entrants, the sponsoring company gets to sell goods and service.

A contest promotion can bring an emotional commitment on the part of the recipient like perhaps no other kind or promotion. In many cases, people have paid their own airfare to fly to sweepstakes promoters to claim an expected prize...even when they haven't won. To a proportion of American consumers, these contests become an obsession—the height of emotional involvement. That's really a marketer's dream.

Here are some of the ways a prize promotion can advance your strategic short- and long-term goals.

- Create new business and repeat traffic
- Prize promotions and games are one of the most effective ways to build immediate traffic and get quick return on your promotional dollar. When a fast-food company like McDonald's runs a contest they get a strong response from people who haven't been to McDonald's in a while. They also get a great deal of increased business and traffic from their existing customer base.

Prize promotions can also spike sales for retailers and packaged good products. M&M's created a Find-The-Impostor M&M's sweepstakes. They hid a gray M&M in randomly selected packages. When a person bought the candy they would look for the impostor M&M. If they found it, they would collect the prize. (If they ate it accidentally, they were probably out of luck.) The excitement filtered down to all distribution chains.

Build Brand Awareness

A strong promotion can liven up even the dullest of products. It can make an existing product shine like new and introduce a new product with great effectiveness. Benson & Hedges created a prize promotion for their cigarette which was just a tad longer (a millimeter) than other brands. The promotion established the brand in consumer minds immediately. This was important, because TV advertising for cigarettes had been banned. The promotion kept the product story alive in consumers' minds.

Separate Your Product from the Others

Prize promotions may be what you need to separate your product from me-toos and commodity products. Suppose your product is butter or you grew figs. There is really not a great deal of difference between your product and others. Instead of fighting it out with your competitors in a price war, a prize promotion can be a defining force in making a consumer choose your product over the competition's.

Make Your Advertising Message Work Harder, Create New Value and Garner Publicity

A strong prize promotion will not only bring people into a given store, it can help you get more shelf space and display space for your point-of-sale material. Because of the news value of a prize promotion, you can gather great media coverage. M&M's got worldwide coverage on it's "Name the New M&M's Color promotion"

Hype Your Product to Salespeople

A prize promotion can renew a salesperson's interest in the brand. A prize promotion can be just what you need to jolt the indifference of salespeople. To them, it's a break from the same old same old. It brings in new life and keeps salespeople hyping your product. Create prizes for your retailer's salespeople. It can make your promotion doubly effective.

Increase Direct-Mail Response

Putting a sweepstakes in a with a direct mail offer increases response rates drastically, not only for huge magazine companies, but for smaller companies. Bio-Organics was a small health products provider. It created a sweepstakes (obviously not the size and scale of the magazine contests) and it gave a big jolt to sales.

Stimulate Learning

A cleverly run contest can actually get people to read through your literature and reinforce its key points. *Psychology Today* was faced with a difficult task when they tried to pitch their magazine to advertisers. Media buyers had thought they knew all about the magazine and its demographics. *Psychology Today* created a sweepstakes whereby people had to answer five questions that were interspersed throughout the media kit. By doing this, *Psychology Today* was able to disseminate new information to its advertising clients.

Reinforce a Benefit

Just like Benson and Hedges did with its sweepstakes, acquaint your customers with your products by making the sweepstakes a mnemonic for the benefit.

Build a Mailing List

Include a prize promotion with your warranty card or ad and people will give you all sorts of information. The information you can get can be vital in segmenting and customizing your sales pitch to a particular market.

Research, and Discover New Uses and Benefits for Your Product

A prize promotion can be a vital research tool for getting into the hearts and minds of consumers. It's an excellent way to gather market information. The Eberhard-Faber Pencil Company developed a program of monthly contests to find out how people were using their various pencils. They came up with enough new products and benefits to guide their advertising and segmentation strategy for year. Similar programs were run by Campbell's Soup for new recipes, and Lehn & Fink for uses for a new cleaning product.

Stimulate Interest in a Trade Show

A prize promotion can lure people to a booth or even to the trade show. In one campaign for a trade show, the trade show's sponsors placed money in specially marked envelopes and hid them in various booths around the show. The attendees had to search the show to find which booths had the money. It was quite exciting.

You can also draw people to your booth with small contests and sweepstakes. Here's a quick hint. Hold the drawing when your chief competitor is about ready for its big pitch.

Localize Your Advertising

Seed your national campaign with local prizes. A national contest can filter down to the local level providing you recruit local businesses to take part. For instance, you can run a national sweepstakes and have local businesses tie prizes into the program. Localize your prizes for a particular area. Give tickets through (and to) a local theater. Have a local music store deliver CDs. Localizing a promotion creates excitement all around.

You can also use prize promotions to test an advertising program's appeal.

Yes, half of all advertising is wasted—but which half?

Several years ago a sponsor was trying to gauge the audience appeal of a proposed long term buy. The sponsor was trying to figure out which type of program would appeal to the largest number of customers. The company sponsored a different type of program each week. At the end of the program a key word was mentioned. The entrants were asked to write a short letter indicating their choice of programming and to include one of the key words in the essay. By tracking the key words they were able to tell which type of programming worked best.

Here's what a prize promotion won't do

Like all forms of advertising, prize promotions are not be alls or end alls. They are a means to make your fully planned marketing strategy work better. Prize promotions are simply another tool in your marketing mix. Prize promotion won't fix a faulty marketing program or one that has under-allocated funds. Here are some more basic limitations of a given prize promotion.

- It usually won't build brand loyalty unless a successful contest is run year after year with a sustained theme.
- It won't, usually, create an image for you. It can however, reinforce an image that has been promoted.
- It won't compensate for a small advertising budget or insufficient marketing and promotional allocations. It can help support a theme, however, and make your money work harder by stirring consumer interest.
- It can't take the place of product sampling. But it can make your sampling much more memorable and effective.

A contest can be a strong way to gauge media and message appeal when the number of entrants a particular ad pulls in is counted. It's hardly scientific but it's quick and relatively cheap.

Create Traffic and Build Relationships with Internet Travelers

People go on the Internet to have fun and explore new sites. Contests, sweepstakes and scavenger hunts are highly effective in drawing customers to your site and making them come back time and time again.

Planning Is Essential

While once the exclusive domain of food and packaged good manufactures, prize promotions can be used in almost every business from mom and pop hardware stores to multi-line conglomerates. The scope and scale of the promotion may be different but the primary objective is to increase sales.

It takes a complete look at your company's aspirations to come up with a winner. Saying "let's have a contest" doesn't carry as much weight as when Mickey Rooney used to say in the thirties—"let's put on on a show." A contest should not be run for its own sake. It should be designed to reach specific goals. The theme, game type, and prize structure should work hand in hand with your marketing ambitions and thrust.

A primary objective in any prize promotion strategy is to graphically create or reinforce a demonstrable difference in your product or to build traffic. But building traffic is not always a good thing. Getting the wrong people to come to your store can be a considerable waste of your resources. Your prize promotion should appeal to people who are or will be ready, willing and able to buy your product in the very near future. That's one reason your media selection for your promotion is so important. Your goal is to target worthy customers, not just people who are playing for the sake of playing.

A very successful prize promotion was created for Revlon's Chaz Cologne for men. The prize was a very prestigious sports car. Contestants received a game card with a lucky number. They checked their number on displays in retail stores. The contest was so strong, people would drive for miles seeking out stores that displayed the promotion. This promotion benefited Revlon in several ways.

- It created awareness for what was then a new product
- It brought traffic in Revlon's retailers
- It created a strong motivation for retailers to stock the display...and the products.

Here are the steps you need to take to establish a prize promotion strategy.

Define Your Objectives and Recognize the Competition

As mentioned above, there are a great many objectives you can satisfy when you have specific goals for your promotion. Do you want to introduce a new product, make dealers happy, or establish a product benefit? A prize promotion can help you satisfy all three. What sales volume are you aiming for? How will the prize promotion help you get there? How—and we're talking specifics here—will your prize promotion help you obtain a better share of market?

You also need to keep a watch on your competitors to determine what kind of prize promotions they are running. If they are giving away a mansion in the country, you will have to rethink your grand prize of a trip to Disneyland. However, if your competition is not doing anything similar, your trip to Disneyland can look very strong to a prospective entrant. A great deal depends on where you want to go and what your competition will do to keep you from getting there.

Choose the Right Type of Game

There are many kinds of sweepstakes and games. A critical choice is to find the type that fits in with your image and resources. A nationwide game with high-value prizes takes a great deal more manpower and resources than a local drawing but both can get a lot of bang for the buck. An important decision is whether you couple the game with a coupon promotion or other collateral material—or let your game carry the entire selling message on its back.

Your Budget

Contests can be expensive or cheap. Obviously the most expensive prize promotions draw the greatest number of consumers. But there are many hidden costs—in time, money and manpower—for even the most modest promotions.

Prizes usually come out of your advertising budget. If you can give away goods you make, you can obviously lower the cost of prizes, but there are other budget considerations in developing a prize promotion. These essentials include judging organizations, prize fulfillment centers, legal fees, customer communications, collateral advertising and administration.

Name That Theme

The theme you choose is probably the most vital choice you are going to have to make. Think carefully about the message you want to get across. Sweepstakes based on anniversary themes are always strong. If you can match the prize with your advertising theme you will have developed a selling message with excitement.

Here Are Some of the More Popular—and More Effective—Types of Prize Promotions.

Sweepstakes

Sweepstakes are the most widely used prize promotion. Raffles and lucky numbers are also forms of sweepstakes. Sweepstakes generally require little consumer involvement (which can be a drawback) except, perhaps, to mail in an entry form or boxtop or to check out a lucky number at a retail store or in an ad. Instead of numbers you can have a consumer match a special symbol. This can be a logo or package design, or a mnemonic for a key product benefit. Alternatively, you can have consumers make a phone call. That's how M&M's drew umteen millions of entrants for their "Name the New M&M's Color" promotion. You can also use the Internet to have people enter electronically. Winners are chosen at random.

Besides causing excitement, you get information about the customer which you can use to create a database or to segment customers.

The nice thing about a sweepstakes promotion is that the ideas are limited only by your imagination and your budget. They can be fun or fancy. Cheap or expensive. They can cover a limited or wide-ranging market area. The negative is that they can be overdone—there is tremendous competition in the sweepstakes area and only the most creative ones stand out.

Examples of Successful Sweepstakes

- A major credit card company offered free charges for a year. Whenever consumers used their credit card, they were automatically entered in the drawing.
- AT&T used a sweepstakes to promote collect phone calls. Whenever a consumer made a collect call, they were automatically entered in the drawing.
- Current events can be great themes for sweepstakes. When Mark McGwire was on his home run tear, several companies created sweepstakes around the feat. People who correctly guessed how many home runs McGwire would hit, were entered in prize drawings.

If you use current events as your theme you should plan and execute quickly to make it timely.

Games

Games, where people have to actively do something to play, get more emotional involvement from consumers than sweepstakes. Lately, the most popular games are borrowing the format of state lotteries. You supply a scratch-off game card or game piece and the consumer hopes for a winner. In a variance, you supply a number of game pieces and have consumers attach the pieces to a master game sheet. Of course, there are a lot more filler pieces than winners, but to consumers, hope is eternal.

When running a game promotion, it's important to "seed" the game with small prizes, coupons and discounts to keep contestants motivated. It's similar to state lottery and slot machine motivational strategies. Research shows that many small rewards keep people returning in hopes of winning the grand prize. It's instant gratification. By offering a small prize, say a free serving of French fries, consumers get the feeling of having won something.

Instead of a game sheet or cards at the point of sale, you can put game pieces inside of boxes, on cups, in free-standing packages—just about anywhere that consumer can find buried treasure.

A word about losing pieces. In a scratch-off contest, one company used the following copy for non-winning pieces. "You're a Loser." This is not the kind of message a consumer wants to hear. Create a line like "Thanks for playing. Please try again" or something a bit more uplifting. Coupons on losing pieces can be effective too.

Examples of Successful Games

- A small tourist town in New Mexico holds a "Find the Rattlesnake Contest" every year. Plastic rattlesnakes are hidden in various stores around the town for people to find. Many small prizes are given away in addition to one large prize. (My son won an ice cream soda and a small stuffed animal—he wanted to go back every year.)
- Many Internet companies run scavenger hunts. People surf the web looking for key words and objects. A prize goes to the first person who finds all.
- McDonald's most profitable game is a cross-promotion with Parker Brothers. Consumers gets a game card with popular symbols from the game, Monopoly. When all the right cards are collected, consumers get a prize.

Skill Games

Games that ask a consumer to make up a slogan or complete an essay like "I love Skirkadidle because..." offer the greatest consumer involvement. There are some limitations though. Because skill is needed, less people are going to take the time and effort to enter. You will normally get only one-tenth to one-hundredth the entries you would get if you ran a sweepstakes. People tend to think you need to be a teacher or writer to amass the skills needed to win. You will also get unsolicited letters from lawyers and players telling you that their essays were better. Judging and being fair to entrants can be problematic because when entrants are tied, you may have to give out two or more prizes.

Examples of Successful Skill Games

- For several years Guinness, the beer company, gave away a real Irish pub to the person who could best extol the virtues of Guinness Ale. The promotion was so successful that the contest was covered by media worldwide.
- Edmund Scientific ran a promotion to name a new telescope. They received thousands from people who read their catalog. (I lost but I think my name was the best—sour grapes.)
- San Jose State runs the Bulwer-Lytton fiction contest. They invite readers to submit an opening sentence to "the worst of all possible novels." It's not really a promotion in the strictest sense of the word, but it's fun and may stir your creative juices. It was named after the guy who wrote "it was a dark and stormy night" that the popular Peanuts cartoon character, Snoopy, likes to have fun with.

Puzzles

Puzzles can be fun and if the puzzle is really challenging and fascinating it might stir up excellent media coverage and word-of-mouth. A drawback is that only seasoned puzzle solvers or people with a special knowledge of your puzzle may want to enter. You also require someone who can create puzzles that only a few people might solve or all. One company created a scratch-off puzzle which was supposedly random. Unfortunately, many people figured out the "random" pattern and the company had to give away a great many prizes. Unless you are incredibly knowledgeable and sure of the promotion, it might be best to shy away from puzzle promotions.

Examples of Successful Puzzles

- A publisher came out with a mystery book in which clues were included throughout the book. The first reader who solved the mystery received $10,000. The book made the *New York Times* best-seller list.
- A small shopping newspaper—the *Pennysaver*—includes humorous fake ads among its real classifieds. The first person who calls in with the fake wins a small prize.

- To show how valuable and rare their beverage was, one liquor company hid a case of their product in a far off land. They got a year's use of the contest and drew heavy media coverage.

Themes and Contest Content

There are as many themes as there are contests. The best themes are those that evolve from your advertising message or product benefit. The most successful themes are those that point to luck or the chance to make a dream real. Similar dreams can be achieved by both the marketer and the entrant when a theme closely matches your marketing and promotional strategy.

Strategic Necessities for Your Prize Promotion

Here are the basic necessities for any prize promotion and the communication strategies you need.

- Inspire the entrant. Motivate the entrant continuously. The strongest word in any prize promotion is "Win." Say it loud. Print it big. Use it as many times as you can in your ads.
- Make sure you are identified as the sponsor. Make your name part of the headline. You're not running the promotion to have fun or to be altruistic. You want to make money, sell and get great visibility.
- Create a clever and motivating name for your event. It should encompass all areas of the promotion. The successful name ties-in every aspect of the promotion.
- Describe and highlight the grand prize. This is your entrant's dream and the reason he or she is entering the contest. It should generate the most excitement so give it the most space or the largest amount of air time. Make your visual strong. People don't want to read about the grand prize. They want to see it.
- Have many smaller prizes. Having many prizes makes it seem that there is a greater chance to win something. State the number of prizes in the promotional piece conspicuously.
- Entrance requirements are important. Tell consumers exactly how to enter. Make it clear and plain.

- Tell consumers the rules. The rules are probably the least fun of your promotion, but if you don't state the rules clearly you could have trouble legally and publicity wise. A list of legal requirements is at the bottom of this chapter.

A Checklist to Make Sure Your Contest and Theme Can Fulfill Your Objectives

- It should be a natural fit with your product. It should get across your promotional message simply and strongly.
- It must fit the media. If you are doing a catalog mailing, make it part of the order form. Call attention to it throughout the catalog.
- Keep it simple. Consumers won't wade through your material figuring out the rules. The basic benefit, theme and rules of your contest should be able to be communicated in a sentence or a headline.
- It should "naturally select your prospects." The goal is to attract those people who are most likely to buy your product.
- Make it publicity friendly. Try to create something so exciting that the media can create a story about it.
- Keep it timely. Tie it in with an event that people know about and respond to.

Prizes

Prizes depend on your goals and your budget. Obviously the most popular contests are the ones that have the biggest prizes. The most enduring prizes are variances on the money theme. You can offer cash for life, bonds, merchandise credits, free rent for a year, etc.

Prizes should appeal to a person's mercenary side. A prize like a donation to a certain charity or a foundation doesn't usually draw well.

Travel prizes always seem to work well, whether the sponsor is an airline or something totally unrelated to the travel industry. For travel prizes, the dollar outlay is rather small but trips and vacations have a highly perceived "dream value."

Cars, houses and boats appeal to almost everyone because of their dream value. But most people who win something super-exorbitant take the cash, since all gifts are taxable.

You don't have to sell the company to finance a prize promotion. Appropriate and motivating prizes can be created for just about any category. Rewards for the *Pennysaver* fake ad are about $5.

The Key Numbers

According to Jeffrey Feinman, in the book *Sweepstakes, Prize Promotions, Games, and Contests,* here's a breakdown on the number of entries you can expect from a typical contest:

- newspaper entry forms - 1 percent
- magazine entry forms - 2 percent
- direct mail - 5 percent (the major magazine sweepstakes programs usually pull much higher)
- free standing "take one" displays - 5 percent
- free standing newspaper inserts - 6 percent

Don't Forget to Publicize the Winner

Your promotion doesn't end the day the winner is chosen. The winners of your prize have high promotional value. Winners are big news, especially in news-hungry small towns. Several magazines have written stories about the winners of the Guinness contest. Lottery winners are posted on the front page of many newspapers.

Invite the media to the drawing or prize ceremony of a winning prize. Contests like "Win a Bit Part in a Movie" or "Five Minutes of Free Supermarket Shopping" are a natural for media attention. The publicity is usually local in scope but some promotions—like the Most Disgusting Sneaker in the World, sponsored by Odor Eaters—achieve national and sometimes worldwide coverage.

Legal Stuff you Have to Know

You know that mouse type you see in back of a contest entry form? It's there for a reason. Both federal and state governments look closely to see that contests are not fraudulently or mimics lotteries. If you run a prize promotion, consult closely with your attorneys. Here are some current legal guidelines adapted from Feinman's book.

1. *Purchase not necessary.* Never, ever make purchase of your product necessary. State that "no purchase is necessary" clearly and unequivocally.
2. *How to enter without purchase.* Clearly disclose alternate means of entering the contest.
3. *Prize disclosure.* Prizes and the chances of winning must be disclosed. If a cash substitute is available, it must be disclosed.
4. *What are the odds of winning?* The odds of winning each prize must be disclosed. If the odds are based on the number of entrants, this must be disclosed also.
5. *Who is judging or selecting winners?* You must specify what kind of judging or drawing there will be and who is doing it. If the winner's lucky numbers are decided on before the sweepstakes has commenced, that must be disclosed also.
6. *Reasons for Disqualification.* Specify every factor that can lead to a disqualification, i.e., photocopied entries, poor handwriting, etc.
7. *Eligibility.* Specify all people who can't enter or win the contest, i.e., age limits, professional and personnel affiliations.
8. *Limit of Entries.* You can't stop a person from entering as often as he or she wants, but you can allow only one entry per envelope.
9. *Addresses.* Tell where to get entry blanks and how to request a list of winners.
10. *Void where illegal.* Yup, you've got to mention all states or localities where the contest is illegal.
11. *Deadlines.* Specify postmark deadlines, receipt of entry deadlines, and the contest's end date.
12. *Sponsor's Liability.* Specify what the sponsor's liabilities are and are not, i.e., who is responsible for the taxes, delivery of prizes.

CHAPTER TWENTY

Exploring Alternative Marketing and Sales Strategies

There was a highly unusual sight in the pristine ski slopes of Vermont. A group of people, allegedly normal, dressed as giant popcorn bags, handed out samples of a new popcorn. In the summer these people, dressed in the same not-so-subtle garb, prowled beaches and handed out samples to the area's surfers and swimmers. The product was Smart Food Popcorn, and this simple, albeit weird marketing ploy led to a huge business that was eventually sold to snack giant Frito-Lay.

The Oreck Vacuum Cleaner Company graces its ads and direct-marketing efforts with the president holding a bowling ball with a vacuum hose.

There are a great many marketing ideas out there if you follow the "inner marketer" strategy. Eat and breathe marketing. Every path you take, every person you come into contact with is either a marketing opportunity or a bridge to a marketing opportunity. Here is a cornucopia of marketing strategies and ideas. All have proven successful.

Direct-Mail Marketing

Because of the dual-income household, people have less leisure time to spend wandering through malls or hunting hard-to-find goods. Whether the product is baby clothes, or cookies, hardware or seafood, there's no end to what consumers will buy through the mail.

Direct mail is a form of direct marketing which uses one or more advertising media to affect a measurable response and transaction at any location. Direct marketing has evolved into more than a fancy term for mail order. It is an aspect of the total marketing picture, a full-fledged distribution channel and a marketing strategy.

Benefits of Direct-Mail Marketing

Direct mail's advantages over traditional "face-to-face" marketing are legion.

1. Large numbers of people can be sold on a highly individual customer basis, rather than on a mass consumer basis, eliminating low-margin competitive pressures.
2. Direct marketing can send a "demographic store" to reach target consumers anywhere they live, unlike "geographic stores" of the retail system which must tailor their product lines to prime prospects who are typically located within a limited geographic area.
3. The direct-mail company exercises complete control over product throughout the purchase and delivery to the buyer or end user. This allows a substantial control over profit, and a greater share of profit. Few "loss leaders" are needed.
4. Target prospects are reached without middleman dependency. An unmediated transaction between customer and vender is created with true knowledge of customer purchase behavior.
5. Promotional messages, communications, deals and target markets are constantly tested and refined toward an optimal effect. This offers total control over the sales process.
6. Most sales are paid for in advance with checks or credit cards. No credit or slow pay problems. A completely accountable, data-driven system is created and implemented.

The Basic Strategy for Direct-Mail Marketing

The basic plan for direct-mail marketing is to acquire an active customer database through the use of small space ads and test mailings. Then exploit the existing customer base 4-12 times a year. Access this customer base aggressively with the objective of increasing the frequency and amount of purchase. Your current customers will offer you the greatest profit. Acquiring new customers can be your biggest expense. Successful direct marketers typically count on one or two major sales periods and four lesser sales period per year.

Be patient. It can take two or more years to realize profits from a brand-new catalog.

Finding the Best Mailing List

A proven axiom of direct marketing is that the best list to use is one consisting of consumers who have recently purchased a product identical, or similar, to the one you are trying to sell. Experimenting with various lists is critical. Look for customers who spend a great deal of money in a particular category. For instance, if a prospect is a woodworker and buys from catalogs that sell woodcrafting tools, that person would be a great target for a woodworking magazine.

You can also build a profit stream by selling your list of customers, particularly if you update it frequently.

Look for the Market Niche

Specialized products that appeal to smaller markets have the best chance of success. That's why you see so many catalogs catering to children, cooking aficionados, animal lovers and many other special-interest segments. Going after a small target market is the best plan for success. The more closely you target your customers, the better off you will be. Choosing your target markets carefully and testing your lists constantly are the keys to success.

Choose a Growing Market Area

If you're looking for a growth opportunity, keep initial costs in hand. Choose a market with at least 100,000 prospective customers at the outset and a good potential for future growth.

The One Percent Rule of Thumb in Direct Marketing

A one percent response rate is considered reasonably good when prospecting for new customers. The number of customers you send to and the ultimate selling price of your products, including markups, should be controlled to allow you to at least break even initially.

Your Catalog

Catalogs reflect the identity of the products you sell. Experiment with artwork, different paper stocks and informational copy to see which pulls best. Use at least 10 percent of your mailing list each month to try new ideas.

Get Into Other Catalogs

Getting into someone else's catalog is a less expensive way to start out in the direct-mail channel. Write a letter to a catalog company that interests you and include a photograph or sample of your product. Describe your product fully and specify why it fits in the prospective catalog.

Catalogs Work for Retail Stores

Mail order is also good for companies that have a retail presence. You don't need a large inventory investment. You probably have the makings of a mailing list from your own customer database. You have established relationships with suppliers.

Keep Everything in Control

Money goes fast in direct marketing. Every aspect of your program, including mailings and customer service, have to be top notch. Two-day delivery and 800 numbers times are just about required for entrance into the market these days. If you can't offer a particular service, chances are your competitors will. Offering customers something different and offering it in a unique and entertaining manner is the secret to direct-mail success.

Creating the Perfect Direct-Mail Piece in Eleven Easy Steps

There are as many theories about direct mail as there are direct-mail companies. The main trick is to keep your communications hard-hitting and flowing. Here are the eleven steps to a successful direct-mail piece.

1. *Target your audience carefully.* Sales are directly related to how accurately you can identify your most likely customers.
2. *Use the letter structure mentioned in Chapter 4 (in the section on written communications).* Use the "you" word as often as you can. Direct Marketer Bob Serling, in his book *Direct Marketing Hotseat*, suggests you use "you" four times as often as you use "I."
3. *Send your letter under the "President's" signature.* People prefer to deal with the person in charge. Build and foster your relationship with your customer in all your sales materials.
4. *Make a charter offer.* People like getting in on the ground floor of an enterprise. Charter offers have strong pulling power.
5. *Create a continuity program.* Perhaps the "Fruit of the Month Club." You can be sure of sales every month. Start your customers slowly with a trial membership so they can see how the program works without making a large investment.
6. *Offer multiple versions of the same product.* A "good"—"better"—"best" (or best buy) strategy or a "standard"—"deluxe"—"super-deluxe" strategy allows people to make choices. Use these variances instead of a "take this product it or leave it" offer.
7. *Make your envelope work for you.* Put a message on it like "Here's some inside information." Words like "free" "new" "announcing" and "important dated material" also motivate people to open the envelope.
8. *Use reply cards and make the 800 number large.* Make it easy for people to order or call for more information.
9. *Use odd-sized envelopes and experiment with textured papers.* They make your mailing piece stand out from the crowd.
10. *Test one variable at a time and use the results of the mailing for future mailings.* Keep close track of who's buying from what ad.
11. *Remember, consumers have not actually touched the product.* They're taking your word that the product is good and will be delivered in a timely manner. Offer free help lines and a super-strong guarantee.

Paragon Public Relations in Evanston, IL sent out press releases about a contest to discover and honor an unknown entrepreneur. Paragon was flooded with entrants. The agency achieved fast credibility and great press coverage. It helped build Paragon's image in a hurry.

Piggy-Back Your Distribution

Invoice inserts. Many companies have developed direct-mail programs that use other peoples' mailing materials. Staples office supplies, for instance, will allow you to add a small selling piece to its invoices. Credit card companies have similar programs.

Many book companies will allow you to place your offer in with book shipments.

Mail-order companies, like record clubs and specialty foods companies, will allow you to piggy-back on its catalog mailings and invoices. Check the demographics and buying habits of customers before committing any money.

Many publishers have developed index cards that they send to their customers in decks of fifty or more.

Some are quite reasonably priced.

To learn more about these mailings and to find specialized lists of vendors who can do your mailing for you, contact the *DM News* website at http://www.dmnews.com.

Food & Beverage Marketing magazine developed a contest for the Brand Manager of the Year. It helped them develop an extremely loyal readership.

A Potpourri of Successful Marketing Strategies

Americans are the most imaginative marketers in the world. Here are more successful marketing strategies that have worked well for various companies. Tailor them to fit your needs.

The Humble Cassette Strategy

While a basic marketing strategy may fit on the head of a pin, sometimes you have to meet with your customers in a quiet room where you can explain your product and the rationale behind it slowly and candidly. You can deliver your message via video- or audiotape (an audiotape is a lot cheaper to produce). Several counter-culture businesses have grown to be million-dollar concerns with a simple half-hour cassette presentation. They're great for businesses that take the muiltilevel route to success or for any business where you have to contact and motivate a great number of people.

Here's how it works. You give out the tapes for free to interested people. In bulk, they should cost only a few pennies to produce and distribute. Those people give them out to other people. Pretty soon, it starts getting geometrical and the numbers go wild.

The message should be meaningful and interesting. If the product sells, you can offer a commission to people based on the sales the cassette brings in. Use code numbers to keep track of each cassette.

Your Employees as Marketers

Everybody in your organization is or should be a marketer. Have your telephone people or customer service people sell a product with each new phone call. One online information company uses its tech-support personnel to create a profit center by having them switch happy customers to new services when they end a phone call. The pitch should be short and sweet and able to be said by rote. Keep it under 30 seconds. By the way, the online company's tech-support people hate making the solicitation.

Hold Button Selling

Even your telephone hold button can create profits. Develop a short outgoing message to people hanging on the phone waiting for a real live human.

The Information Connection

Many communities have telephone information services that tell you the time, where to get free legal advice, and so on. Use these services to deliver your sales message. It can put you in touch with people who have the interests and demographics of people you target. There are hundreds of information lines, from soap opera recaps to stock market info.

When you sponsor a line, callers hear your message before they get the info. These services offer the flexibility to update or change your message easily and quickly. You can also use these services to tie in a seasonal event or promotion. Some services also offer direct connect capabilities.

When they touch a button, callers are directly connected to your place of business.

Transit Advertising and Promotions

The transit industry has come a long way since selling small car and bus cards. Now you can rent the inside of an entire fleet of buses for your own product. Mass transit delivers a highly targetable audience of captive customers. The message should be quick and easy to remember.

Get Really Close to Your Customers

Annie Withey is president of Annie's Homegrown, a pasta company. Customers are her only concern. She's fanatic about customer relationship. She takes customers' calls directly and answers all mail on her website. She'll constantly query customers about the quality of her Macaroni and Cheese and whether they were intrigued by a certain promotion.

She encourages word-of-mouth marketing by sending discount coupons to customers' friends. Customers also receive bumper stickers promoting the company's environmentally conscious message. She has given out over 30,000 stickers.

Slowly Annie Withey has built up a database of 75,000 customers, many of whom enthusiastically spread the message about her products. Considering her competition is the likes of Lipton, Kraft and Golden Valley, she's done well in keeping the company afloat and very profitable.

Suggestive Selling

Use your product or other people's products to move your merchandise. You can do it with suggestive selling.

This is one tactic that's particularly good to get your salespeople involved in. For instance, if you rent video tapes, you might have your people ask if they would like to buy some popcorn for the movie.

You might attach stickers to your video tapes, or create badges with a selling suggestion like "Enjoy some Act II popcorn with your movie."

Suggestive Selling Through Related Companies

A subset of the suggestive selling strategy is to let related companies do your selling for you. PPP is a company that sells a line of toilet-training aids for tykes. Judi Cohen, the president of PPP, talked a toilet seat manufacturer into letting her include a cute sales piece with each toilet seat they sold. Suggestive selling through other merchants is a great idea for companies on limited marketing budgets because you can leverage a small amount of money. If PPP had advertised in *Parenting* magazine, for example, Ms. Cohen would have had to spend a huge amount of money on a hit or miss proposition. To get other manufacturers to do your bidding for you, cut them in on a small piece of the action—or return the plug in your own sales materials.

The Cause-Related Marketing Strategy

You can garner great publicity, cement customer loyalty and create enormous good will when you sponsor a local cause that you believe in. American Opthalmic, in Winter Park, Fl partners with a local Meals on Wheels to serve the elderly. When they make trips to Meals on Wheel Centers, American Opthalmic checks vision and makes helpful presentations about eyecare for the elderly. The company makes money when people sign up for full exams or require surgery. The owner of America Opthalmic says his reach out programs account for 25 percent of sales.

On a larger scale, Otis Elevator is a sponsor for the Special Olympics. But it does more than sponsor. Its employees help with the games and festivities. Besides creating strong visibility, Otis Elevator estimates that company morale has jumped 15 percent since the sponsorship started.

Use Pushcarts to Push Sales

The old-time pushcart is back, and all spiffed up for a new selling venue. You don't see them on streets often these days, but peddlers can ply their wares in enclosed malls.

Pushcarts in a local mall can help you boost sales without paying for long-term space or expensive decorating and fixtures.

United Vision Group, in Ossining, NY built its business by using pushcarts in New York malls. After it decided they didn't want to be a seasonal selling company they stepped up to free-standing kiosks and eventually into permanent stores. But the pushcarts were the key that enabled them to slowly grow. Their carts still account for 60 percent of the business.

Pushcarts can also be a strong research tool. Use them to try out new products and pitches without having to make a long-term commitment.

Catalogs with Every Sale

Your best customer is one who is already satisfied. Reach customers when they are most receptive. Use your product to build an ongoing relationship by enclosing additional brochures, useful information and, of course, coupons.

Natural Ovens of Manitowoc WI writes an informative newsletter about bread and gives it out with every loaf they sell. The newsletter draws thousands of responses. Snapware in California makes reusable plastic canisters. They include a catalog and a hangtag in all products.

Use Seminars to Educate and Sell

Develop a seminar for your product or service. Seminars can bring you credibility and sales because you are speaking with people on your own terms. You become the expert. When you hold a successful seminar for your product, the resulting sales can even pay for the seminar itself. It's a great way to develop word-of-mouth promotions and even to line up potential distributors.

In New Mexico, there is a town called called Rio Rancho. It can be called the city built on seminars. The developer, Amrep, offered free seminars on buying land that (naturally) pitched the growing area of New Mexico. What started as a scheme to sell tiny plots of land, slowly became a thriving community with a main drag that includes McDonalds, Burger King, Pizza Hut and any other franchised fast-food outlet you can think of.

There are two variances on the seminar scene that can even help you save seminar costs. Line up similar but noncompeting companies; charge them to speak to your audience and place their product. Or you can contact other companies that produce seminars and offer your speaking service. Local Chambers of Commerce and trade magazines can give you a list of upcoming speaking opportunities.

Author's Note

Thank you for reading *Winning Marketing Strategies*. This book will always be a "work in progress." If you have any ideas for future editions, or if you have an unusual strategy that worked for you, please contact me at:

Barry Feig's Center for Product Success
6217 Antigua, Suite H
Sandia Mountains, NM 87111
Phone: (505) 237-9342
E-mail: Newmex@aol.com

I look forward to hearing from you.

Index

A

B

C

G

H

I

J

K

L

M

N

O

P